Rwanda After Genocide

In the 1994 Rwanda genocide, around one million people were brutally murdered in just thirteen weeks. This book offers an in-depth study of post-traumatic growth in the testimonies of men and women who survived, highlighting the ways in which they were able to build a new, and often enhanced, way of life. In so doing, Caroline Williamson Sinalo advocates a new reading of trauma: one that recognises not just the negative, but also the positive responses to traumatic experiences. Through an analysis of testimonies recorded in Kinyarwanda by the Genocide Archive of Rwanda, the book focuses particularly on the relationship between post-traumatic growth and gender and examines it within the wider frames of colonialism and traditional cultural practices. Offering a striking alternative to dominant paradigms on trauma, the book reveals that, notwithstanding the countless tales of horror, pain and loss in Rwanda, there are also stories of strength, recovery and growth.

CAROLINE WILLIAMSON SINALO is Lecturer in World Languages at University College Cork. Awarded her PhD from the University of Nottingham in 2014, she has published numerous articles on the lives and experiences of Rwandan genocide survivors, notably on the topic of post-traumatic growth. Her PhD, funded by an AHRC Collaborative Doctoral Award, was carried out in partnership with the Aegis Trust charity, and involved spending a year working in Rwanda at the national archive. Her collaboration with the Aegis Trust has since continued and she has twice received Aegis Research, Policy and Higher Education (RPHE) funding. Williamson Sinalo's research has also been supported by the Irish Research Council (IRC).

Rwanda After Genocide

Gender, Identity and Post-Traumatic Growth

CAROLINE WILLIAMSON SINALO
University College Cork

CAMBRIDGE
UNIVERSITY PRESS

CAMBRIDGE
UNIVERSITY PRESS

University Printing House, Cambridge CB2 8BS, United Kingdom

One Liberty Plaza, 20th Floor, New York, NY 10006, USA

477 Williamstown Road, Port Melbourne, VIC 3207, Australia

314-321, 3rd Floor, Plot 3, Splendor Forum, Jasola District Centre, New Delhi - 110025, India

79 Anson Road, #06-04/06, Singapore 079906

Cambridge University Press is part of the University of Cambridge.

It furthers the University's mission by disseminating knowledge in the pursuit of education, learning and research at the highest international levels of excellence.

www.cambridge.org
Information on this title: www.cambridge.org/9781108444590
DOI: 10.1017/9781108591478

First published 2018
First paperback edition 2020

A catalogue record for this publication is available from the British Library

ISBN 978-1-108-42613-8 Hardback
ISBN 978-1-108-44459-0 Paperback

Contents

Figures

Tables

Acknowledgements

I would like to thank my colleagues in University College Cork's French Department and School of Languages, Literatures and Cultures for their consistent intellectual and moral support throughout this project. In particular, I will mention my Head of the Department, Dr Patrick Crowley, as well as my colleagues and friends Dr Kate Hodgson and Professor Paul Hegarty. I would also like to express my appreciation for all colleagues involved in the Violence, Conflict and Gender cluster in UCC's Centre for Advanced Study in Literatures and Cultures (http://casilac.ie/violence-conflict-and-gender/) for our many stimulating and inspiring encounters: Nicoletta Mandolini, Professor Nuala Finnegan, Dr Silvia Ross, Dr Alan Gibbs, Dr David Fitzgerald, Dr Amanullah De Sondy and Professor Vittorio Buffachi.

For my time in Rwanda, I am heavily indebted to Dr James Smith for his collaboration in parts of the project, and for introducing me to the work of Aegis Rwanda. I am grateful to all Aegis Rwanda staff, but particularly Freddy Mutanguha, Yves Kamuronsi, Claver Irakoze, Paul Rukesha, Fabrice Musafiri, Yvonne Umugwaneza, Diogene Mwizerwa, Jean Paul Mugiraneza, Martin Niwenshuti, Shannon Scully, Aline Umugwaneza, Emery Rutagonya, Marie Gasagire and Adelaide Umugwaneza. All of them welcomed me to the team, helped me with my research, provided me with access to the testimonies, helped me to translate and proofread them, shared with me their expert knowledge and became my friends. For our endless conversations about Rwandan history, culture and politics I would like to thank Maggie and Phil Ziegler. I am also grateful to Jacques Mutabazi and Chantal Umutesi for teaching me Kinyarwanda, assisting me with data analysis and contributing various ideas through our discussions.

For funding different aspects of the project, I would like to thank the Arts and Humanities Research Council, the Irish Research

Council and the Aegis Research, Policy and Higher Education Programme.

Other intellectual contributions to the project came from Professor Nicki Hichcott, Dr Catherine Gilbert, Dr Kathryn Batchelor, Professor Dirk Moses, Dr David Mwambari, Professor Stef Craps and Dr Phil Clark. I am thankful to all of them.

For their endless moral and emotional support, I am thankful for my family members, Sarah Kay, Will Williamson and Emily Kay Goodman, and friends, Fuchsia Fishbourne, Maja Halls Brosnan, Rita Martins Rodrigues and Gill Sorensen.

I am especially grateful to my husband, Chikondi, for supporting and inspiring me everyday.

Finally, I would like to thank all the survivors who had the bravery to share their stories.

Preface

Before the arrival of Europeans, conflict rarely took place between the Tutsi and Hutu in Rwanda. Wars generally pitted the Banyarwanda as a group against outsiders and, with the same language, religion and cultural practices, the terms Hutu and Tutsi did not refer to distinct ethnic groups, as such, but to political status and occupation.[1] The racialisation of these groups came with the arrival of German, and later Belgian, colonists who believed the Tutsi to be racially superior to the Hutu. Such divisions were further reinforced by the colonial policy of introducing identity cards in the 1930s which explicitly stated the individual's ethnic group. Alongside these reforms, the Belgians established Tutsi supremacy by reserving educational opportunities for Tutsi and replacing all Hutu in power with pro-European, Tutsi chiefs.

In the 1950s, a sense of injustice and inferiority among the Hutu, in combination with their numerical predominance, began to draw sympathy from Flemish missionaries and a Hutu counter-elite began to emerge. Anti-Tutsi rhetoric grew in intensity and the Belgian authorities began switching their allegiances to the Hutu majority, replacing Tutsi chiefs with Hutu ones. Following the 1959–61 revolution, the Parmehutu Party was elected to power with Grégoire Kayibanda as president.[2] Parmehutu propagated a pro-Hutu racist ideology, claiming that Hutu held the racial right to rule Rwanda. Despite a growing number of killings and human-rights violations, this government was perceived by Belgium – and later France – as

---

[1] The Hutu majority make up about 85 per cent of the population and are traditionally land-working famers. The Tutsi make up around 14 per cent of the population and are traditionally pastoralists. The third ethnic group of Rwanda, the Twa, represents just 1 per cent of the population and are traditionally hunter-gatherers and potters.

[2] Parmehutu, or Parti du Mouvement pour l'Emancipation Hutu, was the political party established by Grégoire Kayibanda to counter Tutsi supremacy.

democratic because the notion of ethnic majority was equated with democratic majority. Over the next few decades, the government reversed the ethnic hierarchy that had been established during the colonial period and corruption concentrated access to resources, opportunities and power into the hands of a tiny Hutu elite. Several outbursts of anti-Tutsi violence in the 1960s resulted in bloodshed and many Tutsi were driven into exile in surrounding countries.

During his presidency, Kayibanda relied heavily on people from his southern home town of Gitarama where, in return, he concentrated economic resources. In the face of increasing poverty, Hutu from the north of the country began to criticise the regime. Kayibanda lost control in a northern coup d'état on 5 July 1973 which placed Juvénal Habyarimana in power. At the time, the coup was immensely popular as it reduced ethnic violence and government corruption. In the early days, the regime also saw an improvement in Hutu–Tutsi ethnic relations and intermarriage became more common. However, in the late 1980s, Habyarimana faced a similar economic crisis to Kayibanda in 1973. Then, in 1990, the Rwandan Patriotic Front (RPF) – consisting mostly of Tutsi refugees from Uganda – invaded northern Rwanda and sparked a civil war. Seeing this as a propaganda opportunity to abate the growing discontent, Habyarimana deflected criticism of his regime onto all Tutsi. In an attempt to retain power, the government fostered policies of ethnic hatred and fear of the RPF and all Tutsi. Habyarimana used racist propaganda and incited hatred through radio broadcasts, popular magazines, newspapers, songs and even school textbooks. Tutsi were portrayed as inherently evil; foreign conquerors who wanted to enslave the Hutu people. Under intense international pressure, a ceasefire was called and the Hutu government signed a power-sharing agreement with the RPF as part of the Arusha Accords. However, by the time Habyarimana's plane was shot down on 6 April 1994, plans for the genocide of the Tutsi were already in place.

Hutu extremists blamed the RPF for the plane crash and a killing campaign ensued. Hundreds of thousands of ordinary people participated in the genocide and victims were frequently raped, tortured and slaughtered by their neighbours. As soon as the killings began, the RPF rekindled the civil war and won within three months, establishing a new government. But, by the time the RPF won the civil war, as many as three-quarters of the Tutsi population had perished, as well as thousands of moderate Hutu.

Over the thirteen-week period of genocide, the death toll reached around one million people, most of whom were brutally murdered using machetes and other farm tools. In the immediate aftermath, a further two million Hutu – perpetrators and others – fled to neighbouring Zaire in fear of retribution and around 600,000 Tutsi refugees returned from neighbouring Uganda, Tanzania and Burundi. While the influx of Tutsi refugees created an increase in criminality at home, the outflow of Hutu refugees led to a security threat as members of the former regime began retraining their army and threatened to launch a full-scale invasion. Meanwhile, the people that made up the rest of the Rwandan population were psychologically traumatised. There were Tutsi and Hutu survivors who had lost their families, friends and property; thousands of children who had lost their parents; perpetrators of the genocide who had blindly followed orders and now lived in fear of being arrested or killed; and killers who had believed in the genocidal ideology. To make matters worse, the country's economy was non-existent. In short, the genocide left Rwanda and Rwandans devastated.

This book offers an in-depth analysis of post-traumatic growth in the testimonies of men and women who survived. Post-traumatic growth describes the ways in which survivors of trauma are able to build a new way of life that they experience as superior to the life they had before in significant ways – a phenomenon that has been recognised throughout history and across cultures. However, scholars in both the humanities and the psychological sciences have placed much emphasis on the negative cognitive, behavioural and emotional reactions to traumatic events which have been interpreted as pathological. In this book, I argue that Western concepts such as Post-Traumatic Stress Disorder (PTSD), belatedness, unknowability and unrepresentability may have limited useful application in a post-colonial, post-genocide context such as Rwanda and may even exacerbate, rather than remedy, the problems of trauma survivors. In addition, because of their exclusive focus on negative outcomes following trauma, both the medical model and trauma theory could be regarded as incomplete. This book advocates a new reading of trauma; one that recognises not just the negative, but also the positive, responses to traumatic experiences. Taking testimonies recorded in Kinyarwanda by the Genocide Archive of Rwanda as its corpus, the book focuses particularly on the relationship between post-traumatic growth and gender.

The trauma of experiencing genocide can have devastating social and psychological effects. Research has shown that depression and anxiety as well as emotional problems of guilt, shame, anger, substance abuse and conflicts within relationships are all common consequences of trauma. However, research also shows that, in the struggle to rebuild lives, there is often the possibility of positive changes for individuals and their communities. It may seem paradoxical to suggest that the genocide could have resulted in such positive transformations, but research in other contexts suggests it is a real possibility. Through a discursive analysis of survivors' testimonies, this book reveals that, although there are countless tales of horror, pain and loss in Rwanda, there are also many stories about strength, recovery and growth. It identifies how growth is manifested, how gender affects processes of post-traumatic growth and how growth might be facilitated in the socio-cultural context of Rwanda.

Through its focus on the voices of individual Rwandans who have given their testimonies to the Genocide Archive of Rwanda, this book differs from other books on the Rwanda genocide. Many Africanists working on post-genocide Rwanda rely on historical or political documentation produced by government or other elite institutions. Others base their research on interview material. The testimonies on which this book is based offer a new perspective on the genocide because the interviews are carried out by fellow survivors rather than by Western researchers and by providing an environment in which survivors feel comfortable speaking freely, these testimonies challenge many of our received understandings of Rwandans. For example, Rwanda is often portrayed as a place where a culture of silence prevails. Contrary to this popular perception, however, I show that Rwandan men and women are willing to speak out and actively shape public discourse on such issues as the government, ethnicity, pre-genocide history, the genocide and the role of the international community.

Introduction

Rutagarama's Story

Rutagarama, a Tutsi survivor from Rwanda's Southern Province, survived an apocalyptic attack at Mugina parish. After withstanding the militia for several days, he, alongside other Tutsi, was ordered to evacuate the church where they were hiding, remove his clothes and sit in the grounds. The Tutsi women were told to leave while the men sat undressed, each with a militiaman 'behind them carrying a machete'.[1] On the leaders' whistle blow, the killers began to slaughter the Tutsi men, hacking them down with their machetes. A blow to the head left Rutagarama unconscious. He later woke up among corpses. When he tried to stand, he kept falling back to the floor, realising that his assailant had tried to cut his body 'into two pieces'. As he lay among the cadavers, waiting for someone to come and finish him, someone stole 100 Rwandan Francs from his underwear (the equivalent of 60 US cents).[2] Eventually the *Interahamwe*[3] arrived to search the corpses and Rutagarama begged one of them to kill him: 'Please, use anything. I feel dead but I'm not. Get something and just hit my head', he pleaded. The man went off to search the bodies for money but did not return.

Some other people came to bury the corpses, one of whom noticed that Rutagarama was still alive and covertly warned him to leave or

---

[1] All testimonies cited in this book come from the Genocide Archive of Rwanda. Retrieved from: www.genocidearchiverwanda.org.rw/ (accessed 4 December 2017).

[2] According to Marie Béatrice Umutesi, during the genocide 500 Rwandan Francs were worth $3. Marie Béatrice, *Fuir ou mourir au Zaïre: le vécu d'une réfugiée rwandaise* (Paris: L'Harmattan, 2000), p. 57.

[3] Literally 'those who fight together', the *Interahamwe* began as the youth wing of former President Juvénal Habyarimana's political party, the Mouvement Révolutionaire National pour le Développement (MRND), but became the primary militia group involved in killing Tutsi during the genocide.

risk being buried alive. Unable to walk, Rutagarama crawled to a nearby sorghum plantation, looking, as he describes it, 'like a wild animal'. After crawling around, he notes how 'blood mixed with mud on my clothes while crawling through the soil ... I was a frightful sight. Everyone who saw me was in shock. They would stop and stare and wonder, "Is this an animal or a human being?"' Tutsi men were dehumanised to such an extent that when a policeman saw Rutagarama in this state, his reaction was not one of compassion, but of fear as he warned others around saying: 'Be careful. This person may be an *Inyenzi* [Rwandan Patriotic Front (RPF) soldier] in disguise'. By this point, Rutagarama 'had completely lost all hope'. 'Life was over for me', he concedes.

Burizihiza's Story

Burizihiza is from Sahera Sector which is also in the Southern Province. When the killers started arriving in her area, she found a hiding place at the University Hospital of Butare. But she was eventually picked up by the local Burgomaster who enslaved her. Instead of killing her, the Burgomaster explained that it would be Burizihiza's 'special' task to witness how the Tutsi would die. She was told that, once this 'work' was finished, they would kill her too. At the time, Burizihiza had her three children with her – the extremists killed her daughter and threw her two sons to be eaten by dogs. She later found her sons who had been severely mauled by the dogs, but were still alive. She hid them near a cowshed in a large pot used for brewing Rwandan beer.

Living at the Burgomaster's house, Burizihiza saw the brutal torture and killing of many people. Her brothers were killed and she was forced to drink their blood. Her mother was laid out naked and stabbed in the vagina with a sword which was then used to stir her insides. Burizihiza saw one woman raped by a group of men, who then put hooks inside her body and pulled out her intestines. Another woman, who was heavily pregnant, was speared in the uterus. The spear was pushed in so deep it came out of her mouth.

Throughout the genocide, Burizihiza was kept by the Burgomaster as a sex slave. One day, she was attacked by some Hutu women who believed that she was kept alive because of her sexual value. These women tried to force dried herbs into her vagina to destroy her sexuality so that the Burgomaster would have to kill her. She was saved by another Hutu man, but only in exchange for him raping her. Eventually, the Burgomaster, along with other perpetrators, fled the area to escape the advancing forces of the RPF and Burizihiza was able to survive.

A Gendered Genocide

It would be difficult to overestimate the scale and impact of the 1994 Rwanda genocide. In a period of just three months as many as one million people were brutally murdered, leaving a legacy of destruction, fear and distrust. Although the violence committed during the genocide affected all Rwandans, women and men suffered in different ways. Indeed, the genocide was as much a crisis of gender as it was one of ethnicity.[4] There had been an expansion of cash crops over the course of the twentieth century, which deprived Tutsi and Hutu men of potential land for cultivation.[5] In the late 1980s when the global price of coffee collapsed, economic downturn resulted in high unemployment and exacerbated the problems of overpopulation, land scarcity and incompetent governance. Although ethnicity conditioned access to resources such as government jobs, education and land, as Villia Jefremovas observes, 'for most peasants, both Hutu and Tutsi, the privileges accorded by ethnicity were meaningless. It was still a minority within the elite group that profited from ethnic affiliations'.[6] According to Marc Sommers, drought, displacement and food and land shortages combined with the invasion by the RPF and ensuing civil war 'made poor, unemployed male youth easy pickings for those organising the genocide'.[7] Exploiting the weaknesses of young Hutu men, the orchestrators of the genocide were able to persuade them to participate by promoting the *Interahamwe* through idealised masculinities and by referring to the killing as 'work'.[8] The need for employment among Hutu men was so great that the concept of work

---

[4] Adam Jones, 'Gender and Genocide in Rwanda', *Journal of Genocide Research*, 4. 1 (2010), 65–94 (p. 66).

[5] Ibid., pp. 66–7.

[6] Villia Jefremovas, *Brickyards to Graveyards: From Production to Genocide in Rwanda* (Albany, NY: State University of New York Press, 2002), p. 74.

[7] Marc Sommers, 'Fearing Africa's Young Men: The Case of Rwanda', *Conflict Prevention & Reconstruction, World Bank Social Development Papers*, 32 (2006), 8.

[8] Jones, 'Gender and Genocide in Rwanda', pp. 67 and 68.

even governed the way the genocide was carried out. As Adam Jones highlights, killers kept a 'strict regimen' and would carry out the massacres during the same hours that governed the labour of the formal economy.[9]

While Hutu men suffered from unemployment, insecurity and the remnants of an inferiority complex created during the colonial period, Tutsi masculinity was also in crisis by April 1994. The invasion of the Tutsi-led RPF rebels in 1990 had spawned a climate of fear and vengefulness. This anger was targeted primarily at Tutsi men who came to be perceived as the enemy within and became the objects of a witch hunt.[10] As Alison Des Forges writes, following the invasion of the RPF, the 'elite worked to redefine the population of Rwanda into "Rwandans", meaning those who backed the President, and the "ibyitso" or "accomplices of the enemy", meaning the Tutsi minority and Hutu opposed to him'.[11] In propaganda, the RPF Tutsi rebels and their 'Tutsi accomplices' were depicted as 'creatures from another world, with tails, horns, hooves, pointed ears and red eyes that shone in the dark'.[12] Although Tutsi women were targeted by genocidal propaganda and violence, they were actually considered 'less Tutsi' than Tutsi men because of the patrilineal transference of ethnicity.[13] Women could, therefore, be 'liberated' from their ethnicity through rape and forced marriage. According to Erin Baines, while women and girls were often 'spared' until the final stages of the genocide, 'Tutsi men and boys, including male infants, were among the first to be killed' because they 'represented the future enemy'.[14] Indeed, in Jones's view, the extermination of males served as a kind of 'vanguard for the genocide as a whole, an initial barrier to be surmounted and "threat" to be removed, before the remainder of the community is consigned to violent death'.[15] This was certainly the case in Rutagarama's story where the women were spared so that

---

[9] Ibid., p. 90.
[10] Ibid., p. 70.
[11] Alison Des Forges, *Leave None to Tell the Story: Genocide in Rwanda* (Human Rights Watch Report, 1999), p. 3.
[12] Gérard Prunier, *The Rwanda Crisis: History of a Genocide* (London: C. Hurst & Co., 1997), p. 141.
[13] Jones, 'Gender and Genocide in Rwanda', p. 75.
[14] Erin K. Baines, 'Body Politics and the Rwandan Crisis', *Third World Quarterly*, 24. 3 (2003), 479–93 (p. 487).
[15] Jones, 'Gender and Genocide in Rwanda', p. 70.

the killers could proceed to execute the men. He reports the killers saying they would not kill women. 'But', he continues, 'this was a lie. They wanted to ... [first] rape them'.

Tutsi women and girl children were not killed in as large numbers as Tutsi men, but they were targeted for their gender. In Christopher Taylor's view, the genocide was an attempt to re-establish the ideal Hutu state as imagined through the idealised image of the 1959 Hutu revolution.[16] In part, it aimed to reclaim patriarchy and male dominance in rejection of the political and social advances that had been made by women during the 1980s and early 1990s. In Taylor's opinion, Hutu extremists held ambivalent attitudes towards Tutsi women. On the one hand, Tutsi women were loathed for 'their potential subversive capacity to undermine the category boundary between Tutsi and Hutu'.[17] On the other hand, Taylor suggests that as a result of old colonial stereotypes of Tutsi superiority, Tutsi women were irresistible to Hutu men.[18] This cognitive dissonance harboured by Hutu men, in combination with the desire to restore patriarchy, resulted in a form of 'sexual terrorism' reserved for Tutsi women.[19] Thus while men were mostly killed outright, women were frequently raped and tortured sexually. As sexual violence became incorporated into the genocidal programme, *Interahamwe* known to be infected with HIV were often summoned to commit this act. As in Burizihiza's story, sexual violence also took on a symbolic meaning. Women's bodies were mutilated, their breasts cut off, their vaginas pierced with sharp objects or burnt with acid and their faces disfigured. Pregnant women had the foetuses cut from their bodies. Like Burizihiza, many women had their lives saved in exchange for

[16] Christopher Taylor, 'A Gendered Genocide: Tutsi Women and Hutu Extremists in the 1994 Rwanda Genocide', *Political and Legal Anthropological Review*, 22. 1 (1999), 42–53 (p. 42).

[17] Taylor observes how Tutsi women were seen as the permeable boundary between the Hutu and Tutsi ethnic groups. It was much more common in pre-genocide Rwanda for Tutsi women to marry Hutu men than for Hutu women to marry Tutsi men. Official ethnic identity (as marked on the identity cards) was determined by the father and therefore the children of a Hutu man married to a Tutsi woman would be considered Hutu and would thus benefit from having Hutu citizenship despite being considered racially impure by Hutu extremists. Taylor, 'A Gendered Genocide', p. 50.

[18] Ibid.

[19] Ibid.

becoming 'wives' or sex slaves to Hutu men. Because of their com-modified value as sexual objects, however, fewer women than men were killed in the genocide.

Can Living through Genocide Lead to Positive Change?

The examples of Rutagarama and Burizihiza are but two of the thou-sands of stories of horror and tragedy lived by Rwandan men and women in 1994. It may seem abhorrent to suggest that anything good could result from such disaster and yet, positive changes can be observed in both of their testimonies. A term commonly used to describe positive changes following a traumatic event is 'post-traumatic growth', where individuals establish new psychological constructs and build a new way of life that is experienced as superior to their previous one in important ways. This process is thought to arise from the need to adapt one's worldview in order to accommo-date traumatic experiences that violated previously held beliefs.[20] It should be made clear that the notion of post-traumatic growth does not imply the absence of distress, pain or suffering.[21] Indeed, for most survivors, growth and pain coexist. Post-traumatic growth should also be distinguished conceptually from related notions such as resilience and recovery.

According to Georges A. Bonanno, 'many people are exposed to loss or potentially traumatic events at some point in their lives, and yet they continue to have positive emotional experiences and show only minor and transient disruptions in their ability to function'.[22] Such an 'ability to maintain a stable equilibrium' following a violent or life-threatening experience is what Bonanno refers to as 'resilience'.[23] Similar to resili-ence is the concept of 'recovery'. According to Bonanno, this notion 'connotes a trajectory in which normal functioning temporarily gives way to threshold or subthreshold psychopathology (e.g., symptoms of

---

[20] Lawrence Calhoun and Richard Tedeschi, *Facilitating Posttraumatic Growth: A Clinician's Guide* (Mahwah, NJ: Lawrence Erlbaum Associates, Inc. 1999), p. 2.

[21] Ibid., p. 20.

[22] George A. Bonanno, 'Loss, Trauma, and Human Resilience: Have We Underestimated the Human Capacity to Thrive after Extremely Aversive Events?', *American Psychologist*, 59. 1 (2004), 20–8 (p. 20).

[23] Ibid., p. 20.

depression or post-traumatic stress disorder [PTSD]), usually for a period of at least several months, and then gradually returns to pre-event levels'.[24] The concept of post-traumatic growth differs from both resilience and recovery. Like recovery, it often involves a period in which functioning is significantly disrupted, but post-traumatic growth is not simply a return to a pre-trauma state. Instead it refers to the experience of subjectively higher levels of psychological or social functioning. Such a concept, by no means, legitimises the violence and trauma caused by the genocide, but it does recognise the capacity of humans to adapt and change in times of adversity. To illustrate the differences in the ways people respond to trauma, Stephen Joseph draws on the metaphor of a tree in a storm:

The tree is buffeted by the wind, but it stands firm and unbending. When the storm has passed, it appears not to have been affected. Some people, too, seem to weather stressful events, emerging unscathed emotionally. They are like the tree that stands unbending in the wind. Such people are said to be *resistant*. Another tree bends in the wind. It does not break, and when the wind dies down, the tree returns to its original shape. In much the same way, there are people who bend with the strain of life adversity, but quickly bounce back to their original state. In other words, they *recover* ... A third tree bends in the wind. But instead of springing back to its original shape when the wind abates, it is permanently changed. Lashed by the winds, this tree has been altered, and its shape will never be the same again. In time, it grows around its injuries, and new leaves and branches sprout from the trunk where old growths were severed. Scars, gnarls and misshapen limbs give the tree a unique character for the rest of its life span. It is no less of a tree than it used to be, but it is different. There is a group of people who, like the third tree, grow following adversity. They may remain emotionally affected, but their sense of self, views on life, priorities, goals for the future and their behaviours have been reconfigured in positive ways in light of their experiences.[25]

Such positive reconfigurations may be observed in Rutagarama, Burizihiza and many of the other men and women whose testimonies form the corpus studied in this book.

---

[24] Ibid.
[25] Stephen Joseph, *What Doesn't Kill Us: The New Psychology of Posttraumatic Growth* (London: Hachette Digital, 2011), pp. 71–2 (emphasis in the original).

Corpus and Methodological Considerations

In the aim of identifying how the genocide affected the lives of genocide survivors, this book examines a total of forty-two audio-visual
testimonies (including nineteen men, twenty-three women) recorded
in Kinyarwanda and translated into English and sometimes French.
All the corpus testimonies come from the Genocide Archive of
Rwanda which was established by the Aegis Trust in association with
Rwanda's National Commission for the Fight against Genocide
(CNLG).[26] The Aegis Trust is a Nottinghamshire-based non-governmental organisation which works to prevent genocide. It runs the UK
Holocaust Centre and was selected by the Rwandan Government to
establish and run the Kigali Genocide Memorial Centre, which
opened on the tenth Anniversary of the Rwandan Genocide in April
2004. The Genocide Archive of Rwanda forms part of the Memorial
Centre and is located on the same site. With the collaboration of
Ibuka (Kinyarwanda for 'Remember'), the umbrella group for genocide survivor organisations, the testimonies were collected by the
archive from survivors wishing to volunteer to give their testimony.
Participating men and women come from a range of geographical
locations and vary in age and profession. Besides a requirement of
being able to read and write in order to understand and sign the
release form prior to giving their testimony (a factor which could
indicate a certain level of education and therefore socio-economic status), the archive maintains that there are no criteria for selecting survivors. It could be argued, however, that survivors who come
forward to testify are exceptional in some way. For instance, those
who found the mental strength and narrative abilities to translate the
psychological and physical violence they suffered into words could be
more likely than others to exhibit post-traumatic growth. Other survivors may experience very little or even no post-traumatic growth. On
the other hand, the principle concern of this book is to examine
how – not how much – post-traumatic growth occurs in Rwandan
survivors. Therefore, even if survivors in the corpus have experienced
relatively high levels of growth compared to others, this does not
directly affect the validity of the study.

---

[26] For the Genocide Archive of Rwanda website, go to: www.genocidearchiverwanda
.org.rw/ (accessed 4 December 2017).

The survivors who testify for the Genocide Archive of Rwanda may also be exceptional because they do so through a medium overseen by Ibuka and the Aegis Trust; a factor which could imply that the testimonies are skewed ideologically in favour of the government. Many scholars are critical of the Rwandan government for its authoritarian regime and the lack of free speech in Rwanda, particularly the freedom to criticise the government.[27] It is well-documented that dissident Hutu politicians and members of civil society have been killed, arrested or removed from leadership positions.[28] The lack of free speech has also been observed among Tutsi genocide survivors who, according to Filip Reyntjens feel that they have become 'second-rate citizens who have been sacrificed by the RPF'.[29] For example, genocide survivor, Joseph Sebarenzi, was formerly the Speaker of the National Assembly but resigned on 6 January 2000 under pressure from certain members of the RPF. He then fled the country, fearing for his life.[30] Tutsi survivors involved in civil society have also faced

---

[27] Timothy Longman and Théoneste Rutagengwa, 'Memory, Identity, and Community in Rwanda', in *My Neighbour, My Enemy: Justice and Community in the Aftermath of Mass Atrocity*, eds. Eric Stover and Harvey M. Weinstein (Cambridge: Cambridge University Press, 2004), pp. 162–82 (p. 162); Gérard Prunier, *From Genocide to Continental War: The 'Congolese' Conflict and the Crisis of Contemporary Africa* (London: Hurst Publishers Ltd., 2009), p. 23; Filip Reyntjens, 'Rwanda, Ten Years On: From Genocide to Dictatorship', *African Affairs*, 103. 411 (2004), 177–210 (p. 208).

[28] Alison Des Forges and Timothy Longman, 'Legal Responses to Genocide in Rwanda', in *My Neighbour, My Enemy*, eds. Stover and Weinstein, pp. 49–68 (pp. 61–2); Helen Hintjens, 'Reconstructing Political Identities in Rwanda', in *After Genocide: Transitional Justice, Post-Conflict Reconstruction and Reconciliation in Rwanda and Beyond*, eds. Phil Clark and Zachary D. Kaufman (London: Hurst and Co., 2008), pp. 77–99 (p. 88); Timothy Longman, 'Limitations to Political Reform: The Undemocratic Nature of Transition in Rwanda', in *Remaking Rwanda: State Building and Human Rights after Mass Violence (Critical Human Rights)*, eds. Scott Straus and Lars Waldorf (Madison: University of Wisconsin Press, 2011), pp. 25–47 (p. 30); Longman and Rutagengwa, 'Memory, Identity, and Community in Rwanda', p. 162; Susan Thomson, 'Whispering Truth to Power: The Everyday Resistance of Rwandan Peasants to Post-Genocide Reconciliation', *African Affairs*, 110. 440 (2011), 439–56 (p. 442); Lars Waldorf, 'Instrumentalising Genocide: The RPF's Campaign against "Genocide Ideology"', in *Remaking Rwanda*, eds. Straus and Waldorf, pp. 48–66 (pp. 52 and 57–8).

[29] Reyntjens, 'Rwanda, Ten Years On', p. 180.

[30] Sebarenzi was not technically a 'survivor' as he left Rwanda in 1992 to join the RPF but he is considered an 'interior Tutsi' rather than a former Tutsi refugee. Reyntjens, 'Rwanda, Ten Years On', p. 181.

government intimidation and harassment. In the in the late 1990s, Ibuka became increasingly critical of the Rwandan government's neglect of genocide survivors, particularly the lack of economic opportunities for survivors.[31] Following these criticisms, the former prefect of Kibuye Prefecture was assassinated in 2000 and his brother, Ibuka's vice president, Josué Kayijaho, tried to leave the country but was detained by government officials.[32] He was eventually permitted to leave the country and was then joined by another of his brothers who was the executive secretary of the Fond d'assistance aux rescapés du genocide (FARG) along with Bosco Rutagengwa, the founder of Ibuka, and Anastase Muramba, Ibuka's Secretary-General. According to Timothy Longman, a member of the central committee of the RPF, Antoine Mugesera, subsequently took over the presidency of Ibuka and the organisation has since 'largely followed the RPF line'.[33] As Paul Gready notes, many civil society organisations now 'act as mouthpieces for the government' and have become 'monitory and control devices' used to 'prevent independent civil society from emerging'.[34] Reyntjens goes so far as to say that '"civil society" is controlled by the regime'.[35]

    Given that it was chosen by the Rwandan government to establish and manage the Kigali Genocide Memorial Centre and the Genocide Archive of Rwanda, the Aegis Trust also has to toe the government line if it is to maintain its relatively privileged position.[36] Such a position must be taken into account when analysing the testimonies collected by the organisation. However, the archive is given a degree of autonomy from governmental control as the primary purpose of the testimonies is to provide survivors with an outlet through which they may express themselves without coercion or intimidation from others. Although survivors with dissenting views may be more reluctant to come forward, this is not imposed by the archive. Indeed many survivors appear willing to criticise the government in their testimonies

---

[31] Longman, 'Limitations to Political Reform', p. 30.
[32] Ibid.
[33] Ibid., p. 31.
[34] Paul Gready, 'Beyond "You're with Us or against Us": Civil Society and Policymaking in Post-Genocide Rwanda', in *Remaking Rwanda*, eds. Straus and Waldorf, pp. 87–100 (p. 90).
[35] Reyntjens, 'Rwanda, Ten Years On', p. 185.
[36] For example, the exhibition in the Kigali Genocide Memorial Centre is consistent with the government's official narrative of the history of the genocide.

(discussed in more detail in Chapter 4). Moreover, as Chapter 5 shows, the problem with the Aegis Trust's involvement is not so much that it forces survivors to comply with the government's view, but rather that the charity imposes a European narrative on the testimonies. With access to the original Kinyarwanda transcripts, however, I was able to analyse and identify editorial intervention made by the Aegis Trust in published versions of the testimonies.

Despite the potential limitations of basing my analysis on testimonies that are collected by this organisation, there are also a number of benefits to using this archival material. The interviews are conducted in Kinyarwanda by survivors working for the Genocide Archive of Rwanda using open-ended questions which encourage survivors to speak at length about their experiences before, during and after the genocide. There is very little intervention from the interviewer, whose questioning generally focusses on gaining as much detail as possible about events rather than trying to steer the survivor towards or away from certain topics. There is also a great benefit to the fact that these interviews were conducted by fellow Rwandan survivors. For example, Susanne Buckley-Zistel notes from her field research in the Nyamata region, that her position as an outsider, and more importantly as a foreign researcher, may have limited the responses she was given in interviews as interviewees may have hidden their true beliefs or feelings.[37] As discussed in Chapter 5, Rwandans often harbour feelings of resentment and mistrust towards outsiders which may affect data gathered by Western researchers.[38] Indeed, the testimonies themselves challenge the notions of 'silence' and 'secrecy' in Rwanda that have been observed by some scholars. For example, in addition to the lack of freedom of speech discussed above, Buckley-Zistel found in her interviews with convicted *génocidaires*, Tutsi returnees[39] and Tutsi survivors of the Nyamata district in Kigali, that although individuals were willing to discuss the genocide itself, many were silent on

---

[37] Susanne Buckley-Zistel, 'Remembering to Forget: Chosen Amnesia as a Strategy for Local Coexistence in Post-Genocide Rwanda', *Africa: The Journal of the International African Institute*, 76. 2 (2006), 131–50 (p. 133).

[38] For a discussion on the perceptions of outsiders among staff members at the Aegis Trust, see Caroline Williamson, 'Accessing Material from the Genocide Archive of Rwanda', *African Research and Documentation*, 120 (2013), 17–24.

[39] Tutsi refugees who fled from previous outbreaks of violence and returned to Rwanda in 1994, mostly from Uganda, Burundi, Zaire and Tanzania.

historical matters, particularly the causes of the genocide and previous episodes of violence and tension between Hutu and Tutsi. According to Buckley-Zistel, the omission of this history is a form of 'chosen amnesia' which is 'essential for [the] local coexistence' of these various groups.[40] Other scholars suggest that silence is imposed on the Rwandan population by the government which 'seeks full control over people and space'.[41] The archive testimonies reveal that survivors are willing to discuss their lives openly and are even critical of the government, suggesting that this notion of silence, whether voluntary or imposed, is dependent on context.

Having worked closely with the archive and the Aegis Trust since 2010, including one year spent as an assistant at the archive, I have full access to all archive content.[42] The reason I have limited my corpus size to forty-two testimonies is not based on the content of any particular testimony, but because I wanted to include only testimonies with full Kinyarwanda transcriptions and English or French translations, which is not the case for all testimonies housed in the archive. As I have argued elsewhere, the quality of translation can vary, therefore, I chose to prioritise a rigorous and robust analysis based on the original transcripts rather than extend my sample but rely on translations alone.[43] Of the forty-two corpus testimonies, seventeen (eleven women, six men) are from an exhibition called 'Witness for Humanity', developed by the Aegis Trust for the Shoah Foundation at the University of Southern California, collected in 2011; and twenty-five (twelve women, thirteen men) are from the digital archive, collected between 2004 and 2007.[44] These testimonies have been

[40] Buckley-Zistel, 'Remembering to Forget', p. 131.
[41] Filip Reyntjens, 'Constructing the Truth, Dealing with Dissent, Domesticating the World: Governance in Post-Genocide Rwanda', *African Affairs*, 110. 438 (2010), 1–34 (p. 2).
[42] Although the testimonies are all available to members of the public who visit the archive, the archive has put in place a stricter accessibility policy on its website, requiring that users register in order to access a wider range of content. However, this policy was put in place for the protection of witnesses rather than to restrict information.
[43] For a discussion of the translation issues in the archive testimonies, see Caroline Williamson, 'Posttraumatic Growth at the International Level: The Obstructive Role Played by Translators and Editors of Rwandan Genocide Testimonies', *Translation Studies*, 9. 1 (2016), 33–50.
[44] For The Shoah Foundation website, go to: https://sfi.usc.edu/ (accessed 4 December 2017).

exhibited in Kinyarwanda and English and/or French by the archive. Some of them have also been published in English as a book of edited testimonies by the Aegis Trust, edited by Wendy Whitworth and entitled: *We Survived: Genocide in Rwanda*.[45] Because the testimonies are already in the public domain, I have not anonymised them. All Rwandans have a Kinyarwanda name and a Christian name; I use the Kinyarwanda name because it is the one most frequently used among Rwandans themselves.

My analysis relies on the Kinyarwanda transcripts in consultation with indigenous Kinyarwanda-speakers and with the help of the English/French translated texts. Given the variable quality of translation, all extracts cited in this book are my own translations of the Kinyarwanda transcripts. Where relevant, particularly in Chapter 5, I also discuss the original Kinyarwanda syntax and vocabulary. Paying particular attention to discursive features used by genocide survivors (agency, deixis, silence, implicit assumptions, lexical choices and other rhetorical structures such as metaphor and euphemism) the book offers a comprehensive study of post-traumatic growth in Rwandan men and women. In doing so, I advocate a new reading of trauma texts through the lens of post-traumatic growth; one that seeks to de-victimise and re-humanise trauma survivors. Through my analysis of genocide testimonies, I hope to demonstrate that such a reading is not only possible but necessary.

Theoretical Context and Overview

In both the humanities and the psychological sciences, there is a tendency to focus on the negative emotional, cognitive and behavioural consequences of psychological trauma. Within the psychological sciences, such negative outcomes have tended to be interpreted as pathological and labelled 'post-traumatic stress disorder' (PTSD).[46] Scholars in the humanities have drawn on this medical model, also

---

[45] Wendy Whitworth, *We Survived: Genocide in Rwanda* (Laxton, UK: Quill Press, 2006).

[46] Stephen Joseph and P. Alex Linley, 'Positive Psychological Perspectives on Posttraumatic Stress: An Integrative Psychosocial Framework' in *Trauma, Recovery, and Growth: Positive Psychological Perspectives on Posttraumatic Stress*, eds. Stephen Joseph and P. Alex Linley (Hoboken, NJ: John Wiley & Sons, Inc., 2008), pp. 3–20 (p. 4).

attending primarily to trauma's undesirable side effects. Trauma theorist Cathy Caruth, for example, emphasises the unknowability of trauma. In *Unclaimed Experience: Trauma, Narrative and History*, Caruth highlights 'a certain paradox' of trauma in that 'the most direct seeing of a violent event may occur as an absolute inability to know it'.[47] Similarly, Shoshana Felman describes traumatic experiences as 'acts that cannot be constructed as knowledge nor assimilated into full cognition'.[48] For Caruth, Felman and other trauma theorists, the direct expression of extremely traumatic events is ultimately impossible because of the inadequacy of language to represent the unrepresentable 'excess' of trauma.[49] In Chapter 1 of this book, I argue that Caruth's insistence that trauma can never be 'fully known'[50] or referenced directly is particularly frustrating in a Rwandan context where survivors are encouraged to 'move on' and adopt silence as a form of coping.[51] As Burizihiza sees it, survivors like her have a duty to provide an accurate account of historical events: 'There are things we can do for our country,' she states. 'There is the truth that we have to speak out so that our country can have true justice. That information is needed from survivors.' While many Rwandans are fighting to have their voices heard, the idea that they will never be able to know or understand their experiences may, in fact, reinforce society's demands for silence and perpetuate survivors' state of victimhood. Chapter 1 also demonstrates that an event-based understanding of trauma, as conceptualised by the medical model, fails to capture the complexity of trauma experienced in a post-colonial, post-genocide society like Rwanda, and its imposition may constitute a continuation of, rather than a remedy to, trauma. In addition, because of their exclusive focus on negative outcomes following trauma, both the medical model and trauma theory could be regarded as incomplete. Research suggests that, in addition to

---

[47] Cathy Caruth, *Unclaimed Experience: Trauma, Narrative and History* (Baltimore: Johns Hopkins Press, 1996), pp. 91–2.

[48] Shoshana Felman, 'Education and Crisis, or the Vicissitudes of Teaching', in *Testimony: Crisis of Witnessing in Literature, Psychoanalysis and History*, eds. Shoshana Felman and Dori Laub (New York: Routledge, 1992), p. 5

[49] Caruth, *Unclaimed Experience*, pp. 4–5; Felman, 'Education and Crisis, or the Vicissitudes of Teaching', p. 5.

[50] Caruth, *Unclaimed Experience*, p. 6.

[51] Jennie Burnet, *Genocide Lives in Us: Women, Memory and Silence in Rwanda* (Madison: Wisconsin University Press, 2012), p. 78.

the negative consequences, many individuals also experience positive changes in the wake of tragedy.[52]

Chapter 2, and subsequent chapters, introduce the concept of post-traumatic growth and demonstrate its application to post-colonial trauma testimonies. In Chapter 2 I show how Rutagarama, like other men survivors, has experienced significant changes in his identity. Before the genocide, he perceived himself as an invulnerable warrior who was eager to fight. But after being reduced to an animalistic, dehumanised form, any sense of his previously felt invulnerability was shattered. In its place grew a new identity; one which embraces Rwandan culture and language and rejects European ideas that previously divided the country. While this ideology of *Rwandicity*, or *Ndi Umunyarwanda*, receives much criticism in the West because of its association with the Rwandan government, I argue that it is also being adopted and adapted from the bottom up, allowing men to rebuild a constructive identity. Because of its focus on revalorising indigenous values, culture and language, it may also be considered a form of post-colonial post-traumatic growth, providing a response to structural, chronic forms of trauma caused by colonialism. Despite experiencing extreme bodily mutilation, Rutagarama strives to live, to work and to build a family. He now spends his time speaking to survivors' groups, urging young men and women to 'be committed and rebuild [their] life'.

Burizihiza also experienced positive changes since the genocide. But as women lived dissimilar experiences to men during the genocide, the ways in which they experience post-traumatic growth also differ. Like many women, Burizihiza lost her husband and most of her family, devastating her interpersonal relationships. Because of this loss, however, she had to take on roles that would have been socially unacceptable for women before the genocide. Women from all social groups joined cooperatives and organisations for mutual support, many of which have become important and powerful institutions in Rwandan civil society, advocating for legal and political changes.[53] Burizihiza co-founded an association of genocide widows from Mukura (Southern Province) named ABASA. She recognised that a significant problem that continued to traumatise these widows was

---

[52] For an overview of developments in the field, see Lawrence G. Calhoun and Richard G. Tedeschi, eds., *Handbook of Posttraumatic Growth: Research and Practice* (Mahwah, NJ: Lawrence Erlbaum Associates Publishers, 2006).

[53] Burnet, *Genocide Lives in Us*, p. 220.

that many of them had become financially dependent on the very men who had killed their families and raped them. Many widows were even living with their former rapists because they had nowhere else to go. Despite the danger of reprisals and the enormous stigma that surrounds victims of sexual violence, Burizihiza has had the courage to talk about these problems in public. She states in her testimony: 'I will keep on saying what I know [about those who committed rape ...] There is no day I will hide it.' Burizihiza's outspoken performances on television and radio eventually attracted the attention of the Rwandan First Lady, President Paul Kagame's wife, Jeannette Kagame, who helped Burizihiza to arrange for more housing to be built in the area so that genocide widows no longer had to share a house with former members of the *Interahamwe*.

The expansion of women's roles in civil society also gave them the skills and experience necessary for entering politics. After her work with ABASA, Burizihiza became the Elected Representative of Genocide Survivors in the Mukura Sector and received an African Women of Empowerment Award. Whenever she has the opportunity, she continues to speak out about issues of genocide and rape, despite the fact that this is putting her life in danger.[54] Chapter 3 examines post-traumatic growth in the testimonies of women like Burizihiza and reveals that their stories share many similarities. As Jennie Burnet notes, Rwandan women broke taboos 'not because they sought liberation from gender oppression but because they had no other choice'.[55] Although there is a heavy burden of responsibility, as a result of their traumatic past, it is clear that some women have also gained an enhanced sense of self-reliance and independence. Adopting David Bakan's theory of basic human motivation which highlights the two fundamental drives of agency and communion,[56] I argue that Rwandan women have experienced a decrease in communion but an increase in agency, which has resulted in a more individualist culture among Rwandan women.

---

[54] As a result of her outspoken comments about sexual violence and genocide, as well as her denouncement of people in positions of power, Burizihiza has to live in a military camp in Butare and has had numerous attempts made on her life.

[55] Burnet, *Genocide Lives in Us*, p. 6.

[56] David Bakan, *Duality of Human Existence: An Essay on Psychology and Religion* (Chicago: Rand McNally, 1966), pp. 14–15.

Moving beyond analyses of individual post-traumatic growth, Chapter 4 explores the ways in which men and women pursue the drives of agency and communion collectively. Little attention has been paid to the concept of collective post-traumatic growth and where scholars have addressed it, they have flagged factors such as cohesion and group identity as positive collective responses to trauma. Social psychologists, on the other hand, tend to interpret group cohesion as consistent with processes of in-group enhancement, which go hand-in-hand with out-group derogation. I argue that increased group cohesion is, therefore, likely to be disruptive rather than helpful in a context like Rwanda where conflict arose between groups within the same country. In Chapter 4, I present a model of collective post-traumatic growth which posits that if a group has comparable motivations to its constituent individuals, then to achieve positive social change, its drives of agency and communion must be satisfied. I use this model to investigate the differing ways in which men and women survivors seek to satisfy these drives at the societal level through the rebuttal of dominant ideologies that stigmatise sur-vivors (agency) and through processes of reconciliation with the Hutu population (communion). While there are some similarities in the ways men and women pursue these objectives, there are also some significant differences. The chapter identifies a trend of relatively high levels of agentic growth in women and relatively high levels of com-munal growth in men, which is perhaps surprising in the face of the-ories such as Bakan's prototypically agentic men and communal women;[57] or Carol Gilligan's separated men and connected women.[58] But it does support Alice Eagly's view that gender differences in social behaviour are linked to social context rather than sex.[59] The results of the analysis suggest that women are leading the way in terms of holding the government to account, but that this may be because they feel less satisfied with the political system.

Building on the model proposed in Chapter 4, Chapter 5 examines processes of collective post-traumatic growth at an international level

[57] Bakan, *Duality of Human Existence*, pp. 140–2.

[58] Carol Gilligan, *In a Different Voice: Psychological Theory and Women's Development* (Cambridge, Massachusetts: Harvard University Press, 1993), pp. 234–5.

[59] Alice Eagly, *Sex Differences in Social Behaviour: A Social-Role Interpretation* (Hillsdale, MI: Erlbam, 1987), p. 140.

through survivors' engagement in dialogue with the world beyond Rwanda. For this chapter, I examine the corpus testimonies that have been published in *We Survived*.[60] The chapter analyses how survivors' attempts to communicate with – and contest the dominant perceptions of – the world beyond Rwanda are manipulated in this published text. By comparing the published versions of their testimonies with the translations of the original Kinyarwanda versions, I examine editorial practices adopted in the book and identify a number of tendencies including the general domestication of the texts, the removal of orality, the correction (and sometimes insertion) of errors, the linearisation of the narrative and the reduction in length by means of cutting text that describes life before and after the genocide, the portrayal of survivors as 'nicer' than in the original versions, the removal of gendered dimensions of the genocide and the censoring of criticisms of outsiders. Chapter 5 demonstrates that, while the words of both men and women are altered in the published text, criticisms of the international community are censored to a greater extent in the testimonies of women compared to men. I discuss the implications of these findings and how they might influence our interpretations of other testimonial texts available in the West. I also refer back to trauma theory's insistence on the unrepresentability of trauma discussed in Chapter 1 to highlight, once again, how damaging such a concept can be in a context where survivors, particularly women, have to fight to be heard.

Advantages of Post-Traumatic Growth Theory

Despite revealing some of the limitations of post-traumatic growth theory – such as its over-reliance on individuals and events – the book also highlights some of its benefits. In addition to offering a more complete understanding of trauma than the medical model by accounting for negative and positive responses to trauma, the theory of post-traumatic growth may be more cross-culturally valid. According to Derek Summerfield, 'Western trends towards the medicalisation of distress' assume that PTSD is 'a universal human response to [traumatic] events'.[61] However, as Allan Young highlights, the 'psychiatric malady',

---

[60] Whitworth, *We Survived*.

[61] Derek Summerfield, 'Cross Cultural Perspectives on the Medicalisation of Human Suffering', in *Posttraumatic Stress Disorder: Issues and Controversies*, ed. Gerald Rosen (Chichester: John Wiley, 2004), pp. 233–47 (p. 241).

PTSD, 'is not timeless, nor does it possess an intrinsic unity'.[62] Rather it is a 'historical product' of the West that is 'glued together by the practices, technologies, and narratives with which it is diagnosed, studied, treated, and represented'.[63] In cross-cultural settings, Summerfield warns that Western 'psychiatric universalism risks being imperialistic' by assuming that certain types of knowledge are superior to others.[64] The medical model thus threatens to undermine traditional healing systems.

Similarly, the paradigm of trauma studies, which draws on the medical model, has also been accused of neglecting and marginalising the traumatic experiences of non-Western cultures.[65] Despite claims by Caruth that 'trauma itself may provide the very link between cultures',[66] Stef Craps argues that trauma theory has failed to live up to the 'promise of cross-cultural ethical engagement'.[67] In his view, this is because trauma theorists have tended to focus on event-based models of trauma in Western contexts, particularly the Holocaust, while disregarding everyday forms of traumatising violence such as racism, sexism, homophobia and other types of structural oppression.[68] Craps also questions the preference among trauma theorists for 'fragmented, non-linear anti-narrative forms' of expression.[69] Such forms are deemed to reflect the 'psychic experience of trauma', but, citing Andreas Huyssen, Craps reminds us that the aesthetics and ethics of 'nonrepresentability' are not themselves neutral.[70]

Post-traumatic growth theory was developed in the West and, like trauma theory, it recognises the value of constructing narratives as a means of understanding one's traumatic experience.[71] However, rather

---

[62] Allan Young, *The Harmony of Illusions: Inventing Post-Traumatic Stress Disorder* (Princeton, NJ: Princeton University Press, 1995), p. 5.

[63] Ibid.

[64] Summerfield, 'Cross Cultural Perspectives on the Medicalisation of Human Suffering', p. 242.

[65] Stef Craps, *Postcolonial Witnessing: Trauma Out of Bounds* (London: Palgrave Macmillan, 2013), p. 2.

[66] Cathy Caruth, ed., *Trauma: Explorations in Memory* (Baltimore: Johns Hopkins University Press, 1995), p. 11.

[67] Craps, *Postcolonial Witnessing*, p. 2.

[68] Ibid., p. 4.

[69] Ibid., pp. 4–5.

[70] Ibid., pp. 4–5 and 40.

[71] Scholars and practitioners in the field of post-traumatic growth are increasingly seeing the value of narrative exposure therapy as a tool for facilitating growth. Joseph, *What Doesn't Kill Us*, p. 171.

than advocating a particular form or genre of narrative, post-traumatic growth theorists emphasise the importance of a person-centred interpretation of events. In Lynne McCormack's view, such an approach may have cross-cultural validity because it is supportive of individuals' lived experience and avoids imposing diagnostic labels based on a discourse of individual psychopathology.[72] Having said that, post-traumatic growth theory is only beginning to be applied in non-Western contexts and this book is the first to offer a qualitative, text-based approach and is also the first self-consciously post-colonial application of the theory. By attending to the interpretations of ordinary Rwandans and gaining an understanding of how they experience post-traumatic growth, the book concludes by providing insights into how positive changes may be promoted in a manner that is culturally and politically sensitive. As Richard Tedeschi and Ryan Kilmer suggest, listening to people's narratives for evidence of strengths, interests and hopes as opposed to focusing on deficit and dysfunction may ultimately facilitate positive change, enhance health and well-being as well as reduce future needs for formal mental health services.[73]

More broadly, I believe that the failure to recognise the ability of survivors like Rutagarama and Burizihiza to rebuild their lives and, in some cases, experience a higher level of psychological or social functioning, is to miss the full story. To assume that individuals cannot adapt and change following adversity is to deny survivors a sense of agency, dehumanising them and perpetuating their state of victimhood. In privileging the voices of ordinary Rwandans, this book seeks to counter common Western stereotypes about Rwandan survivors as passive, silent victims caught in an endless spiral of tragedy by demonstrating that survivors are agents with the ability to rebuild their lives, reject dominant ideologies, criticise the government and challenge the role of the West.

---

[72] Lynne McCormack, 'Primary and Vicarious Posttraumatic Growth Following Genocide, War and Humanitarian Emergencies: An Interpretative Phenomenological Analysis', Thesis submitted to the University of Nottingham for the degree of Doctor of Philosophy (2010). Retrieved from: http://etheses .nottingham.ac.uk/2142/1/FINAL_THESIS_-_corrections_%26_dedication_18 .11.10.pdf (accessed 4 December 2017), p. 41.

[73] Richard G. Tedeschi and Ryan P. Kilmer, 'Assessing Strengths, Resilience, and Growth to Guide Clinical Intervention', *Professional Psychology: Research and Practice*, 36. 3 (2005) 230–7, (p. 235).

1 | *Defying Silence, Defying Theory*

The dominant approach to trauma in humanities research is known as trauma theory, an area of cultural studies that emerged in the early 1990s. Among the most influential theorists is Caruth, whose work attempts to reconcile understandings of PTSD with Freudian psychoanalysis and post-structuralism. The most enduring aspects of her work include trauma's belatedness and its unrepresentability. According to Caruth, the 'enigmatic core' of trauma lies in 'the delay or incompletion in knowing, or even seeing, an overwhelming occurrence'.[1] Caruth argues that trauma survivors experience post-traumatic repetitions of the event which are 'unavailable to consciousness but intrude repeatedly on sight'.[2] This, in her opinion, suggests 'a larger relation to the event that extends beyond what can simply be seen or what can be known, and is inextricably tied up with the belatedness and incomprehensibility that remain at the heart of this repetitive seeing'.[3] The paradox at the heart of Caruth's theory is that trauma 'is marked not by a simple knowledge, but by the ways it simultaneously defies and demands our witness' and, as such, must be 'spoken in a language that is always somehow literary: a language that defies, even as it claims, our understanding'.[4] The ubiquity of these ideas has been such that Susannah Radstone refers to 'the rise of what is becoming almost a new theoretical orthodoxy'.[5] More recent scholarship has, however, called into question many aspects of Caruth's trauma theory, including its shaky empirical foundations, its narrow understanding of what constitutes 'traumatic', its

---

[1] Caruth, *Trauma: Explorations in Memory*, p. 5.
[2] Caruth, *Unclaimed Experience*, p. 92.
[3] Ibid., p. 92.
[4] Ibid., p. 5.
[5] Susannah Radstone, 'Trauma Theory: Contexts, Politics, Ethics', *Paragraph*, 30. 1 (2007), 9–29 (p. 10).

Eurocentrism and its prescriptivism in terms of how trauma should be represented.

Trauma theory has drawn heavily on the medical model and the concept of PTSD. Traumatic events often produce negative responses in people, although not in all cases.[6] These responses can include distressing emotions such as anxiety and depression as well as anger, irritability, sadness, guilt and fear. Troubling thoughts, such as repetitive, ruminative and intrusive event-related thoughts are another common feature of the cognitive aftermath of a traumatic event. In response to these distressing emotions and thoughts, survivors of traumatic experiences may engage in problematic behaviours, such as social withdrawal or the consumption of legal or illegal drugs, or they may experience sexual difficulties or partake in aggressive behaviour. The aftermath of a traumatic experience may also result in physical reactions such as fatigue, muscle tension and aches, difficulties with breathing, feelings of jumpiness or difficulty sleeping.[7] The medical model holds that these responses constitute 'symptoms' of a 'disorder' or 'pathology' known as post-traumatic stress disorder or PTSD. But as noted in the Introduction to this book, the PTSD concept has been criticised by some scholars as a human-made product of the West.

The idea of PTSD originated in scientific and clinical discourses of the nineteenth century and developed further following America's involvement in Vietnam and the consequent rise in traumatic responses among veterans involved in this war. When it was eventually included in the 1980 American Psychiatric Association's (APA) *Diagnostic and Statistical Manual of Mental Disorders* (DSM-III), PTSD gained even greater public awareness as it had achieved what Craps refers to as 'disease status'.[8] Yet as Richard McNally points out, '[T]he very fact that the movement to include the diagnosis in the DSM-III arose from Vietnam veterans' advocacy groups working with anti-war psychiatrists prompted concerns that PTSD was more of a political or social construct rather than a medical disease discovered in nature.'[9] Yet because

---

[6] Bonanno, 'Loss, Trauma, and Human Resilience', p. 12.
[7] Calhoun and Tedeschi, *Facilitating Posttraumatic Growth*, pp. 5–10.
[8] Craps, *Postcolonial Witnessing*, p. 23.
[9] Richard J. McNally, 'Conceptual Problems with the DSM-IV Criteria for Posttraumatic Stress Disorder', in *Posttraumatic Stress Disorder: Issues and Controversies*, ed. by Gerald Rosen (New York: John Wiley & Sons, Inc., 2004), pp. 1–14 (p. 1).

of the proliferation of the concept and its diagnosis, PTSD has gained a momentum of its own so that 'what was essentially a socio-political as much as a medical category acquired official status'.[10] Alan Gibbs expresses concerns about the prevalence of PTSD, pointing to Ian Hacking's concept of 'looping',[11] the notion that 'people begin to change their behaviour and conform to ways in which they have been defined and treated by dominant social forces'.[12] 'In other words', he writes, 'an iatrogenic circuit reinforces the strength of PTSD as increasing numbers of people fall within its reach.'[13]

Not only is the medical basis of PTSD questionable, but as Gibbs convincingly demonstrates, Caruth's arguments, which draw on this concept, 'are based around logical gaps and lacunae'.[14] Specifically, he shows that: '[W]hat we encounter in Caruth's writing is a series of slippages where initial conjecture is transformed into certainty, which then becomes the basis for subsequent, largely unsubstantiated arguments.'[15] Moreover, referring to the work of Ann Kaplan and Richard McNally, Gibbs contends that there is no neuroscientific evidence to support Caruth's central arguments of amnesia, belatedness or the unknowability of trauma. Citing Kaplan, he points out that it is quite possible for 'trauma to be in conscious memory'.[16] Indeed, amnesia of traumatic events 'is actually rare in sufferers' experience'.[17]

In addition to its unconvincing empirical foundation, another criticism levelled against trauma theory and PTSD is the narrow understanding of what constitutes a traumatic experience. The DSM-III description of PTSD stresses that the 'syndrome' is caused by an event that 'would evoke significant *symptoms* of distress in most people'.[18] According to Craps, '[Q]ualifying stressors, such as rape, military

---

[10] Ibid., p. 4.
[11] Ian Hacking, 'Making Up People', *London Review of Books*, 28. 16 (2006), 23–6.
[12] Alan Gibbs, *Contemporary American Trauma Narratives* (Edinburgh: Edinburgh University Press, 2014), p. 4.
[13] Ibid., p. 4.
[14] Ibid., p. 6.
[15] Ibid., p. 8.
[16] As cited in ibid., p. 12.
[17] Ibid., p. 13.
[18] American Psychiatric Association (APS), *Diagnostic and Statistical Manual of Mental Disorders (DSM-III)* (Washington, DC, 1980), p. 238 [my emphasis].

combat, earthquakes, airplane crashes, or torture were those deemed to be "generally outside the range of usual human experience".'[19] Descriptions in subsequent versions have 'broadened with almost each successive version of the DSM',[20] leading to what McNally refers to as 'a conceptual bracket creep'.[21] Despite this broadening, however, Craps argues that even the most recent DSM definition is still 'narrow enough to make some important sources of trauma invisible and unknowable'.[22] In particular, he cites the work of Laura Brown, who argues that the DSM tends to ignore 'the normative, quotidian aspects of trauma in the lives of many oppressed and disempowered persons'.[23] Brown contends further that 'the range of human experience becomes the range of what is normal and usual in the lives of men of the dominant class; white, young, able-bodied, educated, middle-class, Christian men. Trauma is, thus, that which disrupts these particular human lives, but no other'.[24] In Craps' view, this narrow focus on singular events experienced by an individual psyche tends to 'leave unquestioned the conditions that enabled the traumatic abuse such as political oppression, racism, or economic domination'.[25] This means that 'problems that are essentially political, social, or economic are medicalised, and the people affected by them are pathologised as victims without agency, sufferers from an illness that can be cured through psychological counselling'.[26] Drawing on the work of Frantz Fanon who discusses the psychological impact of colonialism and racism, Craps argues that there are other forms of trauma that are 'everyday' or 'insidious' rather than punctual, unusual events.[27] The tendency to overlook notions such as 'insidious trauma', 'oppression-based trauma', 'post-colonial

---

[19] Craps, *Postcolonial Witnessing*, p. 24.

[20] Ibid., p. 25.

[21] McNally, 'Conceptual Problems', p. 4.

[22] Craps, *Postcolonial Witnessing*, p. 25.

[23] Laura S. Brown, *Cultural Competence in Trauma Therapy: Beyond the Flashback*, (Washington, DC: American Psychological Association, 2008), p. 18.

[24] Laura S. Brown, 'Not Outside the Range: One Feminist Perspective on Psychic Trauma', in *Trauma: Explorations in Memory*, ed. by Cathy Caruth, (Baltimore, MD: Johns Hopkins University Press, 1995), pp. 100–12 (p. 101).

[25] Craps, *Postcolonial Witnessing*, p. 28.

[26] Ibid., p. 28.

[27] Ibid., p. 29.

syndrome' and 'post-traumatic slavery' and other forms of 'collective ongoing, everyday forms of traumatising violence' is also linked to Craps' argument that trauma theory is fundamentally Eurocentric.[28]

As Craps explains, trauma theory was a 'product of the so-called ethical turn affecting the humanities'.[29] He highlights how Caruth herself noted the need for a 'new mode of reading and of listening' because 'history, like trauma, is never simply one's own...history is precisely the way we are implicated in each other's trauma'.[30] In Craps' view, however, 'the founding texts in the field (including Caruth's own work) largely fail to live up to this promise of cross-cultural engagement'.[31] For example, he notes that 'most attention within trauma theory has been devoted to events that took place in Europe or the United States, especially the Holocaust and, more recently, 9/11'.[32] Craps suggests that there is a general 'blindness to, or lack of interest in, the traumas visited upon members of non-Western cultures'.[33] Craps's arguments are informed by Susannah Radstone, who shares the opinion that 'it is the sufferings of those, categorised in the West as "other", that tend not to be addressed via trauma theory'.[34] Similarly, Judith Butler argues that 'forms of racism instituted and active at the level of perception tend to produce iconic versions of populations who are eminently grievable, and others whose loss is no loss, and who remain ungrievable'.[35] 'Those whose lives are not "regarded" as potentially grievable, and hence valuable, are made to bear the burden of starvation, underemployment, legal disenfranchisement, and differential exposure to violence and death.'[36] When Western trauma 'specialists' do engage with non-Western groups through humanitarian intervention, there is a tendency to import 'Western-style trauma programmes...as a basis for interventions in the lives of war-torn populations' which potentially

---

[28] Ibid., p. 4.
[29] Ibid., p. 1.
[30] Caruth, *Unclaimed Experience*, pp. 9, 25.
[31] Craps, *Postcolonial Witnessing*, p. 2.
[32] Ibid., p. 9.
[33] Ibid., p. 12.
[34] Radstone, 'Trauma Theory', p. 25.
[35] Judith Butler, *Frames of War: When Is Life Grievable?* (London: Verso, 2010), p. 24.
[36] Ibid., p. 25.

ignore or undermine traditional beliefs about trauma.[37] Similarly, Michael Rothberg observes that when trauma theorists approach non-Western literature, there is a tendency to 'import individualising and psychologising modes on the terrain of collective violence', leading to 'character-based' readings of 'Postcolonial Trauma Novels'.[38]

Not only is trauma theory Eurocentric in its individualising, event-based view and in its ignoring of non-Western traumas, but also in its prescriptive nature. According to Craps and Gert Buelens, trauma theory's insistence on the unspeakable, unrepresentable quality of trauma has led to a belief that 'traumatic experiences can only be adequately represented through the use of experimental, (post) modernist textual strategies'.[39] Indeed, Gibbs describes what he sees as an 'identifiable canon of approved trauma literature' which usually involves 'fragmented, non-linear chronologies, repetition, shifts in narrative voice, and a resultantly decentred subjectivity'.[40] 'A key ethical element of trauma theory', according to Gibbs, 'is the insistence that only silence is acceptable in the face of unspeakable horror.'[41] As Theodor Adorno famously stated, 'to write poetry after Auschwitz is barbaric'.[42] He later qualified this statement, writing that 'when even genocide becomes cultural property in committed literature, it becomes easier to continue complying with the culture that gave rise to the murder'.[43] He means here that by representing the Holocaust, it may be integrated into a form of collective memory and, therefore, become something that we can come to terms with, rendering it disposable as a human reality. In a similar vein, Claude Lanzmann clings 'to this refusal of understanding as the only possible ethical and at the same time the only possible operative attitude'.[44] In Lanzmann's view, 'fiction is a transgression', indeed he advocates 'un interdit de la représentation' (an interdiction of

---

[37] Craps, *Postcolonial Witnessing*, p. 22. See also Summerfield, 'Cross Cultural Perspectives', pp. 233–47. This is also the case in Rwanda, see the Conclusion to this volume.

[38] Michael Rothberg, 'Decolonising Trauma Studies: A Response', *Studies in the Novel*, 40. 1–2 (2008), 224–34 (p. 230).

[39] Stef Craps and Gert Buelens, 'Introduction: Postcolonial Trauma Novels', *Studies in the Novel*, 40. 1–2 (2008), 1–12 (p. 5).

[40] Gibbs, *Contemporary American*, pp. 26 and 27.

[41] Ibid., p. 19.

[42] Theodor W. Adorno, *Prisms*, trans. by Samuel and Shierry Weber (Cambridge: MIT Press, 1987), p. 34.

[43] Theodor W. Adorno, 'Commitment', in *Can One Live after Auschwitz: A Philosophical Reader*, ed. by Rolf Tiedemann, trans. by Rodney Livingstone and others (Stanford, CA: Stanford University Press, 2003), pp. 240–58 (pp. 252–3).

[44] Cited in Gibbs, *Contemporary American*, p. 19.

representation).[45] The only 'critically-approved aesthetic' of trauma writing is one that attests 'to the inevitability of belatedness' and 'the assertion that trauma is aesthetically unrepresentable'.[46] Yet this genre, in Gibb's view, 'betrays a Western bias in favour of avant-garde forms'.[47] Moreover, just as PTSD diagnoses may lead to a 'looping' effect, Gibbs argues that 'literature of the trauma genre exists in a vicious circle with the reinforcing criticism, which looks approvingly on every new literary text that emerges to reconfirm the theories'.[48]

More recently, scholars are beginning to move away from trauma's 'Euro-American conceptual and historical frameworks'.[49] Rothberg's concept of 'multidirectional memory', for example, brings together the Holocaust, slavery and colonialism as singular, yet relational, histories.[50] Similarly, Craps has recast trauma studies from a post-colonial perspective. He argues that, '[T]rauma theory should take account of the specific social and historical contexts in which trauma narratives are produced and received, and be open and attentive to the diverse strategies of representation and resistance which these contexts invite or necessitate.'[51] Other scholars have begun to follow the lead of Craps, Buelens and Rothberg by examining traumatic experiences in non-Western contexts.[52]

---

[45] Claude Lanzmann, 'Holocauste, la représentation impossible', *Le Monde*, 3 March 1994, p. 12.

[46] Gibbs, *Contemporary American*, pp. 24, 25.

[47] Ibid., p. 25.

[48] Ibid., p. 34.

[49] Rothberg, 'Decolonising Trauma', p. 225.

[50] Ibid., p. 225; Michael Rothberg, *Multidirectional Memory: Remembering the Holocaust in the Age of Decolonisation* (Stanford, CA: Stanford University Press, 2009), pp. 2–7

[51] Craps, *Postcolonial Witnessing*, p. 43.

[52] See, for example: Sonya Andermahr, 'Decolonizing Trauma Studies: Trauma and Postcolonialism', *Special Issue of Humanities* (2015). www.mdpi.com/books/pdfview/book/196 (accessed 4 December 2017); Michelle Balaev, ed., *Contemporary Approaches in Literary Trauma Theory* (Basingstoke: Palgrave Macmillan, 2014); Dolores Herrero and Sonia Baelo-Allu, eds., *The Splintered Glass: Facets of Trauma in the Post-Colony and Beyond* (New York: Rodopi, 2011); Ogaga Ifowodo, *History, Trauma, and Healing in Postcolonial Narratives: Reconstructing Identities* (New York: Palgrave Macmillan, 2013); Jay Rajiva, *Postcolonial Parabola: Literature, Tactility, and the Ethics of Representing Trauma* (New York: Bloomsbury, 2017); Nicole Rizzuto, *Insurgent Testimonies: Witnessing Colonial Trauma in Modern and Anglophone Literature* (New York: Fordham University Press, 2016); Abigail Ward, ed. *Postcolonial Traumas: Memory, Narrative, Resistance* (New York: Palgrave Macmillan, 2015); Jennifer Yusin, *The Future Life of Trauma: Partitions, Borders, Repetition* (New York: Fordham University Press, 2017).

Despite the heavy criticism and the new post-colonial turn in trauma studies, the basics of the paradigm still dominate. Indeed, in an edited collection called *The Future of Trauma Theory*, one of the contributing authors notes her attempt to 'recuperate existing theoretical premises'.[53] In this chapter, I argue that concepts such as PTSD, belatedness, unknowability and unrepresentability may have very limited useful application in post-genocide Rwanda, and may even be detrimental rather than helpful. Specifically, I contend that trauma theory's event-based Eurocentrism misunderstands the Rwandan context, and its imposition may constitute a continuation of rather than a remedy to trauma. I will also show that the idea of unrepresentability is particularly harmful in an environment where survivors are continuously encouraged to 'move on' and adopt silent coping. My overall view is that there is very little, if anything, to 'recuperate' from traditional trauma theory.

Colonial Trauma

At first glance, the genocide in Rwanda may appear to conform to the event-based description of trauma offered by the DSM. It took place over a limited period and represented violence that went far beyond the ordinary, everyday experiences of Rwandan people, leaving many people to suffer the types of emotional, cognitive, and behavioural responses associated with PTSD. But the traumatic experiences of Rwandans date back further than the 1994 genocide. In his *Les damnés de la terre* (The Wretched of the Earth) Fanon spoke of 'les plaies multiples et quelquefois indélébiles' (the countless and sometimes indelible wounds) inflicted by colonialism.[54] He viewed colonialism as the 'négation systématisée de l'autre, une décision forcenée de refuser à l'autre tout attribut d'humanité' (systematised negation of the other, a frenzied determination to deny the other person any attributes of humanity) which forces the people it affects to 'se poser constamment la question: "Qui suis-je en réalité?"' (constantly ask themselves the question: 'In reality, who am I?').[55] Like other colonised peoples, Rwandans suffer the psychological legacy of colonialism. As Gérard

---

[53] Ananya Jahanara Kabir, 'Affect, Body, Place: Trauma Theory in the World', in *The Future of Trauma Theory: Contemporary Literary and Cultural Criticism*, eds. Gert Buelens, Sam Durrant and Robert Eaglestone (London: Routledge, 2014), pp. 63–75 (p. 64).

[54] Frantz Fanon, *Les damnés de la terre* (Paris: François Maspero, 1961), p. 236.

[55] Ibid., p. 237.

Prunier observes, 'African social and cultural ways of doing things were neither taken into account nor questioned [by colonists]; they were simply made obsolete.'[56] The domination of African cultural identity continued well beyond independence. Des Forges reminds us that the French system 'exercised enormous control over African policy' and former President Juvénal Habyarimana tried to impress the French by his 'assimilation of French values'.[57] Claudine Vidal refers to a 'fourth ethnic group'[58] of Rwanda, the *bourgeoisie*, which espoused Christianity and European culture but remained 'totalement dépendente [sic] du maître étranger' (totally dependent on the foreign master).[59] According to Vidal, this *bourgeoisie*:

adopte ses valeurs [européennes], copie du mieux qu'elle peut sa civilisation. Elle n'en reçoit pourtant que les miettes: quelques modes vestimentaires, des rudiments de culture, des meubles, des fêtes... Peu de choses, juste assez pour se démarquer de la masse, mais trop peu pour égaler les Européens.

(adopts [European] values; copies as best it can their civilisation. In return it receives nothing but a few scraps: some clothing styles, some rudimentary culture, a bit of furniture, parties... Very few things, just enough to distinguish itself from the masses, but too little to match the Europeans.)[60]

Unfortunately, the impact of colonialism in Rwanda went way beyond the 'systematic negation' of indigenous culture. By the time of independence, the entire society had been re-engineered by the Belgians on the basis of a pernicious form of scientific racism known as the Hamitic hypothesis. This now-discredited theory regarded the Hutu and Tutsi identities as a fundamental social division between distinct racial groups. Ethnic groups had not had much significance before the European arrival, but the colonists perceived the Hutu and Tutsi as racially distinct groups and issued identity cards to all Rwandans mentioning their ethnic group. These cards were then used to discriminate against the Hutu people, who were considered inferior to the Tutsi by the Europeans. In other words, the 'modern' Rwanda created by the Belgians translated artificial racial divisions 'into real administrative

---

[56] Prunier, *From Genocide to Continental War*, p. xxix.
[57] Des Forges, *Leave None to Tell the Story*, p. 116.
[58] Claudine Vidal, 'De la religion subie au modernisme refusé: "Théophagie", ancêtres clandestins et résistance populaire au Rwanda' [Religion subjected to unwanted modernism: 'Theophagy', Clandestine Ancestors and Popular Resistance in Rwanda], *Archives des Sciences Sociales des Religions*, 38 (1974) 63–90 (p. 82).
[59] Ibid., p. 81.
[60] Ibid., p. 82.

policies',[61] resulting in growing resentment and hatred of Tutsi among Hutu. Rwanda may not have been the utopia portrayed by today's leaders,[62] but as Prunier notes, 'there is no trace in its precolonial history of systematic violence between Tutsi and Hutu.[63] Yet by the time of the Hutu revolution (1959–61), ethnic violence reached a peak as hundreds of Tutsi were massacred, while tens of thousands more fled in fear for their lives. As Rwanda made its way to independence, an essentially racist Hutu government was backed by the Belgian authorities.[64] From the late 1950s until the genocide, Tutsi people faced systematic dehumanisation as the Hamitic myth was reformulated by Hutu extremists who emphasised the exploitative nature of Tutsi rule during the pre-colonial period and considered Tutsi to be an 'outsider' group who had invaded Rwanda.[65] The idea that the Hutu were the 'natural inhabitants' of the land formed the basis of the genocidal ideology and propaganda was used to spread lies about the Tutsi, deeming them inherently evil, foreign conquerors.[66]

As I argue in Chapter 2, the post-genocide government has attempted to respond to the identity crisis caused by colonialism, but Rwandan people continue to experience the neo-imperial demonisation of their identities. For example, in an analysis of news coverage of the Rwanda crisis in the United States, Melissa Wall identifies five overall themes:

1. The Rwanda violence was the result of irrational tribalism.
2. Rwandan people are little better than animals, ranging from the barbaric to the helpless and pathetic.

---

[61] Prunier, *The Rwanda Crisis*, p. 38.

[62] Filip Reyntjens, '(Re-)imagining a Reluctant Post-Genocide Society: The Rwandan Patriotic Front's Ideology and Practice', *Journal of Genocide Research*, 18. 1 (2016), 61–81 (p. 63).

[63] Prunier, *The Rwanda Crisis*, p. 39.

[64] Linda Melvern, *A People Betrayed: The Role of the West In Rwanda's Genocide* (London: Zed Books, 2004), p. 20.

[65] The Hamitic hypothesis is the now discredited theory introduced by European colonists. Missionaries and colonial authorities regarded the division between Hutu and Tutsi not only as the fundamental social division but also as a division between distinct racial groups with the Tutsi viewed as a superior race. The Tutsi were classified as a Hamitic 'race' – a sub-group of the Caucasian race – who had arrived in Rwanda from Somalia or Ethiopia and conquered the Hutu and Twa as a result of their natural superiority. This idea was then used against the Tutsi, who came to be considered foreign and therefore illegitimate citizens.

[66] Jefremovas, *Brickyards to Graveyards*, p. 72.

3. The violence is incomprehensible and, thus, is explained through comparison to biblical myths, supernatural causes, natural disasters or diseases.
4. Neighbouring African countries are just as violent and, thus, unable to help solve Rwanda's problems.
5. Only the West is capable of solving Rwanda's problems.[67]

In her discussion of the second theme Wall notes that, '[When] Rwandans were given a voice, it was only within a framework that consistently presented them as pathetic and helpless victims, as insensate, animal-like creatures or as barbaric savages.'[68] Similar themes have been identified in testimonial literature. Madeleine Hron analysed the perpetrator testimonies in Jean Hatzfeld's *Machete Season* and observed that the Rwandans presented in the book were generally portrayed as primitive, rather than psychologically complex.[69] Overall, she concludes that the text reflects Western clichés of Africa as a dark and dangerous place.[70] Similarly, chapter 5 of this book shows a tendency to omit criticisms of the West in published translations of survivor testimonies, making them appear as passive, voiceless victims of inevitable, unstoppable violence.[71] President Paul Kagame also recognises this reductionist tendency in international representations of Rwanda, stating that: '[D]espite accelerating globalisation, our continent is still perceived as a place apart, an alternate dimension of the human experience, at once faceless, passive, and dangerous.'[72] When put in this context, it can be seen that the genocide was in fact a product of a much more complex, chronic form of trauma – caused by colonialism and the destruction of identity – that continues even today.

---

[67] Melissa Wall, 'An Analysis of News Magazine Coverage of the Rwanda Crisis in the United States', in *The Media and the Rwanda Genocide*, ed. by Allan Thompson (London: Pluto Press, 2007), pp. 261–73 (p. 265).

[68] Ibid., pp. 266–7.

[69] Madelaine Hron, '*Gukora and Itsembatsemba*: The "Ordinary Killers" in Jean Hatzfeld's *Machete Season*', *Research in African Literatures*, 42. 2 (2011), 125–46 (p. 141). See Chapter 5 for more discussion of Hatzfeld's work.

[70] Ibid., p. 136.

[71] See also Williamson, 'Posttraumatic Growth at the International Level', p. 36.

[72] François Soudan, *Kagame: Conversations with the President of Rwanda* (New York: Enigma Books, 2015), pp. 127–8.

The Trauma of Western Therapy

The paucity of resources, personnel and infrastructure to 'treat' people suffering from PTSD constitute significant challenges, even if we were to accept the validity of the concept. According to Isaura Zelaya Favila, all of Rwanda's psychiatrists left during the war; there was just one in 2005 and by 2008 only three psychiatrists practiced in the country.[73] While the 'psychiatric infrastructure had never been good', after 1994 it was 'practically nonexistent'.[74] Leaving aside the obvious criticism that trauma programmes established by international NGOs represented a culturally insensitive Western philosophy, these programmes also 'lacked coherence and coordination between, and within, humanitarian, military and political endeavour'.[75] But of course in addition to infrastructural concerns, the main psychosocial trauma and recovery interventions are still dominated by the Western medical model. For example, most programmes are under the coordination of the Ministry of Health and among the main aims of Rwanda's National Trauma Recovery Centre is the provision of '*outpatient clinical* services to severely traumatised children, adults, and families'.[76] But, in my opinion, to treat Rwandan genocide survivors with an event-based understanding is to ignore the chronic trauma of colonialism. Moreover, the imposition of a Western model may even exacerbate, rather than remedy, trauma by assuming the superiority of outside models and negating indigenous treatments and understandings.

During a fieldtrip to Rwanda, I visited a traditional doctor, Muganga (Doctor) Rutangarwamaboko, who is the founder of the Rwandan Cultural Health Centre LTD.[77] Rutangarwamaboko trained in Western clinical psychology at Rwanda's National University in Butare and began his career practicing what he grudgingly refers to as 'conventional' (i.e. Western) psychotherapy. During our meeting at the Centre, he retold an experience which led him to move away

---

[73] Isaura Zelaya Favila, 'Treatment of Post-Traumatic Stress Disorder in Post-Genocide Rwanda' (Global Grassroots Report, 2009). www.globalgrassroots.org/pdf/PTSD-Rwanda.pdf (accessed 4 December 2017), p. 2.

[74] Ibid., p. 3.

[75] Ibid., p. 3. For a more detailed discussion of therapy programmes in Rwanda, see the Conclusion to this volume.

[76] Luc Chauvin, James Mugaju and Jondoh Comlavi, 'Evaluation of the Psychosocial Trauma Recovery Program in Rwanda' *Evaluation and Programming Planning*, 21. 4 (1998), 385–92 (p. 387) [my emphasis].

[77] I spoke with Muganga Rutangarwamaboko during a fieldtrip on 7 July 2016.

from Western models in favour of therapies rooted in tradition. Rutangarwamaboko was working in a hospital as a psychotherapist where he met a 'patient' who was suffering with 'depression'. After much consultation, the man reluctantly spoke but all he could say was that he wanted to leave the hospital as it was 'not the place to cure him'. Rutangarwamaboko eventually discovered the cause of this man's 'depression': he had killed a wagtail. This action constituted a violation of *kirazira* (taboo) because the wagtail is the sacred bird of the *Abagesera* clan. This breaking of taboo was causing him acute psychological turbulence because, as Rutangarwamaboko put it, the man's spirituality had been 'poisoned'.

Taboos are a fundamental part of Rwandan culture that were gradually eroded by colonialism.[78] The genocide itself constituted the ultimate violation of taboo. Before 1994, it had been customary to engage in various ceremonies of linkage. *Kunywana* (drinking together), for example, refers to the ritual of drinking the blood of a friend or neighbour. Participating parties believed they were sharing each other's life, thereby making an *igihango*, a vow or promise of linkage. A similar bonding practice was that of *kugabira*, the giving of cows. Cows (*inka*) hold a sacred position in Rwandan culture and are considered a source of wealth and survival and – like *kunywana* – the gift of a cow implicated two Rwandans in each other's lives. When, during the genocide, neighbours turned on neighbours, friends turned on friends, and family members turned on family members, these bonds were destroyed, constituting extreme *kirazira* (taboo).

Rutangarwamaboko proposes a triadic model for understanding the human being that ties in with the idea of violating taboos. His model consists in a soul, a spirit and a body (see Figure 1.1).[79] The soul is a person's reason; their thoughts and ideas. The spirit is their religiosity; their morality and, above all, their culture. According to Rutangarwamaboko, the breaking of taboos violates a person's culture, thereby poisoning their spirit and causing a troubled soul. This may eventually result in physiological problems in the body, such as psychosomatic aches and pains. To alleviate the pain of the trauma sufferer's spirit, soul and body, Rutangarwamaboko attempts to reconnect people with their

---

[78] This is reflected in the Rwandan expression: *Kiliziya yakuye kirazira* (the Church abolished taboos).

[79] Muganga Rutangarwamaboko's Facebook page can be found at: www.facebook .com/Rwandan-Cultural-Health-Centre-RCHCLtd-324458897613722/ (accessed 4 December 2017).

Figure 1.1 Image of Rwandan Cultural Health Centre logo depicting Muganga Rutangarwamaboko's theory which led him to found Rwandan Cultural Psychotherapy (RCP). Rutangarwamaboko has used this method to cure patients who became unwell from the violation of *kirazira* (taboo) and who were treated unsuccessfully using Western therapies

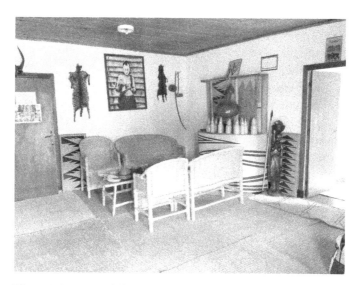

Figure 1.2 Image of the Rwandan Cultural Health Centre (main reception area)

culture (i.e., their spirit). He told me that the disconnection with past traditions and beliefs is such that many Rwandans who visit his Centre fear that it is a satanic place when they see the traditional setting (see Figures 1.2–1.4). But, Rutangarwamaboko insists that the only way to address the long-term trauma of colonialism and identity destruction is to reconnect Rwandan people with their traditions. In his words, 'if you have no culture, you have nothing'.

Figure 1.3 Image of the Rwandan Cultural Health Centre (table with traditional utensils)

Figure 1.4 Image of the Rwandan Cultural Health Centre (display of traditional medicines and devices for preparing them)

Western sceptics may argue that Rutangarwamaboko's model has no empirical basis.[80] However, it seems to me that his model offers a greater degree of understanding of the long-term traumatic experiences of Rwandan people than the Western medical, event-based model. However, it is not only trauma theory's Eurocentrism and narrow understanding of trauma that are potentially damaging in Rwanda. Trauma theory's insistence on trauma's unknowability and unrepresentability is also likely to be harmful in the authoritarian climate of the post-genocide period.

Authoritarian Trauma

Since 1994, the Rwandan government has launched a campaign to eradicate genocide ideology.[81] According to the government, there are no Hutu or Tutsi ethnic groups; there are only 'Rwandans'. While in Chapter 2 I show that the government's ideology is in many ways positive, it is not without problems. New crimes such as 'divisionism' and 'ethnic ideology' have been added to the penal code and, although the use of the terms 'Hutu' and 'Tutsi' is not explicitly forbidden, 'Rwandans interpret these laws as mostly requiring public silence regarding ethnicity.'[82] At least officially, Rwandan society is no longer divided according to ethnicity, however, unofficial divisions and tensions continue to exist between Hutu and Tutsi, moderates and extremists, old and new caseload returnees and even between Tutsi returnees and genocide survivors.[83] The eradication of ethnicity in favour of a single Rwandan identity is, according to many, used by the government to mask the fact that a small group of anglophone Tutsi returnees

---

[80] Western political critics might also argue that his methods echo the government's nostalgia about Rwanda's precolonial past, e.g. Reyntjens, '(Re-) imagining', pp. 63–5.

[81] Helen Hintjens, 'Post-Genocide Identity Politics in Rwanda', *Ethnicities*, 8. 5 (2008), 5–41 (p. 10).

[82] Nigel Eltringham, 'The Past Is Elsewhere: The Paradoxes of Proscribing Ethnicity in Post-Genocide Rwanda', in *Remaking Rwanda: State Building and Human Rights after Mass Violence (Critical Human Rights)*, ed. by Scott Straus and Lars Waldorf (Madison, WI: University of Wisconsin Press, 2011), pp. 269–82 (p. 274).

[83] Heather B. Hamilton, 'Rwanda's Women: The Key to Reconstruction', *The Journal of Humanitarian Assistance* (2000). www.jha.ac/greatlakes/b001.htm (accessed 4 December 2017), p. 12.

monopolises positions of power.[84] In Longman's view, '[T]he RPF now rules Rwanda, and Tutsi enjoy extensive benefits, holding government offices, school positions, and other opportunities far out of proportion to their percentage of the population.' In contrast, the 'majority Hutu now must live in fear of being accused of involvement in the genocide and facing imprisonment'.[85] According to Filip Reyntjens, those who question the official version of events are at risk of being labelled 'divisionist' and considered to harbour 'genocide ideology'[86] while the Tutsi-dominated government attempts to convince the population of its own 'moral rectitude and right to rule'.[87] Thus, to cite Prunier, '"[N]ational reconciliation" [has come] to take on a very peculiar coded meaning. It mean[s] in fact the passive acceptance of undivided Tutsi power over an obedient Hutu mass.'[88]

Yet while the government is predominantly made up of Tutsi, genocide survivors do not exactly benefit from the regime. It is true that the Hutu population is frequently treated as collectively guilty for the genocide,[89] but survivors must bear the weight of collective traumatisation. As Helen Hintjens observes, although 'Tutsi have been elevated [from scapegoats] to victims, [this is] not always a flattering image, nor an easy one with which to live'.[90] Unlike Tutsi returnees, genocide survivors are generally not in positions of political power. They also have limited access to social resources – as Anne-Marie de Brouwer and Sandra Ka Hon Chu observe – with so many of their loved ones dead, survivors have had to forge a solitary path.[91] One might expect the predominantly Tutsi social elite to be sympathetic with Tutsi genocide survivors, but, in Reyntjens' view, Tutsi survivors feel as if they

---

[84] Reynjens, '(Re-)imagining', p. 67.
[85] Timothy Longman, 'Identity Cards, Ethnic Self-Perception, and Genocide in Rwanda', in *Documenting Individual Identity: The Development of State Practices in the Modern World*, ed. by Jane Caplan and John Torpey (Princeton, NJ: Princeton University Press, 2001), pp. 345–59 (p. 346).
[86] According to Reyntjens, alternative historical accounts cannot be articulated, at least not in the public arena, Reyntjens, '(Re-)imagining', p. 64.
[87] Longman and Rutagengwa, 'Memory, Identity, and Community', p. 162.
[88] Prunier, *From Genocide to Continental War*, p. 23.
[89] Nigel Eltringham, *Accounting for Horror: Post-genocide Debates in Rwanda* (London: Pluto Press, 2004), p. 69.
[90] Hintjens, 'Reconstructing Political Identities', p. 87.
[91] Anne-Marie de Brouwer and Sandra Ka Hon Chu, *The Men Who Killed Me: Rwandan Survivors of Sexual Violence* (Vancouver: Douglas & McIntyre, 2009), p. 145.

have been side-lined by the RPF.[92] Described by returnees as *bapfuye bahagaze* meaning 'the walking dead' and often looked upon with suspicion, survivors are generally marginalised.[93] According to Heather Hamilton, they feel as if they are being asked by returnees to 'forget and forgive too quickly'.[94] In turn, survivors have been reported to 'voice resentment against the returnees, including those in government, and criticise them for, among other issues: neglecting the problems of the genocide survivors; falsely denouncing the survivors as genocide "collaborators"; [and] illegally appropriating the land and property of the survivors'.[95] According to Prunier, one RPF ideologue even declared that 'the "interior" Tutsi deserved what happened to them'.[96]

Survivors also face stigmatisation because, as Alexandre Dauge-Roth suggests, they 'embody a disturbing memory, which revives a chapter of Rwanda's history that most people would like to see closed'.[97] In his book on Rwandan testimonial literature, Dauge-Roth discusses how a number of survivors have become aware of their unwanted and disturbing presence in a country that is so desperate to move on. For example, although just nine years old in 1994, an orphan of the genocide presented in Yolande Mukagasana's *Les blessures du silence* (Wounds of silence) states in relation to survivors: 'Personne ne nous aime. Nous sommes devenus un problème de la société rwandaise' (No one likes us. We have become a problem in Rwandan society).[98] Similarly, in *La Fleur de Stéphanie* (Stephanie's

---

[92] Reyntjens, 'Rwanda, Ten Years On', p. 180.
[93] Prunier, *From Genocide to Continental War*, p. 3.
[94] Hamilton, 'Rwanda's Women', p. 12.
[95] After the genocide, women survivors had no legal right to claim the property, land or bank accounts of deceased male relatives, making it easier for returnees to appropriate these assets. Survivors were also viewed with mistrust by returnees who assumed that survivors must have collaborated in the genocide in order to have survived. Human Rights Watch/Africa, Human Rights Watch Women's Project, Fédération Internationale des Ligues des Droits de l'Homme, *Shattered Lives: Sexual Violence During the Rwandan Genocide and Its Aftermath* (New York: Human Rights Watch, 1996), p. 3.
[96] Prunier, *From Genocide to Continental War*, p. 19.
[97] Alexandre Dauge-Roth, *Writing and Filming the Genocide of the Tutsis in Rwanda: Dismembering and Remembering Traumatic History* (Lanham/Plymouth: Lexington Books, 2010), p. 8.
[98] Yolande Mukagasana, *Les blessures du silence. Témoignages du génocide au Rwanda* (Arles: Actes Sud and Médecins Sans Frontières, 2001), p. 110. Cited in English in Dauge-Roth, *Writing and Filming the Genocide*, p. 262.

flower) Esther Mujawayo makes it clear that she shares this awareness of survivors being a disturbance:

Depuis un certain temps, déjà, des politiciens ou des citoyens anonymes nous
suggèrent, par un bruissement de lèvres excédé, qu'"il faut qu'on avance tous
maintenant. Oui, "ça" s'est passé, et on comprend que c'est terrible pour
vous, mais il faut qu'on avance tous maintenant'... Alors, c'est certain, ils [les
rescapés] encombrent. Tu as un pays qui doit avancer et toi, le survivant, tu
es un peu la tumeur qui l'empêche de se prétendre en bonne santé.

(Some politicians and anonymous citizens are suggesting, by an annoyed
smacking of their lips, that 'we must all move on now. Yes "it" happened
and we understand it's terrible for you, but we must all move on'. Certainly
[... survivors] are an encumbrance. You have a country that needs to move
on and you, the survivor, you are a little bit like the tumour that prevents it
from claiming it is healthy).[99]

Further evidence suggesting that there is a certain discomfort surrounding genocide survivors may be found in the testimony of Innocent
Rwililiza in Jean Hatzfeld's *Dans le nu de la vie* (Into the quick of life):

Moi, je vois qu'aujourd'hui il y a toujours une gêne à parler des rescapés,
même au sein des Rwandais, même au sein des Tutsi. Je pense que tout le
monde voudrait bien que, d'une certaine façon, les rescapés aillent se mettre
à l'écart du génocide. Comme si on voulait qu'ils laissent à d'autres, qui
n'ont pas risqué de se faire tailler directement à coup de machette, la tâche
de s'en occuper. Comme si nous étions dorénavant un peu de trop... Nous,
les rescapés, on devient plus étrangers, dans notre propre pays que nous
n'avons jamais quitté, que tous les étrangers et expatriés qui nous regardent
avec les yeux inquiets.

(I see today that there is still uneasiness in talking about survivors, even
among Rwandans, even among Tutsis. I think that everyone would like the
survivors to relinquish the genocide, in a way. As if people wanted them to
leave the task of dealing with it to others, who have never been in direct
danger of being sliced up by machete. As if we were now somewhat super-
fluous... We survivors, we are growing more like strangers in our own
land – which we have never left – than all the foreigners and expatriates
who consider us with such anxiety.)[100]

---

[99] Esther Mujawayo and Souâd Belhaddad, *La Fleur de Stéphanie: Rwanda
entre réconciliation et déni* (Paris: [Éditions] Flammarion, 2006), p. 217.
Cited in English in Dauge-Roth, *Writing and Filming the Genocide*, p. 251.

[100] Jean Hatzfeld, *Dans le nu de la vie: récits des marais rwandais* (Paris: Éditions
du Seuil, 2000), pp. 107, 111. Cited in English in Dauge-Roth, *Writing and
Filming the Genocide*, p. 9.

According to Dauge-Roth, 'survivors like him [Rwililiza] are seen as a parasitic presence today, a disturbance that prevents others from fully embracing the present by obliterating the traumatic legacy of the geno- cide'.[101] In response to the suspicion surrounding them and the pres- sure to 'move on', Burnet observes how survivors have learnt to cope with their violent memories by adopting the culturally appropriate coping mechanism of silence by avoiding crying or sharing their pain- ful memories.[102] Those who do express their pain may be 'labelled "insane", "addled" or "traumatised"'.[103] As the following analysis of testimonies suggests, Caruth's insistence that trauma can never be 'fully known'[104] or referenced directly is particularly frustrating in a context where survivors face multiple forms of stigmatisation and are encouraged to 'move on' and adopt silence as a form of coping.[105]

Stigma and Silence

This stigmatisation of survivors and the corresponding response of silence are closely linked to the government's emphasis on progress and development. Since 1994, the RPF has run an ambitious eco- nomic programme, epitomised by its *Vision 2020*, which aims to transform agriculture, develop an efficient private sector, improve education, health, ICT and infrastructure as well as promote regional economic integration.[106] Rwanda has achieved enviable economic growth every year since the genocide and made significant steps towards achieving its United Nations (UN) Millennium Development Goals. Considering its economy was 'non-existent'[107] in the immedi- ate aftermath of the genocide, the country has made unfathomable progress. In its 2016 Doing Business report, the World Bank ranked Rwanda 62nd worldwide, second in Sub-Saharan Africa and in first place for low-income countries worldwide.[108] In the Africa Prosperity Report by UK-based think tank, the Legatum Institute, Rwanda was

---

[101] Ibid., pp. 8–9.
[102] Burnet, *Genocide Lives in Us*, p. 116.
[103] Ibid., p. 78.
[104] Cathy Caruth, *Unclaimed Experience*, p. 6.
[105] Burnet, *Genocide Lives in Us*, p. 78.
[106] Reyntjens, '(Re-)imagining', pp. 71–2.
[107] Prunier, *The Rwanda Crisis*, p. 327.
[108] World bank, *Doing Business Report*. www.doingbusiness.org/rankings (accessed 4 December 2017).

deemed to have 'the biggest Prosperity Surplus' (i.e., it was the country that has most improved) in Africa.[109] This result, according to the report, 'speaks to the enduring importance of good governance and in particular, rule of law, effective government, and regulation as a means of unlocking prosperity' which has ultimately meant that the country has 'delivered a lot with very little'.[110]

Yet in Reyntjens' view, the government's 'ambitions go far beyond governance and the economy. Indeed, they aim to radically transform social relations, identities, space and the outlook and behaviour of individual Rwandans'.[111] This 'modernising project is being implemented at a fast pace, and it is topdown' with people encouraged to 'kwihutisha amajyambere' (hurry-up progress), epitomised by the motto, 'Birashoboka' (everything is possible).[112] The government's policies are, in Reyntjens' view, 'informed by a condescending attitude towards peasants [whose] poverty is seen as a direct result of their lack of economic acumen and their laziness'.[113] This attitude is echoed generally by the elite. For example, a Kigali banker once told me he believed that 'poverty is a state of mind'. A guide at the Kigali Genocide Memorial Centre informed me that, in the face of this 'narrative of progress', survivors feel unable to complain about their problems. He told me that even during commemoration events, the focus is no longer on remembering the genocide, but on celebrating achievement.[114] He explained that he cannot reveal the level of trauma he is suffering and feels obliged to conceal it. As the following analysis of survivor testimonies demonstrates, this is not an uncommon response. Despite seemingly insurmountable difficulties – orphanhood, poverty, physical disability, sexual violence, HIV/AIDS infection, and the trauma of survivorhood itself – there is pressure on survivors to hide their challenges and sing to the government's song of 'progress'.

---

[109] Legatum Institute, *Africa Prosperity Report* (2016). https://lif.blob.core.windows.net/lif/docs/default-source/publications/2016-africa-prosperity-report-pdf.pdf?sfvrsn=2 (accessed 4 December 2017), (p. 27).

[110] Ibid., pp. 2, 27.

[111] Reyntjens, '(Re-)imagining', p. 72

[112] Ibid., p. 72.

[113] Ibid.

[114] See for example, Eugene Kwibuka, 'Twenty-Two Years Later, Rwandans Talk of Liberation Fruits', *The New Times*, 4 July 2016. www.newtimes.co.rw/section/article/2016-07-04/201387/ (accessed 4 December 2017).

Orphanhood

Kayisire, for example, lost both her parents during the genocide and had to face life as an orphan. Despite her difficulties, Kayisire found it impossible to share her strife with others:

In my studies, at no point did I repeat the year. I completed secondary school even though I had problems like that. But nobody, not even my fellow students, knew that I had such problems. No one could know that I was an orphan because I thought that something called 'an orphan' was like an insult because when you are an orphan you are discredited.

The deliberate concealment of her orphan status is a form of what Erving Goffman refers to as 'passing'. Stigmatising attributes which are not visible or noticeable are described by Goffman as 'discreditable'.[115] Goffman argues that individuals bearing a discreditable stigma must learn to manage information about the stigma by attempting to conceal it so as to promote normal interaction with others.[116] Even while talking overtly about the topic in her testimony, Kayisire refers to her orphanhood first as 'problems like that' then 'such problems' before actually uttering the word 'orphan'.

Physical Manifestations of Genocide

Survivors take similar steps to avoid revealing the physical manifestations of the violence they experienced. During the genocide, Mupenzi was shot in the face which has left her with a lasting disfigurement as well as other enduring health problems, such as headaches, causing her to describe herself as an 'ikimuga' (handicapped person) who 'mpora ndwaye' (is always sick). Just as Kayisire conceals her orphan status, Mupenzi wears a scarf to mask the lower half of her face:

I always wear it [the cloth]. Unless someone asked me to show her or him how my jaw looks. But even if someone asks me to show them, sometimes I don't agree. It depends on who it is... Otherwise, I always put on this piece of cloth.

Disguising her disfigurement using a scarf is an example of what Goffman refers to as 'covering'.[117] In contrast to non-visible,

---

[115] Erving Goffman, *Stigma: Notes on the Management of Spoiled Identity* (Englewood Cliffs, NJ: Prentice-Hall, 1963), p. 57.
[116] Ibid., p. 125.
[117] Ibid., pp. 125–8.

discreditable stigmas, such as Kayisire's orphanhood, stigmatising attributes which are visible, known about or obtrusive (e.g., because they interfere with the flow of interaction, such as a stutter) are described by Goffman as 'discredited'.[118] While individuals bearing a discreditable stigma must implement an information management strategy ('passing') to conceal their stigma, individuals bearing a discredited stigma must adopt a strategy for managing the tension that their stigma causes in social situations. So called 'covering' is when individuals make efforts to prevent their stigma from 'looming large' in order to reduce this tension by making it easier for both the individual and others to draw attention away from the stigma and sustain spontaneous involvement in the official content of the interaction.[119]

Sexual Violence and HIV/AIDS

One form of violence that has left genocide survivors in particularly difficult positions in post-genocide Rwanda is sexual violence. Sexual violence was rampant during the genocide, affecting almost all surviving women in some way.[120] Furthermore, an estimated 70 per cent of all rape victims were infected with the HIV/AIDS virus.[121] Patricia Weitsman argues that rape is a particularly potent form of torture in patriarchal societies like Rwanda because women's standing derives from their relationships to men. In such societies, a woman's value derives from her sexual 'purity' and, once raped, society no longer deems her marriageable or socially acceptable.[122] Survivors of sexual violence have been reported to perceive themselves as dirty, morally inferior and ashamed.[123] HIV infection is also stigmatised in Rwandan society because of its associations with sex and

[118] Ibid., p. 57.
[119] Ibid., p. 125.
[120] Organisation of African Unity, *Rwanda: The Preventable Genocide* (Addis Ababa: OAU, 2000), para. 16.20.
[121] Catharine Newbury and Hannah Baldwin, *Aftermath: Women in Postgenocide Rwanda* (U.S. Agency for International Development, 2000). http://pdf.usaid. gov/pdf_docs/pnacj323.pdf (accessed 4 December 2017), p. 70.
[122] Patricia A. Weitsman, 'The Politics of Identity and Sexual Violence: A Review of Bosnia and Rwanda', *Human Rights Quarterly*, 30. 3 (2008), 561–78 (p. 564).
[123] Donatilla Mukamana and Petra Brysiewicz, 'The Lived Experience of Genocide Rape Survivors in Rwanda', *Journal of Nursing Scholarship*, 40. 4 (2008), 379–84 (pp. 380–3); Weitsman, 'The Politics of Identity and Sexual Violence', p. 382.

promiscuity, which are considered immoral.[124] These negative stereotypes associated with victims of sexual violence can lead to discrimination, causing them to be ostracised and excluded from both their
families and their communities.[125] Amnesty International reports that
this discrimination can result in loss of employment, difficulty in
asserting property rights and a loss of civil and political rights.[126]

Despite the high proportion of women who were raped during
the genocide, the stigma surrounding sexual violence has resulted
in many survivors being reluctant to admit to having been sexually
assaulted for fear of such discrimination.[127] Unfortunately, this
reluctance to come forward results in women survivors being mis-
trusted. As Human Rights Watch discover in their interviews with
Annunciata Nyiratamba of the *Association des Veuves du Génocide
d'Avril* (Association of April Genocide Widows – AVEGA), there is
always the unspoken question asked of survivors: 'What did you do
to survive?'[128] Thus, even if a woman survivor does not openly admit
to being raped, she may not be believed by others in her community
and may, therefore, still face negative stereotyping and discrimination.[129] The stigma associated with sexual violence may be observed
in the following extract from the testimony of Nakabonye in which
she discusses her sister's experiences during the genocide:

– She died after the genocide. She got sick and passed away.
– As they took Antoinette back and forth... Did they rape her?
– They did bad things to her... They killed her badly, though she
  didn't die in the genocide, it's like... She didn't live long after the
  genocide. She died right after the genocide.

[124] Amnesty International, *Rwanda: 'Marked for Death': Rape Survivors Living
with HIV/AIDS* (Amnesty International Report, 2004), p. 25.
[125] African Rights, *Rwanda: Broken Bodies, Torn Spirits: Living with Genocide,
Rape and HIV/AIDS* (African Rights Report, Rwanda, 2004), p. 68; Amnesty
International, *Rwanda: 'Marked for Death'*, p. 7; Hamilton, 'Rwanda's
Women', p. 4; Human Rights Watch, *Shattered Lives*, pp. 72–5; Mukamana
and Brysiewicz, 'The Lived Experience of Genocide', pp. 380–3.
[126] Amnesty International, *Rwanda: 'Marked for Death'*, p. 2.
[127] African Rights, *Rwanda: Death, Despair and Defiance* (London: African
Rights, 1995), p. 749; Hamilton, 'Rwanda's Women', p. 4; Women's
Commission for Refugee Women and Children, *Rwanda's Women and
Children: The Long Road to Reconciliation* (New York: Women's
Commission, 1997), p. 8.
[128] Human Rights Watch, *Shattered Lives*, p. 3.
[129] Amnesty International, *Rwanda: 'Marked for Death'*, p. 25.

- Was her death related to what happened to her during the genocide?
- Absolutely. It is very much related. She got very sick and... She had sworn to never marry. She said, 'I will never marry ever! Why would I marry? Emerthe, you married but have no husband.' She hated herself. She had no more trust in life anymore.
- Was she infected?
- Yes, she was infected. They infected her with incurable diseases. That's what killed her.
- The virus?
- They infected her with HIV. They would come to take her and she would say... They would come and do to her whatever they wanted... At one point, they ordered us to stay in that house... where we are currently staying. 'Stay there. We'll protect you'. They told us. And we stayed. That's where they would find us. And they came in shifts. One group after another. There were so many *Interahamwe*. A single move and you would bump into another *Interahamwe*. And they did whatever they wanted, wherever and whenever they found you.
- Did what happened to Antoinette happen to you, too?
- Yes, exactly.

In this extract, both the interviewer and Nakabonye avoid making direct references to either sexual violence or HIV/AIDS. Although translated as 'did they rape her', the interviewer in fact says, 'baramukoreraga ibya mfura mbi?' which could more accurately be translated as, 'did they commit violence against her?' Nakabonye replies simply that they did 'bad things'. Despite this indirect use of language, it is clear that both Nakabonye and the interviewer know that they are talking about sexual violence. Similar uses of indirect, euphemistic language are found in this extract when Nakabonye and the interviewer talk about HIV/AIDS, referring to Nakabonye's sister as 'infected' with the 'virus' or 'incurable diseases'. It takes several exchanges of indirect language between them before finally Nakabonye uses the word 'HIV' to clarify their discussion. What is particularly interesting about this extract is that, at the end, we see that Nakabonye is in fact telling her sister's story to relay her own experience. The interviewer and Nakabonye engage in a form of collective 'covering', combining indirect language with the story of Nakabonye's sister as a proxy to explain an experience that, in fact, happened to Nakabonye herself. This collaborative effort serves to reduce the tension caused by the stigma surrounding sexual violence and HIV/AIDS and enables Nakabonye to communicate her experience. The 'covering' behaviour used by Nakabonye could also be considered a strategy for avoiding the position of victim as, in addition to the stigma of sexual violence, physical scars and orphanhood, survivors also face negative stereotypes surrounding their survivor status.

Survivorhood

The recognition of this stigma surrounding survivors may be observed in the testimony of Nikuze, who recounts a time when a woman from AVEGA approached her. She explains that her initial reaction was to avoid this woman and to refuse to believe that she could have anything in common with her. Nikuze states: 'She told me she was also a genocide widow. But from the way she was, there was no way I could start conversing with her.' In her account, Nikuze makes it clear that other survivors react to each other in similar ways:

Everybody fights on her own. Ever since I started living there; it was in 1997 or 1998 up to now I haven't seen any kind of co-operation as far as exchanging ideas or any other kind of togetherness between survivors may be concerned. I have never seen it; everyone lives on her own.

This avoidance of other survivors could be interpreted as a form of social withdrawal or social isolation which is a strategy that stigmatised individuals often adopt in order to reduce problematic interactions.[130] In Nikuze's case, her social withdrawal and avoidance of other survivors could be considered a form of disidentification or dissociation from her social identity as a survivor.[131] Indeed, many of the survivors attempt to conceal their survivor identities altogether by adopting the information management strategy of passing. Kayisire,

---

[130] Edward E. Jones, Amerigo Farina, Albert H. Hastorf, Hazel Markus, Dale T. Miller and Robert A. Scott, *Social Stigma: The Psychology of Marked Relationships* (New York: W. H. Freeman and Company, 1984), pp. 200–2.

[131] Jennifer Crocker, Brenda Major and Claude Steele, 'Social Stigma', in *The Handbook of Social Psychology*, ed. by Daniel T. Gilbert, Susan T. Fiske and Gardner Lindzay, 3 vols (Boston, MA: McGraw-Hill, 1998), II, pp. 504–53 pp. 528–30; Goffman, *Stigma*, p. 60.

for example, conceals not only her orphanhood but also her identity as a survivor by lying about the source of her physical scars:

One of [the killers] joked asking about the different ways of killing a snake, then another one said that you hit it on the head.[132] They started hitting me on the head, there is a scar but I lie to people, and tell them that it is a birthmark.

A further inspection of Mupenzi's testimony also reveals that not only does she 'cover' to reduce the tension caused by her discredited stigma of disfigurement, but much like Kayisire, she also 'passes' to conceal her identity as a genocide survivor. As can be seen in the following citation, she refers to her experiences of genocide as an 'accident':

Several things have changed in my life. Before 1994, I hadn't had this accident... In my life today, I am living as a handicapped person. I cannot do anything on my own because I am always sick. I simply live as a handicapped person and I will live like that for my entire life.

Here, rather than presenting herself as a genocide survivor who was injured, Mupenzi presents herself as a person who became sick as the result of an 'accident'. This focus on 'sickness' rather than on the genocide or survivorhood could be interpreted as an example of what Margaret Shih describes as drawing on an alternate identity, where individuals strategically emphasise one identity over another in an attempt to reduce the negative effects of a stigmatised identity.[133]

Overall, survivors seem to adopt a variety of strategies to conceal the impact of the genocide on their lives. In her work on the effects of trauma and victimisation, Ronnie Janoff-Bulman argues that there is no cultural role for survivors except as outsiders. She suggests that victims of violence are often avoided because societies tend to emphasise success and happiness and de-emphasise failure and suffering.[134] The victim of violence, she argues, is an invisible person, an individual who is not culturally acknowledged, a person who is avoided or

---

[132] Extremist propaganda frequently characterized Tutsi as 'snakes' before (and during) the genocide as a means to dehumanize them. Melvern, *A People Betrayed*, p. 227.

[133] Margaret Shih, 'Examining Resilience and Empowerment in Overcoming Stigma', *Annals of the American Academy of Political and Social Science*, 591 (2004), 175–85 (pp. 179–80).

[134] Ronnie Janoff-Bulman, *Shattered Assumptions: Towards a New Psychology of Trauma* (New York: The Free Press, 1992), p. 154.

unnoticed by others.[135] In the Rwandan context, this type of discrimination is recognised by Mujawayo who states 'quand tu sens que la
société veut clore le lourd chapitre du génocide, parfois en trépignant,
tu comprends que les rescapés, eux, resteront en marge' (when you
sense that your society wants to close the heavy chapter of the genocide, sometimes by rushing the process, you understand that survivors
will remain in the margins).[136]

Defying Silence, Defying Theory

Not all survivors yield to the pressure to be silent. Adopting a different stigma management strategy to those above, Sebasoni overtly
defies her stigmatised position as a survivor by saying: 'I do not constitute a burden to the Rwandan society or to the people around me.'
Similarly, Kameya says about survivors, 'We are not a burden to the
country, we are a blessing.' Bukumura sees his physical scar in a very
different way to Kayisire or Mupenzi. He was offered the opportunity
to have it removed, but he refused:

I told those people that my scar would stay as a souvenir of the genocide,
because I personally don't find it easy to forget the genocide. Never. I want
to appear in the history of Rwanda. I will never forget what happened to me
and I will tell it to my grandchildren and my great grandchildren. Whoever
will generate from my family will have to learn that genocide is very bad.
I will expose what it was. The way I am now giving you this testimony.

This need to testify is extremely important to many survivors who
feel that the genocide may be forgotten or denied or that survivors
voices should be silenced. Bampiriye, for example, observes how
'some people who speak about the genocide, tend to underestimate its
destruction'. Like Burizihiza, whose testimony is cited in the
Introduction, Bampiriye urges survivors to speak out about their
experiences and encourages people to 'find the time to talk with survivors'. In her view, 'it would be the greatest mistake to keep quiet
about what happened here in Rwanda'. Kabalisa agrees that 'people
should tell their history'. 'We should speak of what we went
through', he continues, 'we should speak of what we saw...people
must dare to speak out about all that, children need to know that

---

[135] Ibid., p. 154.
[136] Mujawayo and Belhaddad, *La Fleur de Stéphanie*, p. 207.

once upon a time people went wild.' Similarly, Kavubi explains how 'joyful [it is] to know that [his] testimony can be watched by children, grandchildren and great-grandchildren'. 'It is a great thing' he says, 'and I ask people who saw what happened, and who are able to say it, to testify, and if possible contribute so that these testimonies may benefit future generations.' Sole survivors feel particularly compelled to break this silence. As Dusabe explains, 'I must bear witness to the genocide because I am the only survivor in my family.'

This testimonial evidence demonstrates that survivors are fighting to have their voices heard above the noise of colonial identity negation, stigmatisation and authoritarianism. The idea of their trauma being unknowable or unrepresentable, it would therefore seem, is far more damaging than it is helpful. Drawing on Kaplan's work, Lizelle Bisschoff and Stefanie Van de Peer 'insist on the possibility of representing trauma' in an African context.[137] The authors remind us of the proliferation of 'representations of African conflicts by non-Africans, [in] for example, mainstream Hollywood films [which use] African atrocities as a backdrop'.[138] They argue that such representations 'have not been useful in creating multi-faceted views of the continent. Rather they have led to the desensitisation of viewers, promoting voyeurism and a type of "atrocity tourism", both real (for example through physically visiting memorial sites) and imaginary (through reading news articles on Africa or watching documentary news footage on television)'.[139] This 'pervasive Western kind of one-dimensional engagement with Africa', they continue, 'runs the risk of flattening the perception of Africa in a single narrative of war, corruption and devastation.'[140] The authors discuss the responsibilities of art, which they argue include the need to 'address the unspeakable' and 'to transport the spectator/reader/listener into the realm of the experience'.[141] The authors share trauma theory's emphasis on the centrality of 'testimony to the art form, whether it is music, visual art, literature or film' but

---

[137] Lizelle Bisschoff and Stefanie Van de Peer, 'Representing the Unrepresentable', in *Art and Trauma in Africa: Representations of Reconciliation in Music, Visual Arts, Literature and Film* ed. by Lizelle Bisschoff and Stefanie van de Peer (London: I. B. Tauris & Co Ltd, 2011), pp. 3–25 (p. 11).

[138] Ibid., p. 5.

[139] Ibid.

[140] Ibid.

[141] Ibid., p. 13.

oppose its notion of unrepresentability and its prescriptivism.[142] In his discussion of representations of the Rwanda genocide, Dauge-Roth agrees that, through testimony, witnesses may 'reclaim on their own terms the meaning of their survival', enabling survivors to 'move from a position of being subjected to political violence to a position that entails the promise of agency'.[143] Dauge-Roth cites the work of Kalí Tal, who asserts that:

> Bearing witness is an aggressive act. It is born out of a refusal to bow to outside pressure to revise or to repress experience, a decision to embrace conflict rather than conformity, to endure a lifetime of anger and pain rather than to submit to the seductive pull of revision and repression... If survivors retain control over the interpretation of their trauma, they can sometimes force a shift in the social and political structure. If the dominant culture manages to appropriate the trauma and can codify it in its own terms, the status quo will remain unchanged.[144]

Thus, by testifying, survivors are able to contest the status quo and gain a voice with potential transformative power, interrupting the dominant understanding of events among a given audience. Often alienated by denial, survivors use testimony in order to be heard and to have their pain and their histories recognised.[145]

Conclusion

In conclusion, it would seem that concepts such as PTSD, belatedness, unknowability and unrepresentability are of limited use in the Rwandan context and may even exacerbate the problems lived by trauma survivors. Specifically, I contend that trauma theory's event-

---

[142] Ibid., p. 12.

[143] Dauge-Roth, *Writing and Filming the Genocide*, p. 42.

[144] Kalí Tal, *Worlds of Hurt: Reading the Literature of Trauma* (New York: Cambridge University Press, 1996), p. 7. Cited in Dauge-Roth, *Writing and Filming the Genocide*, p. 26.

[145] Phil Clark, *The Gacaca Courts, Post-Genocide Justice and Reconciliation in Rwanda: Justice without Lawyers* (Cambridge Studies in Law and Society, Cambridge University Press, 2010), pp. 272–3; Alexandre Dauge-Roth, 'Fostering a Listening Community Through Testimony: Learning with Orphans of the Genocide in Rwanda', *Journal of Community Engagement and Scholarship*, 5. 2 (2012), http://jces.ua.edu/fostering-a-listening-community-through-testimony-learning-with-orphans-of-the-genocide-in-rwanda/ (accessed 4 December 2017), para. 10 of 23.

based Eurocentrism misunderstands the post-colonial, post-genocide Rwandan context and its insistence on trauma's unrepresentability has the potential to reinforce society's demands for silence and perpetuate survivors' state of victimhood. Moreover, trauma theory's emphasis on these negative consequences of trauma offers not only a pessimistic but also an incomplete view, given that research suggests that many individuals also experience positive changes in the wake of tragedy. Therefore, rather than recuperating existing aspects of trauma theory, I call for a change in paradigm altogether. In the chapters that follow, I will attempt to do this by introducing a reading of trauma texts through the lens of post-traumatic growth theory.

2 | Post-Colonial Post-Traumatic Growth in Rwandan Men

Umugabo arigira yakwibura agapfa (Without autonomy, a man dies)

Rwandan proverb

The Rwandese genocide is an example of an atrociously violent leap into some form of modernity [... albeit one that is] far from the ideological dreams of the West.

Gérard Prunier, 2009, pp. xxxvii and 333

The concept of positive transformation resulting from human suffering has been recognised throughout history and across cultures.[1] The writings and ideas of ancient Egyptians, Greeks and Hebrews as well as many early religions – including Buddhism, Hinduism, Christianity and Islam – have all addressed the possibility of good resulting from trauma and suffering.[2] Positive changes following adversity have also been a recurrent theme in European literature,[3] as well as in the

---

[1] Katie Splevins, Keren Cohen, Jake Bowley and Stephen Joseph, 'Theories of Posttraumatic Growth: Cross-Cultural Perspectives', *Journal of Loss and Trauma*, 15, (2010), 259–77 (p. 262); Tzipi Weiss and Roni Berger, 'Posttraumatic Growth around the Globe', in *Posttraumatic Growth and Culturally Competent Practice: Lessons Learned from around the World*, eds. Tzipi Weiss and Roni Berger (Hoboken, NJ: John Wiley & Sons, Inc., 2010), pp. 189–96 (p. 191).

[2] Calhoun and Tedeschi, *Facilitating Posttraumatic Growth*, pp. 10–11; Joseph and Linley, 'Positive Psychological Perspectives', pp. 7–8; Richard G. Tedeschi, Crystal L. Park and Lawrence G. Calhoun, 'Posttraumatic Growth: Conceptual Issues', in *Posttraumatic Growth: Positive Changes in the Aftermath of Crisis*, eds. Richard G. Tedeschi, Crystal L. Park and Lawrence G. Calhoun, (Mahwah, NJ: Lawrence Erlbaum Associates, Inc., 1998), pp. 1–22 (pp. 3–4).

[3] Joseph and Linley cite examples such as Dante Alighieri's description of his search for his lost love Beatrice, taking him through Hell and Purgatory to reach Paradise in *The Divine Comedy*, as well as Fyodor Dostoevsky's redemption of the murderer Raskolnikov when he embraces the suffering of the prison camps to atone for his actions in *Crime and Punishment*. Joseph and Linley, 'Positive Psychological Perspectives', pp. 7–8.

writings of existential philosophers.[4] However, it was not until the 1990s before systematic attempts were made by psychologists and other researchers to investigate and understand the nature of what has come to be known as 'post-traumatic growth'.[5]

Leading scholars in the field, Lawrence Calhoun and Richard Tedeschi, explain the concept of post-traumatic growth using an earthquake metaphor. In their understanding, 'seismic' events are experiences with the destructive power to produce a severe shaking, and in some cases shattering, of an individual's internal world.[6] The scholars base their 'seismic event' theory on the earlier work of Ronnie Janoff-Bulman, according to which, the foundation of individuals' cognitive-emotional system is made up of basic assumptions about themselves, the external world and the relationship between the two.[7] At the core of these assumptions, people believe that the world is benevolent, safe, predictable and meaningful and that the self is worthy. According to Calhoun and Tedeschi, just as earthquakes produce a significant threat to physical structures, seismic events pose a threat to these cognitive-emotional structures. In the absence of an individual's usual modes of belief about the self and the world, typical means of coping are overwhelmed and the aftermath of such a disaster is frequently marked by significant distress, incredulousness, denial and a struggle to come to terms with post-traumatic reality.[8]

The distressing emotional, cognitive, behavioural and physical responses that are frequently experienced following a traumatic event are usually thought to be symptomatic of psychopathology or PTSD. Stephen Joseph and Alex Linley argue, however, that because clinical psychology has often been placed under the umbrella of

---

[4] See, for example, Søren Kierkegaard, *The Sickness unto Death*, trans. Alastair Hannay (London: Penguin Books, 1989); Rollo May, *Freedom and Destiny* (New York, NY: Norton, 1981); Jean-Paul Sartre, *Being and Nothingness* (New York, NY: Philosophical Library, 1956).

[5] Calhoun and Tedeschi, *Facilitating Posttraumatic Growth*, p. 11.

[6] Ibid., p. 2.

[7] Janoff-Bulman, *Shattered Assumptions*, p. 6; Ronnie Janoff-Bulman and Cynthia McPherson Frantz, 'The Impact of Trauma on Meaning: From Meaningless World to Meaningful Life', in *The Transformation of Meaning in Psychological Therapies: Integrating Theory and Practice*, eds. Mick Power and Chris R. Brewin (Chichester: John Wiley & Sons, Inc., 1997), pp. 91–106 (pp. 92–3).

[8] Leslie A. Morland, Lisa D. Butler, and Gregory A. Leskin, 'Resilience and Thriving in a Time of Terrorism', in *Trauma, Recovery, And Growth: Positive Psychological Perspectives on Posttraumatic Stress*, eds. Stephen Joseph and P. Alex Linley (Hokboken, NJ: John Wiley & Sons, Inc., 2008), pp. 39–61 (p. 42).

psychiatry, the science and practice of clinical psychology have been pervaded by an illness ideology which has led it to become analogous to the practice of medicine and psychopathology.[9] This illness ideology, Joseph and Linley argue, has narrowed the focus of clinical psychology to 'what is weak and deficient rather than to what is strong and healthy.'[10] In their criticism, Joseph and Linley argue that the pervasive illness ideology has separated the study of PTSD from that of post-traumatic growth, rather than developing an integrative perspective for understanding all responses to trauma. For Joseph, the symptoms commonly thought to indicate PTSD – re-experiencing, avoidance and arousal – are, in fact, indicative of the need for cognitive–emotional processing of the trauma-related information and are 'normal, natural cognitive processes that have the potential to generate positive change'.[11] To return to Calhoun and Tedeschi's metaphor, in the wake of an earthquake, a community may later reflect not on what was lost, but on the care that members of the community showed and on the superior nature of what was rebuilt and what was learnt. In a similar vein, individuals may build a stronger sense of self, experience-enhanced interpersonal relationships and make positive changes to their life's goals and priorities as a result of the struggle with a major life crisis.[12]

Post-traumatic growth theory shares with other approaches to trauma an emphasis on narrative. The initial dissolution of cognitive–emotional structures often sets in motion a significant amount of thinking about the event. Initially this ruminative process is automatic and unintentional then, in later stages, it may become effortful and intentional and play a role in developing new schemas.[13] To make

---

[9] Joseph and Linley, 'Positive Psychological Perspectives', p. 4.

[10] Ibid., p. 5.

[11] Stephen Joseph and Lisa D. Butler, 'Positive Changes Following Adversity', *PTSD Research Quarterly*, 21. 3 (2010), 1–8 (p. 2); Joseph and Linley, 'Positive Psychological Perspectives', p. 10.

[12] Tedeschi, Park and Calhoun, 'Posttraumatic Growth', p. 2.

[13] A schema is a mental structure that consists of pre-existing theories about some aspect of the world and may 'vary in level of abstraction and inclusiveness' (Janoff-Bulman, *Shattered Assumptions*, p. 28). Although schemas may change gradually with the acquisition of new knowledge, the theory-driven, rather than data-driven, nature of our cognitive processes means that schemas have a tendency to remain relatively unchanged. Traumatic life experiences, however, have the power to dramatically alter people's self-schemas. Calhoun and Tedeschi, *Facilitating Posttraumatic Growth*, pp. 17–19.

sense of their experience and restore a sense of meaning, control and order, it becomes crucially important for survivors to reconstruct their experience through narrative. This new narrative is likely to diverge greatly from previously constructed life stories because of the ways in which traumatic events challenge previously held beliefs, philosophies of life, goals, perceptions of self and interpersonal behaviour.[14] The result of this struggle with a traumatic life event is frequently personal transformation. Changes occur in different people in different ways and can be both positive and negative.[15] Joseph and Linley's *Organismic Valuing Theory* predicts that, in some cases, the output of this rumination may result in the assimilation of the traumatic event into pre-existing schemas.[16] In other cases, however, this rumination may result in the development of new (positive or negative) schemas. Post-traumatic growth is when individuals positively accommodate their worldview to the trauma-related information.

To explain the ways in which trauma can result in positive changes, Joseph and Linley distinguish subjective well-being from psychological well-being.[17] Subjective well-being, or the hedonic approach, concerns emotions while psychological well-being, or the eudemonic approach, refers to personality development and 'engagement with the existential challenges of life'.[18] The authors suggest that psychological well-being 'comprises dimensions of self-acceptance, environmental mastery, personal growth, autonomy, positive relations with others and having a purpose in life'.[19] Joseph and Linley argue that positive accommodation, or post-traumatic growth, can be understood as changes to one's psychological well-being and therefore, does not imply the absence of distress. Post-traumatic growth is usually associated with changes in three domains: self-perception (e.g., an increased sense of personal strength and self-competence); interpersonal relationships (e.g., an increased compassion for others or a new appreciation for loved ones);

---

[14] Richard Tedeschi, 'Violence Transformed: Posttraumatic Growth in Survivors and Their Societies', *Aggression and Violent Behaviour*, 4. 3 (1999), 319–41 (p. 312).

[15] Ibid., p. 321.

[16] Joseph and Linley, 'Positive Psychological Perspectives', pp. 12–13.

[17] Ibid., p. 11.

[18] Ibid.

[19] Ibid.

and life philosophy (e.g., a new sense of meaning, an enhanced appreciation for life or an increased spiritual awareness).

Although the concept of post-traumatic growth is understood to be universal, the basic assumptions affected by trauma – the cognitive processes that follow and the ways in which growth is manifested – may be culture-specific.[20] In the United States, Tedeschi and Calhoun have identified five dimensions of growth: personal strength, new possibilities, relating to others, appreciation of life and spiritual change.[21] As Tzipi Weiss and Roni Berger note, however, 'studies in other cultures [have] identified between two and five domains of growth' and the nature of these domains may vary.[22] For example, it was found in the Netherlands that feelings of pride are considered growthful while in Japanese culture, where modesty is highly valued, post-traumatic growth is conceptualised as an increased self-awareness of one's weaknesses and limitations and a loss of desire for possessions.[23] Weiss and Berger also note how values, such as self-control and patience, are emphasised in cultures where the family plays a central role.[24] In addition, while spiritual growth is highly valued in American culture, in largely secular societies such as Germany, the Netherlands and Australia, it could be considered irrelevant or even offensive to suggest growth in such a domain.[25] When trying to understand the nature of post-traumatic growth, Calhoun and Tedeschi advocate that both 'primary reference groups' (i.e., one's local community and social networks) and broader domains of culture (i.e., the broad cultural themes that are prominent within a society, country or geographic region)

---

[20] Splevins et al., 'Theories of Posttraumatic Growth: Cross-Cultural Perspectives', p. 262; Weiss and Berger, 'Posttraumatic Growth around the Globe', p. 191.

[21] Richard Tedeschi and Lawrence Calhoun, 'The Posttraumatic Growth Inventory: Measuring the Positive Legacy of Trauma', *Journal of Traumatic Stress*, 9. 3 (1996), 455–71 (p. 460).

[22] Weiss and Berger, 'Posttraumatic Growth around the Globe', pp. 191.

[23] Ibid.

[24] Ibid.

[25] Lawrence G. Calhoun, Arnie Cann, and Richard G. Tedeschi, 'The Posttraumatic Growth Model: Sociocultural Considerations', in *Posttraumatic Growth and Culturally Competent Practice: Lessons Learned from around the World*, eds. Tzipi Weiss and Roni Berger, (Hoboken, NJ: John Wiley & Sons, Inc., 2010), pp. 1–14 (p. 4); Weiss and Berger, 'Posttraumatic Growth around the Globe', pp. 191–2.

should be considered.[26] They also emphasise the importance of the individual's own interpretation of what constitutes growth.[27]

Although scholars are beginning to investigate the phenomenon in different cultures, post-traumatic growth theory contributes to a perpetuation of the Eurocentric, event-based model discussed in Chapter 1. Research frequently uses pre-established self-report scales to measure levels of post-traumatic growth and these have been, for the most part, developed in Western contexts, often on populations of undergraduate students.[28] Such measures are unable to detect culturally specific accounts of individual experiences, they fail to take structural forms of trauma into consideration and, ultimately, they may be as culturally alien to people as Western mental health labels. Rather than relying on pre-conceived domains of growth, I advocate a qualitative, text-based approach to understanding post-traumatic growth, in agreement with Jennifer Pals and Dan McAdams, who suggest that the analysis of narrative accounts 'may constitute the

---

[26] Lawrence G. Calhoun and Richard G. Tedeschi, 'The Foundations of Posttraumatic Growth: An Expanded Framework, in *Handbook of Posttraumatic Growth: Research and Practice*, eds. Lawrence G. Calhoun and Richard G. Tedeschi (Mahwah, NJ: Lawrence Erlbaum Associates Publishers, 2006), pp. 3–23 (p. 12).

[27] Ibid., p. 16.

[28] For example Joseph and Yule's Changes in Outlook Questionnaire (CiOQ) was developed from a population of survivors of shipping disaster in the UK. Stephen Joseph, Ruth Williams, and William Yule, 'Changes in Outlook Following Disaster: The Preliminary Development of a Measure to Assess Positive and Negative Responses', *Journal of Traumatic Stress*, 6 (1993), 271–9; Tedeschi and Calhoun's Posttraumatic Growth Inventory (PTGI), was developed on a population of undergraduate students in the United States, Tedeschi and Calhoun, 'The Posttraumatic Growth Inventory', p. 460; Park, Cohen and Murch's Stress-Related Growth Scale (SRGS) was also developed from a population of undergraduate students in the US, Crystal L. Park, Lawrence H. Cohen and Renee L. Murch, 'Assessment and Prediction of Stress-Related Growth', *Journal of Personality*, 64. 1 (1996), 71–105; McMillen and Fisher's Perceived Benefits Scale (PBS), was developed from a population of adult spectators at a children's baseball game in the United States, Curtis McMillen, and Rachel H. Fisher, 'The Perceived Benefits Scale: Measuring Perceived Positive Life Changes Following Negative Events', *Social Work Research*, 22 (1998), 173–87; and Abraido-Lanza, Guier and Colón's Thriving Scale (TS), was developed from a population of Latina women in the United States suffering from poverty and chronic illness, Ana F. Abraido-Lanza, Carolina Guier and Rose Marie Colon, 'Psychological Thriving among Latinas with Chronic Illness', *Journal of Social Issues*, 54 (1998), 405–28.

most valid way of assessing post-traumatic growth'.[29] This is because 'post-traumatic growth may be best understood as a process of con-structing a narrative understanding of how the self has been positively transformed by the traumatic event and then integrating this trans-formed sense of self into the identity-defining life story'.[30] In my view, reading trauma texts through the lens of post-traumatic growth theory, taking cultural and historical factors into consideration, including long-term, structural trauma, can provide a richer, more nuanced understanding of the experiences of survivors than self-report measures. By analysing the testimonies of Rwandan men who survived the 1994 genocide, I will show in this chapter that such a reading can also enable trauma scholars to move beyond the Eurocentrism of traditional trauma theory and its focus on events, belatedness and unrepresentability.

Gender and Post-Traumatic Growth

The 1994 Rwandan genocide was as much a crisis of gender as it was one of ethnicity. In the 1980s and early 1990s, overpopulation, the collapse of coffee prices and incompetent governance resulted in an economic downturn. In 1990, the RPF, consisting mostly of Tutsi refugees from Uganda, invaded northern Rwanda and sparked a civil war. Seeing this as a propaganda opportunity to abate the growing discontent, Juvénal Habyarimana deflected criticism of his regime onto all Tutsi. In an attempt to retain power, the government fostered policies of ethnic hatred and fear of the RPF and all Tutsi. Habyarimana used racist propaganda and incited hatred through radio broadcasts, popular magazines, newspapers, songs and even school textbooks. At the time, the majority of men – Hutu and Tutsi alike – were living in grinding poverty, but Hutu men were manipu-lated into thinking that their Tutsi counterparts had taken their land, cattle, and money and were encouraged to kill the Tutsi and seize back these assets.[31] Tutsi men, meanwhile, became the objects of this witch hunt as they came to be seen as foreigners who wanted to take

---

[29] Jennifer L. Pals and Dan P. McAdams, 'The Transformed Self: A Narrative Understanding of Posttraumatic Growth', *Psychological Inquiry*, 15. 1 (2004), 65–9 (p. 65.)

[30] Ibid., p. 65.

[31] Jones, 'Gender and Genocide', p. 67.

over Rwanda and oppress the Hutu people. Although the genocide targeted all Tutsi, it was the men who 'were overwhelmingly targeted in the genocide's earliest and most virulent stages'.[32]

Potential differences in the way men and women respond to trauma might be linked to the relationship between gender and victimhood. As Alison Heru argues, the term 'victim' is 'preferentially applied to and adopted by women' because feminine identity is often viewed as synonymous with victimhood in patriarchal culture.[33] For example, in much nineteenth- and early-twentieth-century Western literature, women were revered for their selflessness, and were covertly 'encouraged to find their solution in the extinction of self, the transcendence of personality, the loss of subjectivity and the state of victimhood'.[34] The same could be said for Rwanda where, as Burnet notes, women are 'viewed negatively when they gossip, are loud and overly emotional' and positively 'when they are reserved, submissive, modest, silent and maternal'.[35] Masculinity, on the other hand, tends to be defined as powerful and aggressive; thus, for Heru, victim-status has the potential to negate masculinity. Men who adopt this identity may be considered less manly and encounter prejudice and ostracism.[36] Given that in Rwanda, even the word *umugabo* (man) is synonymous with being 'strong',[37] the impact of victimisation on Tutsi male identity was undoubtedly significant. Through an analysis of their testimonies, it will be seen that pre-colonial notions of male strength and invulnerability were ultimately decimated during the three months of violence in 1994. Since the genocide, however, Tutsi masculine identity has been reconstructed through the ideology of *Ndi Umunyarwanda*, the notion of Rwandanness or *Rwandicity*.

An official *Ndi Umunyarwanda* programme was launched by the Rwandan government in 2013 with the aim of reconciling Rwandans in advance of the twentieth anniversary of the genocide. It consisted

---

[32] Ibid., p. 71.

[33] Alison Heru, 'The Linkages between Gender and Victimhood', *International Journal of Social Psychiatry*, 47. 3 (2001), pp. 10–20, (p. 10).

[34] Ibid., pp. 16–17.

[35] Burnet, *Genocide Lives in Us*, p. 44.

[36] Heru, 'The Linkages between Gender and Victimhood', p. 14.

[37] *Umugabo* can even be applied to women to denote strength. The abstract form of this word, *ubugabo*, equates to English terms such as 'masculinity', 'virility', 'courage', 'ability', 'capability' and 'power'. Alexis Kagame, 'La philosophie băntu-rwandaise de l'être' [Bantu-Rwandan Philosophy of Being], *Académie royale des sciences coloniales*, Mémoire, 8, 20 June 1955, p. 61.

in a set of public meetings in which young Hutu (particularly men) were encouraged to apologise for genocide crimes. According to President Paul Kagame, 'Le but de cette campagne est de mettre l'accent sur ce qui nous unit, la "rwandité", et de faire disparaître ce qui nous divise et qui a causé le génocide' [the point of this campaign is to focus on what unites us, our *Rwandicity*, and eradicate the things that divide us and caused the genocide].[38]

The official *Ndi Umunyarwanda* programme is part of the RPF-led government's campaign to eradicate genocide ideology and foster national unity.[39] The RPF and its policies of unity and reconciliation have received much criticism. While ethnicity is no longer discussed openly, there is an underlying tendency to conflate Hutu with perpetrator and Tutsi with victim (see Chapter 1). In Reyntjens' view, the RPF's top-down de-ethnicisation project may have made ethnic identity more meaningful than before the genocide, given the 'Tutsisation' of public office that is 'hidden under the guise of ethnic amnesia'.[40] Critics of the *Ndi Umunyarwanda* programme argue that it encourages the Hutu population to apologise to the Tutsi in the name of the entire ethnic group (regardless of whether or not they were individually responsible for the genocide) and that this may further exacerbate ethnic divisions in Rwanda.[41]

I propose that the form of *Rwandicity* espoused by the men in my corpus is, in fact, an ideology of Rwandan identity that includes many positive elements which could be considered forms of post-colonial post-traumatic growth.[42] The emphasis of male identity since 1994 is on a shared culture and language and collectively working for one's country. Any trace of a pre-colonial warrior identity appears to

---

[38] François Soudan, 'Paul Kagamé: "Je ne conseille à personne de se mêler des affaires intérieures du Rwanda"' [Paul Kagame: 'I would not advise anyone to interfere in Rwandan internal affairs'], *Jeune Afrique*, 14 April 2014. Retrieved from: www.jeuneafrique.com/Article/JA2778p020.xml1/ (accessed 4 December 2017).

[39] Hintjens, 'Post-Genocide Identity Politics', p. 10.

[40] Reyntjens, '(Re-)imagining', p. 67.

[41] Robert Mbaraga, 'State Pushes Campaign that Critics Say It Is Ethnically Divisive', *The East African*, 16 November 2013. Retrieved from: www .theeastafrican.co.ke/Rwanda/News/Mixed-reactions-to--Ndi-Umunyarwanda-initiative-/-/1433218/2075366/-/6ktcmf/-/index.html. Retrieved 12 August 2015 (accessed 4 December 2017).

[42] The testimonies were collected before the government's official *Ndi Umunyarwanda* campaign, however, the ideology behind the campaign, that of a shared Rwandan identity, has been developing since the RPF came to power.

have been lost with men expressing an aversion to violence. Post-genocide masculinity also emphasises its rejection of colonial and neo-colonial ideas about Rwanda, turning instead to indigenous culture and beliefs: a phenomenon that post-colonial theorists might label 'interior vision'.[43] I also suggest that the adoption of this ideology is not necessarily a renunciation of ethnic identity, nor is it simply the result of top-down government policies. Although one of the men expresses the view that ethnicity is a meaningless form of identification, this was not the case for the others. A number of the men also convey attitudes which are distinct from official understandings and uses of *Ndi Umunyarwanda*, such as their rejection of forced apologies. Despite facing some significant challenges (such as authoritarianism and neo-imperialism), I argue that the ideology of *Rwandicity* may go some way to address the long-term trauma of colonialism and identity destruction.

Based on a close reading of the men's testimonies, three time periods were identified as presenting distinct versions of masculinity in the testimonies: the early stages of the genocide, in which a predominantly warrior/military identity persisted; later stages of the genocide, when men became aware of their vulnerability and the extent of the genocide; and the post-genocide period, during which masculinity has been rebuilt through the ideology of *Ndi Umunyarwanda*. Within each of these broad temporal periods, several sub-themes of gender and masculinity were identified. The analysis that follows will demonstrate how these sub-themes contribute to the construction of masculinity within each temporal period.

Early Stages of Genocide: Persistence of a Warrior Identity

Genocide Viewed As War: 'We Are the Youths Who Are Ready to Fight'

Despite the assault on Tutsi masculinity in the years leading up to the genocide, a warrior identity among Tutsi men nonetheless appears to have been deeply ingrained. The military had played a pivotal role in Rwanda's pre-colonial society, not only as a means of protection and expansion, but also as the very basis of socio-political organisation. While Reyntjens refers to post-genocide Rwanda as 'an army with a

---

[43] Jean Bernabé, Patrick Chamoiseau and Raphael Confiant, *In Praise of Creoleness*, (English and French Edition) trans. Mohamed B. Taleb Khyar (Paris: Editions Gallimard, 1993), p. 91.

state, rather than a state with an army',[44] this was even more the case in pre-colonial times, when every adult male (Hutu and Tutsi) belonged to the army (*ingabo z'uRwanda*).[45] According to Frank Rusagara, war was considered 'a legitimate social function supported by the binding national feeling of Rwandanness through an extensive institutional infrastructure.'[46] Before being conscripted into the army, young male Rwandans would attend *amatorero* (military schools) as a matter of national duty and initiation into adulthood. Here they would learn 'war dances (*imihamilizo*), archery (*kurasa*), shield tactics (*ingabo*), fencing/sword tactics (*kurwanisha inkota*) and the use of different types of spears (*gutera icumu*)'.[47] Young recruits would also be educated in Rwandan cultural values, including discipline (*imyitwarire*), courage (*ubutwali*) and patriotism (*gukunda igihugu*).[48] Perhaps the most important ideal, in Rusagara's view, was that of *ubucengeri* (martyrdom). This was the act of sacrificing oneself by shedding blood – or even dying – for Rwanda, to become *umucengeri* (a martyr). Thus, the aim of the pre-colonial education system was to transform young Rwandan males into patriotic soldiers prepared to fight and die for their country. Many elements of this pre-colonial warrior identity can be detected in men's descriptions of the early stages of the genocide.

For example, at the beginning of their accounts, men frequently refer to the genocide as *intambara* ('war' or 'battle'), and most recount how they began by fighting back against the killers. In Rutayisire's testimony, he recalls attending a meeting of Tutsi at which it was agreed: 'We are the youths that are ready to fight.' For those who were still children at the time, such as Gatare, it was older male family and community members who would fight in their place: 'The youth and men around there would then defend us.' In both cases, the term *abasore* (young men) is translated as 'youths', but the original terminology suggests that those responsible for defence were exclusively male, reflecting Adam Jones's finding that 'gendered role expectations dictated the behaviour of Tutsis' during the genocide.[49]

---

44 Reytnjens, 'Constructing the Truth', p. 2.
45 Frank Rusagara, *Resilience of a Nation: A History of the Military in Rwanda*, (Kigali: Fountain Publishers Rwanda, 2009), p. 43. It is probably no coincidence that the word for army, *ingabo* ('shield' or 'protection'), shares the same base as the word for man with a different prefix (-*in*).
46 Ibid., p. 9.
47 Ibid., p. 48.
48 Ibid., pp. 48 and 91.
49 Jones, 'Gender and Genocide', p. 74.

Perceived Invulnerability: 'We Could Guard Our Sector'

For several of the men, their knowledge of – and skills in – traditional weaponry (archery, use of spears) led them to a perceived sense of invulnerability. As Bukumura, a member of the *Abamere* clan, for example, states, 'we could guard our sector' because 'people in that clan were good at using bows and arrows'. For others, it was the belief in traditional masculine values (strength, courage) which led them to this sense of invulnerability. Karenzi recalls, 'at the time, I thought the people I was fighting with were untouchable since they were strong men who were energetic and who fought with courage'. Similarly, Rutayisire was advised by some RPF soldiers not to leave the Conseil National pour le Développement (National Development Council) (CND) parliament building. Despite their warnings, Rutayisire explains, 'I did not care; I felt old enough, a young man, and I thought there would be no problem. I was motivated to fight for the country, so I went out'. The justification for Rutayisire's invulnerability – being 'a young man' (*umusore*) – suggests that simply being male implies an ability to protect oneself.[50] Rutayisire's reference to fighting for his country also alludes to the pre-colonial martial ideals of *ubucengeri* (martyrdom) and *gukunda igihugu* (patriotism).

In some cases, early victories against the *Interahamwe* reinforced this warrior identity and sense of invulnerability. After a battle in Bisesero, Harerimana reports that the militiamen 'realised that they had lost many of their men. They said, "There must be some *Inyenzi* [RPF soldiers] among them!"'[51] This victory bolstered Harerimana's belief in his

---

[50] In his original words, Rutayisire even switches to the diminutive, *agasore*, meaning 'small young man', but with the extra nuance of being extraordinary, able to overcome obstacles and fight even with limited means. The diminutive of a noun in Kinyarwanda can be formed by adding the prefix *–aka/aga* (plural *–utu*). In some cases, this class of noun can add a pejorative meaning, while in others, it can add a nuance of exceptional value. Kagame, 'La philosophie bantu-rwandaise de l'être', p. 58.

[51] *Inyenzi* is the Kinyarwanda word for 'cockroach'. It was the name adopted in the 1960s by Tutsi exiles living in surrounding countries who had fled the violence in Rwanda and formed an army in the aim of returning. This militarised group eventually struggled to find funding and divided into competing factions (see Rusagara, *Resilience of a Nation*, p. 148). The RPF or *Inkotanyi* were from the next generation of Tutsi refugees and, when they invaded in 1990, the term *Inyenzi* reappeared but as one of the pejorative expressions, alongside *ibyitso* (accomplice) and *inzoka* (snake), to refer to RPF soldiers and all Tutsi. Melvern, *A People Betrayed*, p. 227.

military prowess, and prompted a two-week break in the fighting, with many Tutsi returning to their daily activities. As Harerimana puts it, they believed that 'the *war* was over' (*intambara yarangiye*).

Later Stages: Genocide Is Different to War

While it shares many characteristics with war, genocide also differs in important ways. In Mark Levene's view, the difference is not military or political, but psycho-social. Unlike war, in genocide 'the enemy is not a competitor that must be conquered', but one that 'is a wholly alien "other" – the sinister force behind society's ills – that must be utterly destroyed'.[52] The problem in Rwanda was that the genocide against the Tutsi took place amid a civil war between the Rwandan government forces and the predominantly Tutsi army of the RPF, leading to much confusion, particularly among members of the international community.[53] For Tutsi survivors of the genocide, however, the difference between war and genocide soon became clear.

Tutsi Men Are No Longer *Abagabo*: 'We Are Not Even Soldiers'

Nkezabera tells of how he overheard two people discussing how 'in Murambi, blood [was] flowing, it [was] gushing through the pipes and frothing up'. They were referring to Murambi technical school, where around 65,000 Tutsi were lured by the authorities in the promise of finding safety; a trap which enabled the militia to kill them more efficiently. Around 45,000 people were murdered in a single day at the school and most of those who survived the massacre were murdered the following day at a nearby church.[54] Despite hearing about 'all those corpses lying there', Nkezabera still refers to the events as 'war', however, he realises that this is not a conventional war, but one pitting the state against the civilians: 'the war was so bad and those who started it were the authorities'. This realisation became even clearer as events went on.

---

[52] Mark Levene, 'What Makes Genocide Different from Other Types of War?' Retrieved from: http://clg.portalxm.com/library/keytext.cfm?keytext_id=188 (accessed 4 December 2017).

[53] Melvern, *A People Betrayed*, p. 172.

[54] The school was also the base of the French soldiers during their controversial Opération Turquoise. Today around 50,000 genocide victims are buried there and it is now one of the six main memorials in Rwanda.

Bukumura had initial success in the fighting and reports that, in the early days, 'we were confident that we would conquer them'. But as the genocide progressed, it became apparent that traditional weaponry would be no match for the *Interahamwe* and government forces who bore modern artillery (guns, grenades):

We heard buses coming and people singing, 'We are coming to finish you completely'... They began to trick us by shooting arrows in order to get closer to us. Within no time, soldiers appeared from nowhere. These soldiers were near us and ready to shoot... [They] shot one bullet with a pistol and, immediately after, gunshots followed. All of us got confused and we scattered. That day was when I realised that this was the apocalypse for Tutsi. In fact, I came to realise that Kayumba lost so many people that day. We started running, we got scattered and mixed up. That day people were killed in a big number and in my heart, I thought, 'whoever survives this day will be a real man'.

Bukumura is among the men who at first referred to the events as *intambara* (war), but his vocabulary choice changes here. In the song translated 'to finish you completely', he uses the verb *gutsembatsemba* ('to destroy' or 'exterminate') from which the Rwandan word for 'genocide' (*itsembabwoko*) derives.[55] Bukumura's recognition that this was not war but genocide ('the apocalypse for Tutsi') ultimately modifies his conception of masculinity. While before, being male (*umugabo* or *umusore*) was used interchangeably with military might and invulnerability, here it is reduced to the ability to survive. In fact, the verb used for 'survive' here is *kurokoka* ('urokoka araba ari umugabo'), which might be translated using the more passive phrasing of being 'saved', further emphasising the emasculation of Tutsi men.[56]

Other men demonstrate similar changes in their identity as their stories of the genocide progress. It can be seen that Rutayisire's previous fearlessness and invulnerability had been lost when he recalls correcting a priest for referring to him as 'lieutenant'. 'We are not even soldiers,' he concedes, 'it is just we try to fight for our lives, but none of us went for military training'. In a similar vein, Harerimana acknowledges that being a man no longer has a bearing on one's ability to survive a

---

[55] *Itsembabwoko* is a compound of the verb *gutsemba* (exterminate) and the noun *ubwoko* meaning ethnic group.

[56] *Kurokoka* is a passive form of the verb *kurokora*, 'to save from danger or death'.

genocide. Initially he states that it was only 'the weakest neighbours, women and children, who were being hacked ... if I remember correctly, only people with strength, capable of running, would survive the next day'. But he promptly corrects himself: 'I mean, sorry, even if you could run, it was up to God to save people.'

No One Was Spared: 'Children Called Out Their Mother's Name, They Screamed in Agony'

Traditional views of gender were further distorted through the targeting of women and children during the genocide. Although initially it was predominantly adult and adolescent males who were exterminated, Tutsi women and children were also killed in huge numbers.[57] Other than its scale, this was perhaps the main difference between 1994 and previous incidents of mass violence in Rwanda which had targeted exclusively men.[58] According to Rusagara, in pre-colonial times, 'killing women and children in war was considered taboo and extreme recklessness'.[59] This opinion is shared by many of the men in this study whose revulsion at the killings of women and children is evident. After resisting *Interahamwe* attacks for several days, Rutagarama describes how the militia were eventually successful in breaking into the old chapel of the Mugina Parish, next to where he was hiding:

They started throwing grenades through the windows. We could hear children crying...old women screaming in pain...old men were screaming, too. I was in the main church because I was among those who threw rocks. When they ran after us, we hid in the main church...the new one. They then started killing in that old chapel. Imagine being in a house and knowing that people are being killed in the next. Children called out their mother's name, they screamed in agony; old men and women calling out their sons and daughters... Everyone screamed for help. They hoped that the people they called out for were still alive, but it was over. It was an apocalyptic attack.

What started as a fight between young men degenerated into the extermination of children, old men and women, sons and daughters.

---

[57] Jones, 'Gender and Genocide', pp. 65 and 71.
[58] Christopher Taylor, *Sacrifice as Terror: The Rwandan Genocide of 1994* (Oxford: Berg, 1999), pp. 157–70.
[59] Rusagara, *Resilience of a Nation*, p. 16.

Rutagarama's horror at this apocalyptic experience is particularly accentuated through his repetition of the appalling sounds he heard: 'crying' (*imiborogo, baraboroga*), 'screaming' (*barataka*), 'calling out' (*barahamagara*), 'screamed for help' (*mwadutabaye*).

Rutagarama's feelings of horror combined with powerlessness while witnessing the torture and murder of women and children are shared by other survivors. Ruhurambuga lived in in the province of Gitarama and describes the experience of having to leave his sister-in-law to die an agonising death. After witnessing the murder of his father and older brothers, he too was taken by the killers who beat him, spat in his face and forced him to his knees. After being kicked in the chest, he was whipped 'without pity', then beaten with a hammer. He eventually lost consciousness and when he awoke, he found himself in a pit latrine among other Tutsi who had experienced similar torture. Among the bodies, Ruhurambuga found his brother's wife: 'What they had done to her above [the latrine] I do not know', he explains but 'it seems like she had been raped'. Before throwing her in the hole 'they had broken her hip bones, she was agonising in the shit'.[60] Ruhurambuga tried to save her by untying her and helping her to stand but 'she couldn't manage', he explains. 'They had hit her with hoes and shattered her hips'. 'She cried out', he continues, 'but everywhere had been shattered. I left her because I saw that she had no life left and I needed to fight to get out myself.'

In an even more personal account, Kavubi recounts having to witness the murder of his entire family. Living in Kigali, he was taken by the local Burgomaster to the house of an *Interahamwe* militiaman. 'When we arrived there', he says, 'it was like an abattoir, there was a lot of blood.' 'They hacked my children first,' he explains, and threw them 'in the pit'. He continues:

Then their mum, she couldn't even scream while they were hacking her. They cut her to pieces in front of me. Then her sister, they hacked her and put her next to her sister [his wife] and said, 'Don't put these women in the pit, kill them because if they escape, they may be granted mercy'. Then they said to me, 'We wanted to kill your wife and children first and show you that'.

Having killed all his family, they then hacked Kavubi leaving him with '14 machete scars on [his] body'. They then threw him into the

---

[60] Ruhurambuga uses the Kinyarwanda term 'mabyi' which is a slang word for human faeces.

pit latrine where he could hear 'children crying'. He even reports hearing one woman praying, 'God, what did we do to deserve such a death?' The genocide certainly shattered traditional views of gender by targeting vulnerable groups; but it also did so through the participation of these groups.

Women and Child Killers: 'I Started Seeing Everyone As a Killer'
The general consensus is that women who participated in the genocide were primarily involved in looting, revealing hiding places and generally supporting their menfolk.[61] However, Nicole Hogg found that ordinary women were also directly involved in the killings, to an extent that cannot be considered an aberration.[62] The role of women certainly went beyond the expectations of many non-Rwandans, as one United Nations Assistance Mission to Rwanda (UNAMIR) officer famously noted: 'I had seen war before, but I had never seen a woman carrying a baby on her back kill another woman with a baby on her back'.[63] Their participation also came as a shock in Rwanda, where women killers have been referred to as 'non-women' or even 'monsters'.[64] Many of the men in this study also highlight their horror at the participation not just of women, but of children.

Karenzi, for example, was captured by the *Interahamwe* and forced to dig his own grave. As he dug, the killers contemplated how they would kill him. To Karenzi's surprise, it was a woman who proposed the method: she suggested grinding Karenzi in a coffee trough. 'Let me give you a trough and we will grind him in it,' he reports her saying. His disbelief that such a cruel murder was the brainchild of a woman is evident as he repeats, 'it was the *woman's* idea to crush me', then exclaims, 'there is no worse death than being ground'. Fortunately, Karenzi was able to escape this incident, but he later reports hearing children also 'talking about how they murdered', which made him 'afraid of everyone'. 'I started seeing everyone as a killer,' he recalls.

Like women, children's involvement in the genocide was varied, and did not always involve direct killing. Gatare, for example, was

---

[61] Nicole Hogg, 'Women's Participation in the Rwandan Genocide: Mothers or Monsters?', *International Review of the Red Cross*, 92. 877 (2010), 69–102, (p. 78).
[62] Ibid.
[63] Cited in Des Forges, *Leave None to Tell the Story*, p. 261.
[64] Hogg, 'Women's Participation in the Rwandan Genocide', p. 99.

turned over to the killers by children: 'On the main road, I bumped into two girls. They screamed, saying, "Here is a cockroach. It's a snake!" People came to see what happened and seized me'. Although they were not directly committing violence, the obvious indoctrination of these girls in the genocidal ideology can be seen through their use of such terms as 'cockroach' (*inyenzi*) and 'snake' (*inzoka*). Moreover, in order for them to attract attention, Gatare reports the girls giving the *induru*, the 'cry of alarm' or 'war cry'. Such a choice of vocabulary might imply the systematisation and even militarisation of these girls' involvement, further perverting such concepts as warrior, masculinity and childhood. When the full extent of the genocidal plan was laid bare, these notions were completely obliterated.

Moral Disengagement, Dehumanisation, Mutilation: 'Is This an Animal or a Human Being?'

We have seen that Hutu men were enticed into participating in the genocide through the emphasis on 'work' and other euphemisms – a form of moral disengagement identified by James Waller as a means to 'diminish individual responsibility for perpetrating evil'.[65] Bukumura, for example, remarks how the killers would talk about going 'to work' (*tugiye gukora*), or 'to hunt' (*bakaza kuduhiga*). The hunting metaphor could equally be construed as a form of dehumanisation, another type of disengagement identified by Waller.[66] Interestingly, Bukumura also uses euphemistic language to describe his own daily routine of survival during the genocide; perhaps this is his own form of disengagement. He uses vocabulary such as *akazi* ('work', noun) and *gukora* ('to work', verb) to describe collecting sweet potatoes. He explains how at the end of each day, he and fellow Tutsi survivors would 'give a report' (*dutanga ripoti*) about who had died that day.

For the killers, these forms of disengagement enabled them to carry out all manner of atrocities. The dehumanisation of Tutsi led not only to their mass execution, but to forms of extreme torture and bodily mutilation. For example, Harerimana recounts seeing his cousin having her legs cut off at the thigh; seeing his sister having her

---

[65] James Waller, *Becoming Evil: How Ordinary People Commit Genocide and Mass Killing*, 2nd edn. (Oxford: Oxford University Press, 2007), p. 126.

[66] For example, Bukumura describes people being hunted like 'rabbits'. For Waller dehumanisation is when a distinct group becomes 'stigmatised as alien'. Waller, *Becoming Evil*, p. 207.

pregnant stomach sliced open and the killers removing the foetus; and seeing his brother cut into small pieces, then having his penis removed as a trophy. Several of the men experienced extreme mutilation first-hand.

Rutagarama survived an apocalyptic attack in which the killers tried to cut his body 'into two pieces' leaving him looking, as he describes it, 'like a wild animal' (see Introduction). Kavubi experienced similar injuries: After being hacked with machetes he describes himself as 'like a dead man' who 'couldn't move'. He was left lying in a drain and survived only by drinking 'the water from the drain'. When the killers confronted Kavubi for a second time, they declared that 'killing [him] is killing *Inyenzi*, it is not killing a person'. Similarly, Bugirimfura, one of just 34 to survive the massacre at Murambi, was reduced to a 'thing' by the killers as they discussed the way he had escaped death. Before beating him at one of the roadblocks, he recalls them saying 'look at that blood. They killed it but it has refused to die'.[67] While Rutagarama had 'completely lost hope', after surviving his beating, Bugirimfura felt like he had 'lost [his] mind'. 'I felt useless,' he says, 'I could see all those who died and I felt that I was not any better than those who had to die.'

Desperation, Devastation, Trauma: 'Still I Find Myself Quiet'

Rutagarama and Bugirimfura were not alone in reaching the point of hopelessness. Toward the end of the genocide, Karenzi's endurance had begun to ebb, and he decided to commit suicide. But during the attempt, he fell into a river and landed on a log which injured his leg. He went 'to check if [he] was hurt', then realised the absurdity of his self-concern while in the midst 'of trying to kill [him]self'. This realisation fortunately changed his plans, but Karenzi continued to be conflicted by the choice between life and death. While on the run, he reports hearing 'an inner voice', telling him to 'stop and let them kill you! If it is a dream, when they kill you, you will wake up'. Karenzi eventually found safety, but his problems persisted long after the genocide.

The devastation of the genocide was so great that many of the men faced psychological problems afterwards. Murengezi, for example,

---

[67] The original Kinyarwanda version uses the morpheme '-ki' ('-gi') which comes from the 'thing' class: 'dori *iki gi*citse abantu dore *gi*fite n'amaraso mu mutwe, ubu ba*ki*she cyanga gupfa'.

explains how his trauma manifested itself as an illness. 'I got sick, with a weird sickness I had never heard of before', he explains:

My whole body was itching and I was scratching myself all over. I went to see a doctor and they couldn't give me any medication. The psychologist told me that it's OK to cry when I feel like it and that I could do it as much as I wanted maybe when I am alone... But almost every night, I would remember everything and I would feel like I did not know where I was.

Similarly, on realising the impact of losing his entire family, Uwamungu recalls how he spent 'six months without talking'. He explains that he continues to seek counselling: 'I have never cried. Instead of crying, I can't talk... I have someone I can keep talking to in order to avoid losing my speech. But still I find myself quiet.' Despite experiencing such extreme psychological trauma, the majority of the men in this study have been able to reconstruct their identities in the aftermath of the genocide. Many of these changes are linked to broader political changes in Rwanda.

Post-Genocide Ubugabo: Reconstructing Masculinity through Ndi Umunyarwanda

The RPF government and its policies have faced numerous criticisms from commentators (see Chapter 1). It is well-known that the RPF has carried out revenge killings of Hutu civilians both within Rwanda and during incursions into refugee camps in the Democratic Republic of the Congo (DRC).[68] Moreover, despite the removal of ethnic labels, it is also well-documented that dissident Hutu politicians and members of civil society have been killed, arrested or removed from leadership positions.[69] Those who question the government and its policies are in danger of being labelled 'divisionist' and considered

---

[68] Des Forges and Longman, 'Legal Responses to Genocide in Rwanda', p. 60; René Lemarchand, 'The Politics of Memory in Post-Genocide Rwanda', in *After Genocide: Transitional Justice, Post-Conflict Reconstrucion and Reconcilation in Rwanda and Beyond*, eds. Phil Clark and Zachary D. Kaufman (London: Hurst and Co., 2008), pp. 65–76 (pp. 67 and 71); Prunier, *From Genocide to Continental War*, p. 20.

[69] Des Forges and Longman, 'Legal Responses to Genocide in Rwanda', pp. 61–62; Hintjens, 'Reconstructing Political Identities', p. 88; Longman, 'Limitations to Political Reform', p. 30; Longman and Rutagengwa, 'Memory, Identity, and Community in Rwanda', p. 162; Waldorf, 'Instrumentalising Genocide' pp. 52 and 57–8.

to harbour 'genocide ideology'.[70] As Chapter 1 demonstrates, Tutsi survivors also face difficulties living under the regime, with pressure on them to conceal their difficulties and remain faithful to the government's narrative of progress.

Despite these criticisms of the Rwandan government, the following section will show that the form of *Ndi Umunyarwanda* adopted by the men in this sample includes many positive elements compared with previous dominant ideologies in Rwanda. It will also be seen that this ideology is not simply imposed on Rwandan men by the government, as there are aspects of government policy with which these men disagree. It would seem that these men draw on, but adapt, the ideas that led to the official version of *Ndi Umunyarwanda* to reconstruct their identities, often in positive and constructive ways.

Non-violence: 'Conflicts and Rivalry Only Make Us Move Backwards'

Many of the men were personally saved by RPF soldiers, and some joined that army themselves. Rutayisire notes how, after being saved, 'those who were young men became soldiers', as if this were an automatic step. Where post-genocide masculine identity appears to differ from pre-colonial ideals is that the appeal of war and being a warrior has disappeared. As Rutayisire states:

We did not stay long as soldiers; we asked [to leave] because some of us were still young so we asked to return to school. The main reason we quit the army was because we felt traumatised... We asked to leave the army and some were allowed.

Far from seeking military service and distinction, it is clear that Rutayisire would rather not be a soldier, and his previous perception of his own invulnerability and fighting spirit has been lost. Through his emphasis on being 'young' and 'traumatised', we see that Rutayisire now acknowledges his vulnerability. Moreover, the repeated requests to leave would suggest that his involvement in the army was involuntary. Although many survivors praise the RPF, they do not applaud its role in wars, but in preventing further violence. Harerimana, for instance, argues that 'the government has a role to play in the fight

---

[70] Longman and Rutagengwa, 'Memory, Identity, and Community in Rwanda', p. 177.

against [genocide] in partnership with the people'. Nshimiyimana concurs, suggesting further that, 'conflicts and rivalry only make us move backwards'.

Ubucengeri Through Work, Not War: 'Above All, We Must Work'

In pre-colonial times, failing in the sacrifice of *ubucengeri* (martyrdom) was seen as deeply shameful, as exemplified by the proverb: *wima igihugu amaraso, imbwa zikayanywera ubusa* ('when you deny Rwanda your blood, then the dogs may take it for free').[71] Rusagara compares this proverb to former US President John F. Kennedy's call for patriotism: 'Ask not what your country can do for you, but what you can do for your country.'[72] In the past, *ubucengeri* (martyrdom) was about shedding blood or sacrificing your life for Rwanda. Today the focus is not on *fighting* for your country, but on *working* for it. The sentiment of the proverb, however, remains pertinent, as can be seen in the testimony of Uwamungu: 'It is not only the government's responsibility. All Rwandans need to understand that if we want to build a better future and to avoid what we went through in the past, we will have to work on it.' The importance of working for one's country may be found in several of the testimonies. Gatare, for example, states: 'Above all, we must work towards the prosperity of our families and country. We must work and live in peace with everyone.' The emphasis here is on peace and work. In the original version of his testimony, Gatare repeats the word *imbere* ('first' or 'above all') three times, as if to highlight how fundamental this is. Recognising the challenges of Rwandan development, Karenzi declares, 'there are times when I feel like sleeping, but then I recall that where the rest are walking, I must run. And I pray not to stumble'.

Rejection of European Ideas: 'We Should Eradicate the Ideology Imposed by Colonisers'

Another aspect of post-genocide identity expressed in the testimonies is the belief in the autonomy of the Rwandan nation and an outright rejection of colonial and neo-colonial influence. When Rwanda gained independence in 1962, both the First and Second Republics remained in close contact with Belgium and later France, and European culture dominated.[73] Since 1994, however, many Rwandans have become

---

[71] Rusagara, *Resilience of a Nation*, pp. 5–6.
[72] Ibid., p. 6.
[73] Vidal, 'De la religion subie au modernisme refusé', p. 82.

critical of the West, particularly for the role played by colonial and neo-colonial powers in the genocide. During the twentieth commem-oration of the genocide in April 2014, Kagame pointed to 'le rôle direct de la Belgique et de la France dans la préparation politique du génocide et la participation de cette dernière à son exécution même' [the direct role of Belgium and France in the political preparation of the genocide, and the participation of the latter in its actual execu-tion].[74] Perhaps one of the most overt rejections of the former neo-colonial powers is the shift from French to English as the language of secondary education in Rwanda.[75]

This anti-colonial sentiment is reflected in several of the testimo-nies. Harerimana expresses his belief that the genocide 'ideology [was] imposed by colonisers'. Although the translation uses the term 'ideology', the word used by Harerimana is *imico*, which can mean customs, virtues or norms, but is most commonly translated as 'cul-ture'. This rejection of European ideas and culture is also expressed in the following extract from his testimony:

I think that what led people to attack their neighbours was put there by foreigners... I used to hear my father saying that all Rwandans come from Gihanga. No one ever said if he was Tutsi, Twa or Hutu! Now we are all Rwandans.

Not only does Harerimana reiterate his belief that the ideas behind the genocide were European, but also, he draws on the traditional Rwandan belief about the 'legendary ancestor of the dynasty and of

---

[74] Soudan, 'Paul Kagamé'. The French government has become well-known for its role in the 1994 genocide in Rwanda. Although aware of the preparations for the genocide, in the early 1990s France continued to support the Rwandan government and played an active role in training and arming the Hutu militias. When the genocide started, France's troops arrived to evacuate French citizens, but soldiers stayed to carry out non-combative duties, freeing Rwandan troops for frontline duties and creating a more effective killing machine. Moreover, France's Opération Turquoise provided *génocidaires* with an escape route from the RPF into neighbouring Zaire. Further evidence suggests that not only did France support the genocidal regime, but actively took part in the persecution of Tutsi at roadblocks during their Opération Noroît. More shocking still, testimonial evidence directly implicates French soldiers in the massacres of Tutsi in Bisesero. See Patrick de Saint-Exupéry, *Complices de l'Inavouable: La France au Rwanda* (Paris: Éditions des Arènes, 2004).

[75] This change took place in 2008 after English had already been added as a third official language in 1996. Beth Lewis Samuelson and Sarah Warshauer Freedman, 'Language Policy, Multilingual Education, and Power in Rwanda', *Language Policy*, 9 (2010), 191–215 (p. 192).

all Rwandans'.[76] According to Josias Semujanga, Gihanga was the apical ancestor of all Hutu, Tutsi and Twa. This legend of ancestry was replaced by the European Hamitic hypothesis, but Harerimana's reference to it suggests a revival of indigenous myths.

Unity but Not Reconciliation: 'What is Not Clear to Me is Who to Reconcile with Whom?'

The government's vision of *Rwandicity* is often interpreted as an attempt to eradicate ethnic identity in favour of Rwandan national identity. This view is also expressed by Harerimana:

I wouldn't say that the idea of Hutu and Tutsi has any basis because you are either a Tutsi or Hutu Rwandan. The way I see it, all are one people because all speak Kinyarwanda, they share one language and it is that which unites us as Rwandans. I don't think I've ever understood the concept of Hutu and Tutsi.

While the concepts of Hutu and Tutsi (*ubuhutu* and *ubututsi*) are essentially incomprehensible to Harerimana, Rwandan national identity appears to make sense and is based on unity and the shared Kinyarwanda language. Harerimana is, however, the only man in the sample to share the government's view that ethnic identity is no longer important. Moreover, there are some aspects of the government's ideology which are opposed by the men.

Since the genocide, the government has placed great emphasis on unity and reconciliation. For example, according the Rwandan government, reconciling people involves the 'reinforcing of their unity through the creation of an environment favourable to dialogue and to collaboration'.[77] Thus reconciliation is viewed as interaction and engagement (e.g., dialogue) on the one hand, and unity which may be viewed as working together under a shared identity for a common purpose (e.g., collaboration) on the other. Similarly, the concepts co-occur in the National Unity and Reconciliation Commission's (NURC) definition:

[A] consensus practice of citizens who have a common nationality, who share the same culture and have equal rights; citizens characterised by trust,

---

[76] Josias Semujanga, *Origins of Rwandan Genocide* (New York: Humanity Books, 2003), p. 85.

[77] Cited in Clark, *The Gacaca Courts, Post-Genocide Justice and Reconciliation in Rwanda*, p. 309.

tolerance, mutual respect, equality, complementary roles or interdependence, truth and healing of one another's wounds inflicted by history, with the objective of laying a foundation for sustainable development.[78]

Here unity is reflected in terms such as a 'common nationality', 'the same culture', 'complementary roles or interdependence', but it comes hand-in-hand with reconciliation which is reflected in terms such as 'trust', 'tolerance', 'truth' and 'healing'.

Similar to Susan Thomson's findings that 'Rwandans do not believe in the policy of national unity and reconciliation', many of the men in this sample also express scepticism towards these policies. In her field-work, Thomson found that 'Rwandans can only speak publicly about ethnicity in state sanctioned settings like the *ingando* [re-education] camps and the neo-traditional *gacaca* trials'.[79] In other contexts she found that resistance to government policies is largely 'implicit', involving tacit strategies such as 'staying on the sidelines' (avoiding engagement with local authorities), 'irreverent compliance' (covertly undermining authority) and 'withdrawn muteness' (purposeful and strategic moments of silence).[80] In contrast to Thomson's findings, however, the men in this sample do overtly state their criticisms of the government and its policies of unity and reconciliation. This difference could reflect Longman and Théoneste Rutagengwa's observation that 'Tutsi genocide survivors generally feel freer to speak' compared with Hutu who mostly 'feel limited in their ability to speak freely, particularly to express criticisms' of the government'.[81] Specifically, a number of men in this sample state that while they embrace the concept of unity, they are largely against the government's top-down approach to reconciliation. In his exploration of these issues, Karenzi points out that the 'two words [unity and reconciliation] are quite different'.

[78] Penine Uwimbabazi, Patrick Hajayandi and Jean de Dieu Basabose, 'Forums for Reconciliation in Rwanda: Challenges and Opportunities', *The Institute for Justice and Reconciliation*, Policy Brief, 17 (November 2014), p. 4.

[79] Susan Thomson, 'Whispering Truth to Power: The Everyday Resistance of Rwandan Peasants to Post-Genocide Reconciliation', *African Affairs*, 110. 440 (2011), 439–56 (p. 443). Gacaca is the national system of community courts which was designed by the government to carry out transitional justice using popular participation.

[80] Thomson, 'Whispering Truth to Power', pp. 449–54.

[81] Longman and Rutagengwa, 'Memory, Identity, and Community in Rwanda', p. 162.

In his view, 'reconciliation is rather a big word. What is not clear to me is who to reconcile with whom? Reconciliation is linking two things that separated but used to be one ... [I prefer] to talk about unity because talking about reconciliation is hard'.[82] Similarly, Nshimiyimana believes that reconciliation 'would be a very big step', but 'Rwandans should unite and put their hands together in the development of their country'.

For others, the problem is not the concept of reconciliation, but the role of the RPF in obstructing this process.[83] Bukumura, for example, is open in his criticism of the government on this issue:

After I joined the army, I came to know the truth... OK let's leave this subject. But I see the way they [the authorities] postpone things and if there is no immediate justice in Rwanda, if there is no truth, if there is no trial proceeding, and if there is no clear punishment, which is an important foundation, then I can assure [you] that there will be no reconciliation.

It can be seen that Bukumura views the authorities as impeding processes of truth, justice and ultimately reconciliation.[84] He also cites the government's failure to 'come down to listen to us [survivors]' and its pressure on Hutu people to apologise for their crimes, asking: 'how can you force someone to admit his crimes?' Bukumura recognises the taboo of criticising the government by apologising in advance of making these statements: 'I will excuse myself because I am going to talk about the leaders of this country'. On the other hand, he is clearly vocal in his criticism of the government's handling of reconciliation, just as others are sceptical of the concept altogether. But despite his criticisms of the government, Bukumura nonetheless embraces a certain version of *Ndi Umunyarwanda* as the final message to Rwandans in his testimony is 'to love one another and strive for the improvement of our country'.

---

[82] Phil Clark suggests that the government interprets reconciliation as a process that is 'primarily group-to-group', however, this is clearly a somewhat nebulous concept for Karenzi. Clark, *The Gacaca Courts, Post-Genocide Justice and Reconciliation in Rwanda*, p. 313.

[83] Survivors responses to the government are explored in more detail in Chapter 4.

[84] The profound aims of the justice system after the genocide include truth, peace, justice, healing, forgiveness and reconciliation; where reconciliation is the ultimate objective in which the other five are involved. These are discussed in more detail in Chapter 4.

Post-Colonial Post-Traumatic Growth

In summary, the journey for most of these men involved the transformation from strong *abagabo* – an identity associated with traditional militaristic values of good conduct, strength and patriotism – to dehumanised, animalistic life forms, many of whom were on the verge of suicide. Every element of previously held beliefs about male power and invulnerability was eventually destroyed during the genocide. Yet one of the paradoxes of post-traumatic growth is that vulnerability can lead to strength. As Calhoun and Tedeschi put it, 'people can get stronger by confronting weakness', although the concept of what is considered 'strong' might have to change.[85] Calhoun and Tedeschi suggest that the acknowledgement of vulnerability is a form of 'subtle strength'; one which recognises the value of 'endurance, acceptance, expressiveness and support-seeking – tendencies that may have previously been seen only as vulnerabilities'.[86] Many elements of 'subtle strength', notably the awareness of vulnerability, may be found in the form of masculinity that has emerged since the genocide.

It would appear that the reconstruction of Rwandan masculinity incorporates many growthful elements. Although it draws heavily on the military values of the past, including patriotism, dignity, unity and the importance of a strong army, there is one notable difference: the emphasis on non-violence, rather than on war and aggression. It would seem that the new masculinity in Rwanda recognises and acknowledges the pain and suffering caused by the genocide, and could thus be considered a form of post-traumatic growth or 'subtle strength'.

Another positive aspect of the change in male identity is the rejection of former colonial influences and their ideas. Instead, there is an emphasis on developing one's own country through hard work, unity and a shared, indigenous language. It could be said of Rwanda, then, that it has engaged in a process of what some post-colonial theorists would term 'interior vision'.

Indeed, *Rwandicity* is very similar to the various post-colonial theories that have developed in the Caribbean such as *Indigénisme* in Haiti or *Négritude*, *Antillanité* and *Créolité* in the French Antilles. Just as Rwandans before the genocide, Jean Bernabé, Patrick

---

[85] Lawrence Calhoun and Richard Tedeschi, *Posttraumatic Growth in Clinical Practice* (New York: Routledge, 2013), p. 141.

[86] Ibid., p. 79.

Chamoiseau and Raphaël Confiant argue that, as a post-colonial people, Antilleans are 'dans une attrape de dépendance culturelle, de dépendance politique, [et] de dépendance économique' [caught in the trick of cultural dependence, of political dependence, [and] of economic dependence].[87] For the authors of *Éloge de la Créolité* [In Praise of Creoleness], interior vision is the examination of one's own culture, with 'un regard neuf qui enlèverait notre naturel du secondaire ou de la périphérie afin de le remplacer au centre de nous-mêmes. Un peu de ce regard d'enfance' [a new look capable of taking away our nature from the secondary or peripheral edge so as to place it again in the centre of ourselves, somewhat like the child's look].[88] Given Rwanda's continued dependency on foreign aid, it would seem that a complete escape from outside spectators and influence could not be possible.[89] However, as the men's testimonies suggest, the country does appear to have found a certain authenticity: a new identity based on its own indigenous values, myths, customs and language. As President Kagame puts it:

Rwanda can't be Rwanda without its own traditions. They are the foundation we build upon... Westerners tend to consider their own democratic model as the only viable one...[but] our country is not supposed to become the West. We are different... We've had to make a democracy that is our own, one which suits Rwandans and takes our culture and values into account.[90]

It has been argued that post-colonial theories are 'too theoretical and esoteric, and hence irrelevant to the study of African politics and society'.[91] Rita Abrahamsen argues that such theories have been 'deemed ineffective' in the face of the 'development imperative' because they are 'too preoccupied with textuality and discourse'.[92] She reminds

---

[87] Bernabé, Chamoiseau and Confiant, *In Praise of Creoleness*, p. 14.

[88] Ibid., p. 24.

[89] International aid accounts for over 40 per cent of Rwanda's budget and its economy suffers when Western donors decide to freeze or reduce their donations, often because of Rwanda's involvement in the DRC. 'Aid to Rwanda: The Pain of Suspension', *The Economist*, 12 January 2013. Retrieved from: www.economist.com/news/middle-east-and-africa/21569438-will-rwandas-widely-praised-development-plans-now-be-stymied-pain [accessed 4 December 2017].

[90] Soudan, *Kagame*, p. 98.

[91] Rita Abrahamsen, 'African Studies and the Postcolonial Challenge' *African Affairs*, 102. 407 (2003), 189–210 (p. 189).

[92] Ibid., p. 190.

us, however, of Michel Foucault's interpretation of discourses as 'practices that systematically form the objects of which they speak'.[93] In other words, ideas and understandings (i.e., knowledge) become dominant and gain the power to shape our social reality. What post-colonial ideas can offer, is an alternative to the dominant 'good governance agenda' which, she argues 'rewrites and reinvents the right of Western countries to intervene in Africa in the post-Communist era'.[94] In her concluding remarks, she highlights that, 'by making explicit ... the forms of rationality and the assumptions that underpin "common sense" and that permeate languages and practices... post-colonialism...can help generate possibilities for transforming social and political conditions'.[95] I would suggest that the Rwandan model is a form of post-colonial post-traumatic growth which provides a living example of Abrahamsen's thesis. Moreover, like the methods of Rutangarwamaboko (see Chapter 1), *Rwandicity* may go some way to address the long-term trauma of colonialism and identity destruction. On the other hand, I would not want to offer an overly romantic vision of Rwanda. If *Rwandicity* is to be the post-colonial ideology that will really bring about meaningful change for Rwandan people, then it will have to overcome some significant challenges, including the problems of authoritarianism and neo-imperialism.

Many of the criticisms levelled against the Rwandan government (intolerance, lack of free speech, disrespect for human rights, etc.) are well-founded. And while I praise the ideology of *Rwandicity* for its revalorisation of indigenous culture and language, at the same time its staunch anti-colonial sentiment makes it easy for the government to deflect any criticism from outside by labelling it neo-colonial interference. The intolerance of free speech in Rwanda is not a myth. Indeed, even in a report which lauds the government notes that Rwanda's 'impressive lead could be solidified and widened by lifting the increasing restrictions on free speech, opposition and a free press'.[96] Hintjens makes a convincing point when she highlights that

---

[93] Cited in Ibid., p. 198.
[94] Ibid., p. 203.
[95] Ibid., p. 210.
[96] Legatum Institute, *Africa Prosperity Report*, p. 28.

the 'top-down and authoritarian manner' of the current regime has 'prevented the emergence of potentially more complex forms of political identification'.[97] If *Rwandicity* is to evolve to become multifaceted, flexible and creative, then Rwandans need the right to express themselves freely, even if this means disagreeing with the government.

In addition to these problems of authoritarianism, *Rwandicity* also faces a lingering neo-imperial threat. Rwandan suspicion of outsiders – referred to by Reyntjens as an 'arrogant stance' which leads to 'fraught relations with the world'[98] – is perhaps not unfounded considering the continued neo-imperial demonisation of their identities (see Chapters 1 and 5). The findings of this chapter may, however, contribute towards a more nuanced discussion of post-genocide Rwanda, reading against the prevailing tendency to characterise the country as a tyrannical dictatorship ruling over a terrified and voiceless mass.

The changes outlined here do not imply that Rwanda is free from the problems identified by its critics. In his analysis of Rwanda's young men, Marc Sommers notes that the situation 'is likely not as punishing as before the 1994 genocide' but that the 'plight for the overwhelming majority remains extremely serious'.[99] In Sommers's view, 'Rwanda's contracting social and political environment, and grossly inadequate advocacy for and investment in youth rights and development, threatens to worsen an already dire situation for most of Rwanda's youth population.'[100] What seems clear from my analysis, however, is that in spite of the climate of political authoritarianism, some ordinary Rwandan men are reshaping their own identities. Moreover, the concept of *Ndi Umunyarwanda* seems far preferable to the self-negating strategy of cosying up to a foreign, neo-imperial power to gain support and legitimacy as leaders did in the past. By asserting Rwanda's independence and drawing on Rwandan culture and traditions, the ideology of *Rwandicity* goes some way towards responding to the identity crisis caused by colonialism and could therefore be considered a form of post-colonial post-traumatic growth.

---

[97] Hintjens, 'Post-Genocide Identity Politics', p. 6.

[98] Reyntjens, '(Re-)imagining', p. 69.

[99] Marc Sommers, 'Fearing Africa's Young Men: The Case of Rwanda', *Conflict Prevention & Reconstruction, World Bank Social Development Papers*, 32 (2006), p. 15.

[100] Ibid.

Conclusion

This chapter demonstrates that reading texts through the lens of post-traumatic growth theory does not mean taking an uncritically positive view, but it can provide insight into the ways Rwandans make sense of their own experiences of the genocide and its aftermath. Such a reading leads to quite different conclusions to other studies of post-genocide Rwanda. By taking cultural and historical factors into account, post-traumatic growth theory can help de-victimise and re-humanise trauma survivors rather than imposing diagnostic labels or promoting silence. It also counters common Western stereotypes about Rwandan survivors as passive victims by recognising their agency. The following chapter will take a similar approach to explore the experiences of women survivors.

Acknowledgement

This chapter is derived in part from an article published in *The Journal of Genocide Research*, 2016, copyright Taylor & Francis, available online: www.tandfonline.com/doi/full/10.1080/14623528.2016.1120463

3 | *Rwanda's Women and Post-Traumatic Individualism*

In the wake of a traumatic experience, a person moves through a cycle of appraisals, emotional states and coping. As we have seen, the framework of traditional clinical psychology explains the factors involved in this cycle as indicative of disorder.[1] For Joseph and P. Alex Linley, however, the cycle serves as a way of processing trauma-related information, that is, information with the potential to shatter an individual's assumptions about the self and the world.[2] Joseph and Linley's *Organismic Valuing Theory* proposes that this information may either be assimilated within existing models of the world, or that existing models of the world may accommodate the information.[3] In the case of assimilation, an individual is able to assimilate the trauma-related information into previously held beliefs about the nature of the world and the self through the application of cognitive strategies (such as self-blame).

Accommodation of trauma-related information can be made in either a positive or negative direction. Negative accommodation refers to the depressogenic reaction of hopelessness and helplessness. Martin Seligman's observations of 'learnt helplessness' in animals offer a useful analogy for understanding feelings of helplessness in humans.[4] Seligman and his colleagues trained dogs to jump out of the way of electric shocks. The researchers then raised a barrier so that the dogs could no longer jump out of the way. In a second experiment, the barrier was removed so that the dogs could once again escape the shocks, but rather than jumping, the dogs lay down and

---

[1] Joseph and Linley, 'Positive Psychological Perspectives', p. 11.

[2] Calhoun and Tedeschi, *Facilitating Posttraumatic Growth*, p. 2; Janoff-Bulman, *Shattered Assumptions*, p. 6.

[3] Joseph and Linley, 'Positive Psychological Perspectives', pp. 12–13.

[4] Described in Janoff-Bulman, *Shattered Assumptions*, pp. 142–3. See also Martin E. P. Seligman, *Helplessness: On Depression, Development and Death* (San Francisco: W. H. Freeman, 1975).

passively absorbed them. Seligman and colleagues argue that the dogs had learnt that nothing they did had any effect on the shocks. Similarly in humans, learnt helplessness and hopelessness is the acquired belief that the world is completely random and that individuals are powerless to influence their environment.[5] In contrast, positive accommodation involves the recognition that although negative and random events are possible, there is reason to believe that life is to be lived for the here and now and that it is possible to regain some control over one's life.[6] It is when individuals are able to positively accommodate their worldview to the trauma-related information that post-traumatic growth becomes possible. As noted in Chapter 2, post-traumatic growth is broadly associated with positive changes in the three domains of self-perception, interpersonal relationships and life philosophy.

The fact that growth is observed in these domains gives credence to McAdams' conceptualisation of identity.[7] McAdams draws on David Bakan's theory of basic human motivations, which highlights the two fundamental drives of agency and communion.[8] According to Bakan, agency allows for the existence of an organism as an individual, manifesting itself in self-protection, self-assertion and self-expansion. In contrast, communion involves the participation of the individual in some larger organism of which the individual is part, manifesting itself in contact, openness and union.[9] McAdams suggests that Bakan's position is particularly valuable for 'comprehending the basic motivational themes expressed in both personal myths and human lives'.[10] To this motivational duality, McAdams adds a third component for understanding human identity, namely, the ideological setting.[11] This aspect of identity develops during adolescence and concerns questions

[5] Joseph and Linley, 'Positive Psychological Perspectives', p. 13.

[6] Ibid.

[7] Dan P. McAdams, *The Stories We Live By: Personal Myths and The Making of the Self* (New York: William Morrow & Company, 1993), pp. 70–90.

[8] Ibid., p. 71; Bakan, *Duality of Human Existence*, pp. 14–15. For a similar characterisation of human motivations, see Richard M. Ryan and Edward L. Deci, 'Self-Determination Theory and the Facilitation of Intrinsic Motivation, Social Development, and Well-Being', *American Psychologist*, 55 (2000), 68–78.

[9] Bakan, *Duality of Human Existence*, pp. 14–15.

[10] McAdams, *The Stories We Live By*, p. 71.

[11] Ibid., pp. 80–90.

of goodness and truth; it defines a person's understanding of the universe, the world, society and God. It is, therefore, comparable to Janoff-Bulman's definition of 'basic assumptions'.[12] For McAdams, the ideological setting functions as a context for identity, locating it 'within a particular ethical, religious, and epistemological "time and place"'.[13] He argues that the two superordinate themes in a person's identity, agency and communion, 'characterise fundamental beliefs and values' in an ideological setting.[14]

Traumatic experiences can leave survivors feeling powerless, isolated and without a sense of meaning, suggesting that trauma destabilises these fundamental drives of agency and communion, undermining their ideological belief system (i.e., their basic assumptions). Given that post-traumatic growth tends to manifest itself in the aforementioned domains – self-perception, interpersonal relationships and life philosophy – it would seem that individuals who experience growth are striving to restore these motivations, which in turn helps rebuild a philosophical framework that provides meaning and purpose.

The drives of agency and communion are also important for understanding the broad cultural distinction of individualism/collectivism. In general, cultures that are characterised as individualist promote independence (i.e., agency) while those characterised as collectivist promote interdependence (i.e., communion).[15] Of course, such a binary categorisation of cultures is over-simplistic as all societies exhibit elements of both individualism and collectivism, but some themes (of agency or communion) may be more or less important in different cultures. For example, according to Calhoun, Arnie Cann and Tedeschi, people in collectivist cultures are thought to prefer

---

[12] Janoff-Bulman, *Shattered Assumptions*, p. 6.

[13] McAdams, *The Stories We Live By*, p. 81.

[14] Ibid., p. 87. The individual 'ideological setting' referred to by McAdams, alludes to the idiosyncratic set of basic beliefs that an individual holds about the nature of the world. This will henceforth be referred to using Janoff-Bulman's term 'basic assumptions' or as the individual's philosophical framework. In Chapters 4 and 5 I use the term ideology in accordance with Teun van Dijk's definition, which refers to the socially acquired beliefs, knowledge and other social representations that are shared by members of a given group. See Teun van Dijk, *Ideology: A Multidiciplinary Approach* (London: Sage Publications, 1998), p. 8.

[15] Calhoun, Cann, and Tedeschi, 'The Posttraumatic Growth Model', p. 10.

collective action, seek harmony with others and place emphasis on meeting group expectations and being respected by important others.[16] Similarly, Hazel Rose Markus and Shinobu Kitayama argue that in collectivist cultures, 'a premium is placed on emphasising collective welfare and showing a sympathetic concern for others' as well as 'on interrelatedness and kindness' and the 'ability to both respect and share feelings'.[17] Catherine Raeff observes that individuals from collectivist cultures are thought to view themselves in relation to others and strive to maintain strong interpersonal connections.[18] Goals associated with collectivism include affiliation, communion and engagement with others as opposed to the goals of agency, autonomy and disengagement from others associated with individualist cultures.[19] According to McAdams, the values thought most important in collectivist cultures are group harmony, cooperation, solidarity and interdependency.[20] People from individualist cultures, on the other hand, tend to believe that they can exert more control over events and assume more personal responsibility than people from collectivist cultures (i.e., they value agency). People from individualist cultures tend to define themselves in terms of how they differ from others, their uniqueness and their personal accomplishments.[21] Individualist cultures also tend to prioritise freedom of the self.[22] People are seen as self-sufficient agents endowed with fundamental rights such as the right to life, liberty and the pursuit of happiness.[23] Parents in individualist cultures are thought to emphasise self-reliance and independence, giving their children autonomy

---

[16] Ibid., p. 9.

[17] Hazel Rose Markus and Shinobu Kitayama, 'Culture and the Self: Implications for Cognition, Emotion, and Motivation', *Psychological Review*, 98 (1991), 224–53 (p. 228.) Cited in Catherine Raeff, *Always Separate, Always Connected: Independence and Interdependence in Cultural Contexts of Development* (Mahwah, NJ: Lawrence Erlbaum Associates, Inc. 2006), p. 12.

[18] Raeff, *Always Separate, Always Connected*, p. 12.

[19] Shinobu Kitayama, Hazel Rose Markus and David Matsumoto, 'Culture, Self and Emotion: A Cultural Perspective on "Self-Conscious" Emotions', in *Self-Conscious Emotion: The Psychology of Shame, Guilt, Embarrassment and Pride*, eds. June Price Tangney and Kurt W. Fischer (New York: Guilford Press, 1995), pp. 439–64 (p. 442).

[20] Dan P. McAdams, *The Redemptive Self: Stories Americans Live By* (New York: Oxford University Press, 2006), p. 14.

[21] Calhoun, Cann and Tedeschi, 'The Posttraumatic Growth Model', p. 9.

[22] McAdams, *The Redemptive Self*, p. 278.

[23] Ibid.

and freedom of exploration.[24] Weiss and Berger, who have pioneered cross-cultural research into post-traumatic growth, discuss the interaction between culture and the ways in which post-traumatic growth is manifested. With respect to the individualist/collectivist distinction, the authors discuss how, in highly communal societies such as Spain and Israel, a prominent feature of post-traumatic growth was found to be a greater degree of social cohesion. In contrast, in the Netherlands, a more individualist society, pride was an important aspect of post-traumatic growth.[25]

This chapter presents an analysis of the drives of agency (self-perception) and communion (interpersonal relationships) in the testimonies of Rwandan women. It will be seen that most of the women have experienced some positive changes in the domain of self-perception (agentic growth), but very few of the women present signs of positive change in the domain of interpersonal relationships (communal growth), indeed, most women appear to experience negative accommodation in this domain. These changes may be linked to the specific ways in which women were affected by the genocide and its aftermath which has resulted in a dramatic transformation in women's position in society including changes in gender roles, a significant women's movement in civil society, and an increase in the number of women in political life. This co-occurrence of positive changes in the domain of self-perception and negative changes in the domain of interpersonal relationships, it is argued, reflects what might be expected from an individualist society (i.e., placing emphasis on agency, accomplishment and individual action) rather than from a collectivist society (i.e., placing emphasis on relationships with others, social harmony and collective action). A quantitative analysis of their testimonies also reveals a marked shift from the use of the collective 'we' before the genocide, to the use of the individual 'I' after the genocide, which might also suggest that the genocide may have caused a shift towards individualism among these Rwandan women. While Rwanda is often lauded for its progressive gender politics, the findings

---

[24] Marc H. Bornstein, Joseph Tal and Catherine Tamis-LeMonda, 'Parenting in Cross-Cultural Perspective: The United States, France, and Japan', in *Cultural Approaches to Parenting*, ed. Marc H. Bornstein (Hillsdale, NJ: Lawrence Erlbaum Associated, 1991), pp. 69–90 (pp. 73–4). Cited in Raeff, *Always Separate, Always Connected*, p. 13.

[25] Weiss and Berger, 'Posttraumatic Growth around the Globe', p. 191.

in this chapter suggest that the changes in women's roles do not necessarily reflect an improvement in women's lives given that drives of both agency and communion are thought to be needed for well-being.

Trauma and Rwanda's Women

The genocide had a catastrophic impact on Rwanda's women, but like all Rwandans, the trauma suffered by women dates back far before 1994. In pre-colonial Rwanda, public life was dominated by men and society was largely patriarchal in structure, as reflected in most Kinyarwanda proverbs about women. *Ukurusha umugore akurusha urugo* (the better the woman, the better the homestead) implies, for example, that a woman's place is in the home. Men's authority over women is reflected in the proverbs: *Uruvuze umugore ruvuga umuhoro* (if a woman raises her voice, cut her off with a machete) and *Amafuti y'umugabo nibwo buryo bwe* (a man's mistakes are his own), meaning do not question a man. The proverb *Ingabo y'umugore iragushora ntigucyura* (A woman's army will never bring you home safely) implies the belief that women are not trusted to be in positions of leadership. Finally, *umugore ni umgore* (a woman is a woman) implies that a woman has little importance and cannot be trusted because she is always weaker than a man.[26]

Women could, nonetheless, hold powerful positions within the religious realm of pre-colonial life.[27] In the Kubandwa cults, for example, women could become spirit mediums, priestesses or traditional healers. The Queen Mother also held a powerful position in pre-colonial times, often owning her own land and herds of cattle and influencing royal succession.[28] By centralising the political system and eliminating the overlapping chieftaincies, colonial rule diminished women's roles in marriage and kin groups, thereby reducing the small

---

[26] According to informal conversations with Rwandan colleagues at the Genocide Archive of Rwanda.

[27] Timothy Longman, 'Rwanda: Achieving Equality or Serving an Authoritarian State?', in *Women in African Parliaments*, eds. Hannah Evelyn Britton and Gretchen Bauer (Boulder, CO: Lynne Rienner Publishers, 2006), pp.133–50 (p. 134).

[28] Taylor, 'A Gendered Genocide', p. 51; Longman, 'Rwanda: Achieving Equality', p. 134.

amount of power that women held.[29] In addition, the monetisation of the economy under colonial rule excluded women who remained economically subordinate to their male relatives who controlled economic resources.[30] The introduction of Christianity drove indigenous religions underground and thus diminished women's religious authority.[31] After Rwanda gained independence in 1962, the Hutu government, which was closely tied to the Catholic Church, took little interest in women's issues and women were under-represented in government.[32] The position of women changed little after Juvénal Habyarimana's 1973 coup d'état. In fact, throughout the post-independence period, women were responsible for the maintenance of the household through their agricultural labour, but had severely circumscribed rights.[33] Inheritance, for example, was governed under customary law under which women could not inherit property unless they were explicitly designated as beneficiaries.[34] Indeed, women had virtually no access to property. While men were responsible for cash crops and other commercial enterprises, women's roles revolved around subsistence agriculture. If a woman earned any money from surplus production it would be taken by her husband, making it virtually impossible for women to accumulate wealth. Married women could vote but needed their husband's consent to engage in commerce or buy land.[35] According to Jefremovas, if women wanted to engage in commercial activity, they had to subscribe to various stereotypes (such as loose women, virtuous wives or timid virgins) in order to negotiate the limitations of control over labour, resources and surplus.[36]

In the 1980s and early 1990s, overpopulation, the collapse of coffee prices and incompetent governance resulted in an economic downturn. Driven by economic necessity, women became a dynamic force behind Rwandan civil society and a number of women's organisations

---

[29] Burnet, *Genocide Lives in Us*, p. 50; Longman, 'Rwanda: Achieving Equality', p. 134.
[30] Burnet, *Genocide Lives in Us*, p. 76.
[31] Longman, 'Rwanda: Achieving Equality', p. 134.
[32] Ibid.
[33] Jefremovas, *Brickyards to Graveyards*, p. 86.
[34] Ibid., p. 76; Human Rights Watch, *Shattered Lives*, p. 4.
[35] Jefremovas, *Brickyards to Graveyards*, p. 98.
[36] Ibid., p. 97.

were founded.[37] Under pressure from this nascent women's movement, Habyarimana's government created the Ministry for the Promotion of Women and the Family in order to promote economic development to improve the status of women and children.[38] In the first multiparty government in 1992, Agatha Uwilingiyimana became Minister for Education and was then named Prime Minister the following year, making her the third female Prime Minister in Africa.[39] A year later, when the genocide broke out, Uwilingiyamana became one of its first victims: a death which, according to Cristopher C. Taylor, owed as much to Uwilingiyamana's gender as it did to the fact that she was a member of the opposition.[40]

Other than its scale, one of the main differences between the 1994 genocide and previous incidents of mass violence was the targeting of women. As Taylor argues, the genocide was more than a battle for political supremacy between groups of men, 'it was about reconfiguring gender'.[41] The extremist propaganda that circulated before the genocide targeted Tutsi women very specifically, identifying their sexuality 'as a means through which the Tutsi community sought to infiltrate and control the Hutu community'.[42] Tutsi women were considered more beautiful than their Hutu counterparts, and it was more common for Europeans to marry Tutsi women than Hutu women. This led to excessive jealousy and hatred of Tutsi women who were portrayed as arrogant and dangerous because they would use their sexual prowess to manipulate the United Nations peacekeepers who were deemed supporters of the RPF.[43] One extremist magazine,

---

[37] A number of civil society women's groups were formed during this period such as *Duterimbere*, a women's banking and micro-lending cooperative; *Haguruka*, an advocacy group for women and children's legal rights; and *Réseau des femmes œuvrant pour le développement rural*, an organisation that provided technical assistance to rural women's organisations. Longman, 'Rwanda: Achieving Equality', p. 135; Jennie E. Burnet, 'Gender Balance and the Meanings of Women in Governance in Post-Genocide Rwanda', *African Affairs*, 107. 428 (2008), 361–86 (p. 372).

[38] Burnet, 'Gender Balance', pp. 372–3.

[39] Longman, 'Rwanda: Achieving Equality', p. 136.

[40] Taylor, *Sacrifice as Terror*, p. 32.

[41] Taylor, 'A Gendered Genocide', p. 43.

[42] Human Rights Watch, *Shattered Lives*, p. 2.

[43] Ibid., p. 17.

Kangura, warned Hutu men to be on guard against Tutsi women who, it claimed, were being used by the RPF to conquer Rwanda.[44]

It was partly this propaganda campaign that fuelled the widespread sexual violence committed against women during the genocide.[45] Rape was used as a tool to dehumanise all Tutsi (although often Hutu women fell victim to sexual crimes also). Because of their commodified value as sexual objects, however, fewer women than men were killed in the genocide. Moreover, many men fled in exile after the genocide while others were imprisoned, so the aftermath saw a significant demographic imbalance.[46] In the immediate aftermath, the new Government of Rwanda estimated that 70 per cent of its population was female.[47] As refugees returned to Rwanda from the camps in Tanzania and Zaire this figure was revised downwards to 53.7 per cent.[48] Although the estimated proportion of women in the population of 1996 does not seem substantially higher than the 1991 figure of 51.8 per cent, it should be noted that it comprises the proportion of females in the entire population. By dividing the population into different age cohorts, Hamilton shows that in 1996, of the population aged between 20 and 44, the proportion of women was actually 56 per cent and of those aged between 45 and 64, the proportion of women was in fact 58 per cent.[49] The elevated number of women relative to men of working age resulted in women having to shoulder the greater burden of reconstruction and other economic activities during the post-war period. Furthermore, many women were left as heads of households, solely responsible for the care of orphans as well as their own children.[50]

---

[44] Ibid.
[45] For more on the depiction of women in extremist propaganda, see Binaifer Nowrojee, 'A Lost Opportunity for Justice: Why Did the ICTR Not Persecute Gender Propaganda?', in *The Media and the Rwanda Genocide*, ed. Allan Thompson (London: Pluto Press), pp. 362–72.
[46] Burnet, *Genocide Lives in Us*, p. 65; Hamilton, 'Rwanda's Women', pp. 2–3
[47] Women's Commission for Refugee Women and Children, *Rwanda's Women and Children*, p. 6.
[48] République du Rwanda, *Enquête sociodémographique 1996, Rapport Final (Abrege)* (Kigali, Rwanda: Ministère des Finances et de la Planification Economique, Office de la Population, et Fonds des National Unis pour la Population, 1998), p. 18.
[49] Hamilton, 'Rwanda's Women', p. 2. See also, Burnet, *Genocide Lives in Us*, p. 65.
[50] In 2000, 34 per cent of households were women-headed, an increase of 50 per cent from 1991, Hamilton, 'Rwanda's Women', p. 6.

However, women had previously been financially dependent on their male relatives and now found themselves having to find the time to cultivate enough food for their families and complete their domestic and childcare tasks which in turn reduced the possibility of growing surplus food to sell for profit.[51] Lack of education, training and experience made it difficult for women to find paid employment. This combination of factors meant that those living in female-headed households more frequently suffered from poverty and malnutrition.

In the face of these difficulties, women survivors of the genocide were further troubled by the lack of accountability and justice. After the genocide, the new government announced its intention to prosecute all those involved in the genocide but, with an overwhelming lack of resources, it faced major constraints.[52] Many survivors failed to obtain justice and women in particular faced substantial difficulties.[53] Initially rape and gender-based crimes were only considered as Category 3 crimes and were not moved to Category 1 until 1996.[54] Furthermore, police inspectors documenting genocide crimes were predominantly male which, in addition to the stigma associated with sexual violence, resulted in survivors of sexual violence being even more reluctant to give evidence.[55]

The International Criminal Tribunal for Rwanda (ICTR) was initially feted by lawyers for its judgement in the sexual violence case against Akayesu which led to an expansion of international law on rape, but as Binaifa Nowrojee writes, 'as ground-breaking as the

---

[51] Ibid.

[52] Human Rights Watch, *Shattered Lives*, pp. 88–9.

[53] Ibid., p. 89.

[54] According to the Organic Law (08/96), Category 1 refers to (a) the planners and organisers of the genocide; (b) those who were in a position of authority on the national, prefectural, communal or sectorial level; (c) those who were killers of great renown because of the zeal or cruelty with which they carried out the killing; and eventually (d) those who committed acts of sexual torture. Category 2 covers perpetrators or accomplices of intentional homicide or serious assaults that resulted in death; Category 3 covers persons accused of other serious assaults; and Category 4 covers offences against property. In an earlier draft of the legislation, rape was explicitly included in Category 3. Claire Devlin and Robert Elgie, 'The Effect of Increased Women's Representation in Parliament: The Case of Rwanda', *Parliamentary Affairs*, 61. 2 (2008), 237–54 (p. 249); Human Rights Watch, *Shattered Lives*, pp. 37–8.

[55] Women interviewed by Human Rights Watch indicated that they would report rape crimes to a female investigator but not to a male. Human Rights Watch, *Shattered Lives*, p. 4.

Akayesu judgement is, it is increasingly standing as an exception, an anomaly'.[56] In her research with Rwandan rape victims pursuing justice via the ICTR, Nowrojee writes that 'virtually without exception, [the women] articulate what they see as the failure of this court not only to deny them justice, but to exacerbate the suffering they continue to experience'.[57] Many perpetrators of sexual violence and gender-based crimes have never been prosecuted. Making matters worse, the overwhelmed legal system and overcrowded prisons prompted the government to initiate a liberation process according to the principle of 'faute avouée, faute pardonnée' ('crime confessed, crime forgiven') for certain crimes and thus, large waves of prisoners were released back into society.[58] The large-scale release of prisoners coupled with widespread impunity resulted in many survivors having to live alongside the perpetrators of genocide, further intensifying their psychological trauma.[59] In summary, although the genocide had unspeakable consequences for all those involved, the suffering inflicted on Rwandan women was particularly devastating. As the following analysis will reveal, this was especially the case for their interpersonal relationships.

The Destruction of Women's Interpersonal Relationships: Negative Accommodation

The upheaval caused by the genocide had a profound impact on family structures and interpersonal relationships leaving families and communities torn apart. It created a population marked by distrust as it was frequently neighbours, friends and even family members who killed one another. Networks of friendship and community were shattered which resulted in a higher incidence of land disputes and deprived both men and women of the social support networks that

---

[56] Binaifa Nowrojee, '"Your Justice Is Too Slow". Will the International Criminal Tribunal for Rwanda Fail Rwanda's Rape Victims?', in *Gendered Peace: Women's Struggles for Post-War Justice and Reconciliation*, ed. Donna Pankhurst (New York: Routledge, 2008), pp. 107–36 (p. 110).

[57] Ibid.

[58] Sandrine Ricci, '*La parole mémorielle de rescapées du génocide des Tutsi au Rwanda: vers une (re)construction du sens*' (Montreal: Mémoire, Université Du Québec À Montréal, 2008), p. 14.

[59] Human Rights Watch, *Shattered Lives*, p. 69.

they had previously relied on.[60] There are a few isolated cases of post-traumatic growth in the domain of interpersonal relationships (such as increased self-disclosure and emotional expressiveness or enhanced compassion for others), but in most cases, the genocide appears to have had a catastrophic impact on the interpersonal relationships of women. Most emphasise the destructive nature of the genocide on their relationships and exhibit the depressogenic response of helplessness and hopelessness associated with negative accommodation of trauma in this domain.[61]

Social Isolation and the Destruction of Community

As a result of negative emotions such as distrust and fear with respect to others, social isolation is one observed outcome of the genocide.[62] For example, as seen in Chapter 1, Kayisire lost five siblings and her parents in the genocide and faces the stigma of being an orphan. When her cousins returned from exile in Burundi, they helped pay her school fees but she notes how she avoids sharing her emotional problems with them: 'I had a feeling that I was being a burden to [my cousin], and I don't like involving others in my problems.' Social isolation is also a theme in the testimony of Uwimpuhwe, who survived the genocide at the age of ten:

Not a single member of my family is still alive, I have no one to go to talk to about my problems. Everyone takes care of their own family ... I remember it was in 1998 when I decided never to tell my problems to anyone.

In a similar vein, Kameya describes her post-genocide life in the following way:

It's a life that I cannot describe. It's a life that we lived with hurt and trauma. Another thing is you are closed. You have no one you feel you can approach. I want to approach [others] but you find it menacing. Because of the trauma left behind by those people during the genocide, we could not accept people into our lives.

Here, the genocide's legacy of fear and distrust is demonstrated by Kameya's apparent loss of faith in humanity. This is highlighted in

---

[60] Angela Veale and Giorgia Donà, 'Street Children and Political Violence: A Socio-Demographic Analysis of Street Children in Rwanda', *Child Abuse & Neglect*, 27. 3 (2003), 253–69 (p. 257).

[61] Joseph and Linley, 'Positive Psychological Perspectives', p. 13.

[62] Newbury and Baldwin, *Aftermath*, p. 3.

her shift from speaking about the actions of a specific group ('those people'), to speaking about her inability to accept 'people' in general. Her loss of faith in people is also demonstrated when she describes how she is unable to open up to others because, during the genocide, 'We had seen what a human being really is.' Despite her loss of faith in humanity, Kameya yearns to find someone she can confide in, yet she is unable to find anyone she can trust. Her predicament is repeatedly manifested in the following extract from her testimony through a series of four contrastive pairs (a verbal format consisting in two consecutive items of discourse which contrast with each other in some way):[63]

But there was a time when I didn't know who I really was. <u>There was no one I could talk to, no.</u> *I felt like I was damaged. I felt that I wasn't myself* <u>… I had no one to tell about this ordeal.</u> *I thought that people were of two categories, those who were telling us they [the killers] were going to kill us and those that kill.* <u>I was unable to find someone to tell. I didn't know the other people that were there, they were not the sort of people with whom you could share your problems. The last time we had real communication with them is when we lived at home [in our families].</u> *We were damaged. A time came when I felt that I really wanted to be free of the things I had within me* but <u>I was unable to find a person I could talk to.</u>

Here Kameya repeatedly expresses the emotional burden of her experiences (in italics) followed by a reason preventing her from alleviating herself from this burden (underlined). This repetition of Kameya's inability to find someone to confide in serves to highlight her general sense of hopeless isolation and despair. She eventually finds someone who was absent from the country at the time of the genocide and decides to confide in him. Unable to communicate verbally, she writes her feelings using SMS text messages. She explains how, 'It was like evacuating my mind … I had little information about him I just used him to ease my mind.' Later, however, Kameya discovers that the man's father was one of the most notorious killers during the genocide:

I became very much tortured. I went back to him calling him an *Interahamwe* and asking him why he had listened to me. He told me that

---

[63] Victoria Lee and Geoffrey Beattie, 'The Rhetorical Organisation of Verbal and Nonverbal Behaviour in Emotional Talk', *Semiotica*, 120. 1/2 (1998), 39–92 (p. 61).

his father had changed from Tutsi to Hutu: those were the worst ones, you have no idea what they did.[64] So telling him didn't help me.

Kameya decided to write her story as a book rather than confide in others. This decision begins to improve her psychological state as she explains, 'writing is a cure to a broken heart'.[65] Thus, despite her isolation, Kameya took control of the situation, demonstrating personal agency in the face of despair at destroyed social relationships. As will be seen, this is a common response among women.

The distrust among people after the genocide also resulted in a lack of cooperation or motivation to help others. The widespread poverty that followed the genocide made it extremely difficult for people to help each other as their priority was to help themselves. Nikuze, for example, describes the aftermath stating, 'I saw how everyone just fought for their own lives, no one had the time to fight for others.' In a similar vein, Uwimpuhwe describes her struggle of living in the ensuing poverty and being unable to seek assistance:

People would look at us and feel ashamed because I never used to ask for food even when we were starving to death. We would never beg for food from anyone. I never go to someone and say that 'I, Uwimpuhwe, am hungry'. I just keep silent until people can tell from my appearance that I need something. Because the majority of people listen to your problems yet they are not going to help you. I stopped going to school because there were no people in this world to help others in need.

Clearly, the social stigma associated with orphans, with genocide survivors and with poverty more generally, inhibit Uwimpuhwe from gaining the assistance or cooperation of others. She is thus held at an impasse because, although she may starve to death, she is unable to ask for food because of the shame of begging as well as the reluctance of others to help.

Not only is there an apparent lack of cooperation among the general community but the same is also true among fellow survivors. Kameya, for example, describes how she is unable to trust other

---

[64] Because of the ethnic persecution that took place against Tutsi in the post-independence period, some Tutsi were able to change their ethnic group so as to avoid this persecution. See Longman, 'Identity Cards', pp. 345–7.

[65] Kameya is referring here to her first book, Laetitia Umuhoza Kameya, *Kami yanjye: Urwibutso rwa data* (My Kami: In Memory of My Dad) (Butare, 2009).

people whether Hutu or Tutsi.[66] In the aftermath of the genocide, Kameya concludes, 'We couldn't trust anyone else, just our family members. We expected that every survivor around had betrayed us.' Similarly, Nikuze talks of how she 'used to avoid survivors' because she 'didn't want to be near them'. Even within families, Kameya explains how strained relationships were: 'Survivors could hurt each other. Because they were hurt themselves, they would hurt those close to them. Many families separated as a result of mutual hurt.'

The Difficulties of Living without Family

Dealing with the difficulties of having lost family members is another area in which survivors experience feelings of hopelessness and helplessness. This is particularly the case for children who lost their parents as well as their extended family. Umulisa, for example, lost her entire family apart from a sister. The difficulty she faces can be observed in the following sample from her testimony:

Life is completely difficult, I mean completely. At this time there is no way to earn a living. You find no one to help you, no one to care for you, no one to ask you what you are suffering with. It is a time you feel that life is far from good.

Umulisa's struggle to survive without her family is intensified by poverty and the two factors converge to make her life particularly difficult:

Comparing this life with life before the war, there is a very big difference. Nowadays I may be having a problem but I can't find anyone to talk to about it. I can spend two days without eating, yet before the war, I had never spent even a single day or an hour ... every time I would feel like eating, I would eat. But now I can even spend three days and remain silent. Because there is no one I can share my problem with. Life after the war is very complicated. I would say it is not even a quarter of the life I was leading before the war.

Unfortunately, Umulisa is not alone in struggling with the difficulties of living without a family. Uwimpuhwe also struggles with day-to-day activities as a result of having no family to support her:

When it's time to leave school, we worry thinking about where to go as we dread going back to our so-called home. It is a life where no one comes to say 'hi', and sometimes we cannot even find a way to get to school.

[66] According to Kameya, many of the most powerful and merciless perpetrators of the genocide were in fact Tutsi masquerading as Hutu.

Similarly, as cited earlier, Kayisire describes her difficulty of maintaining motivation at school without the encouragement of her parents: 'I would lament how no one was going to reward me. There was no one to show my report to so I was about to stop going to school.' She also describes the difficulties of having to care for younger siblings on her own:

My brother, when he was in primary, he was traumatised but we didn't know. I was raising them with little skills of doing so. I would punish him for failing in class without asking him what caused him to fail. I was deeply disappointed in him but he was the only boy that survived in our family. He lived with my grandmother so I would find him very dirty and I beat him. We weren't friends anymore because of my beating him ... He confessed the hatred he had for me because of following him up. Unknowingly I was traumatising him. I wanted him to be perfect. But we were too young to know.

Kameya faced similar difficulties in attempting to raise a younger brother without her parents. She tried to encourage her brother to complete his education but, as a result of his trauma, he rebelled against her and would make hurtful remarks about Kameya's future:

I remember, he used to hurt me by saying that, you will soon produce more orphans. Can you imagine? Hearing that repeatedly, I couldn't plan for marriage. There are others among us who couldn't welcome a stranger. They would limit the number of people who could live at their home while married. Beyond that fixed number, you had to get divorced. That is one of the consequences of the genocide. Meaning that you forgot the structure of a family without a nuclear family you can't think about an extended one.

It appears that, for Kameya, losing a family means losing an understanding of love and relationships. Her fear or reluctance to extend her family through marriage is shared by Nikuze ('Since then I haven't thought of getting married again') and Burizihiza ('In my life I never wanted a husband, even now I hate men ... Whenever I see a man I remember what happened to me in the genocide'). The broader consequences of losing family members are further explained when Kameya states: 'But it is personal values not materials that we lost. We don't know how to love. There are lots of things we don't know because we don't have a complete family.'

The pain of living without a family may also be observed in Nishimwe's testimony. Nishimwe was the sole survivor in her family and explains the difficulties of surviving alone:

It is hard for someone who is alone. Because, no one can love you as members of your family can. They have a place in your heart that nobody else can occupy. It's impossible.

Nishimwe moved to Kigali after the genocide and became financially successful, but describes how she is still unable to feel happy:

I built my life, you build yourself, you study, you find a job, you do whatever you want, you live, you can eat, you sleep, you can buy whatever you want, you can talk … you say 'I can travel to wherever' but you feel that you are not going anywhere. You feel you are not a person, that's what I say to other people. Maybe others find it easier, you have a brother or sister who can at least remind you of things, you feel that you can talk to each other, you have a connection to one another, you can share things with each other at home. But when you survived alone, I cannot lie. I cannot lie and say that I am happy.

Like other women in my corpus, Nishimwe gained personal agency and independence ('you can buy whatever you want') in the face of negative interpersonal changes. She has very much been affected by the broader changes in women's roles discussed below. For example, she has remained single and even describes wearing trousers and having her ears pierced; 'things I couldn't [have done] if my father was there'. However, while these changes have enabled her to become autonomous, she remains isolated and experiences negative change in her interpersonal life.

The Difficulty of Living with an Adopted Family

While some survivors faced the challenges of living alone, others had to struggle with life in adopted families. In the aftermath of the genocide, thousands of children were cast out of their family of origin, as family structures ceased to exist and new family structures were forced into existence. Before the genocide, child-headed households were relatively uncommon because even in the event of a parent's death, members of the extended family would generally assume responsibility for the children.[67] By 1998, however, a very large pro-portion of children were living alone (42 per cent) or with peers (19 per cent). Only 20 per cent of Rwandan children were living with their father, 8 per cent with their mother and as few as 11 per cent with both parents.[68] The increase in orphaned children also led to a large number of women taking in children other than their own. In some cases these would be the children of family members or friends, but often the children were unknown.[69] In both child-headed house-holds and adoptive family households, children had to manage com-plex negotiations around issues of identity and grief as well as comprehend their position within the family.[70] Furthermore, many adoptive parents and communities found the behaviour of orphaned children challenging while the children themselves report feelings of being unloved and unwanted.[71] The difficulty of the adopted parent–child relationship is even expressed in the Rwandan proverb, *Umwana w'undi abishya inkonda* (a child of somebody else is not like one's own).[72] These difficulties are reflected in the testimony of Uwimpuhwe. She was adopted by a man who had known her parents and had at first promised to 'take care of [her] like [his] own children'. After living with the family for a while, however, she began to have problems with the man's wife, who used to say to her: 'I cannot handle the kids you brought; they are disobedient, they are … I cannot even name it.' Eventually, the man came to treat them differently to his own children, as can be seen in the following scenario:

He took his daughters to the tailor and made them good clothes then for us he bought us very dirty old clothes. He put those clothes in the closet and called me. He said to me, 'look in the closet there are some clothes, check if they suit your sister and you'. I rushed to the closet and saw the clothes but when I compared them with the clothes that they had given the others [his own children], they were incomparable.

---

[67] Berthe Kayitesi, Rollande Deslandes and Christine Lebel, 'Facteurs de résilience chez des orphelins rescapés du génocide qui vivent seuls dans les ménages au Rwanda (Association Tubeho)', *Revue Canadienne de Santé Mentale Communautaire*, 25. 1 (2009), 67–81 (p. 68).

[68] Comrade, *Socio-Economic Analysis and Conditions of Street Children in Kigali* (Unpublished report, Kigali, Rwanda: Comrade, 1998). Reported in Veale and Donà, 'Street Children and Political Violence', p. 256.

[69] Newbury and Baldwin, *Aftermath*, p. 5.

[70] Veale and Donà, 'Street Children and Political Violence', p. 264.

[71] Ibid.

[72] The proverb literally means that the saliva of another person's child is bitter. Ibid.

Clothing is very important in Rwanda culture as reflected in the Rwandan proverb: *Ntawe ugira ijambo yambaye injamba* (No one can speak publicly wearing torn clothes).[73] Giving such dirty clothes (*ibyamvagara*) is, therefore, particularly insulting to Uwimpuhwe who later gave the clothes to the domestic worker only to be later scolded by her adoptive father who called her and her sister 'difficult children'. She eventually ran away from the adoptive family because of the second-class treatment she received.

In summary, rather than experiencing post-traumatic growth in their interpersonal relationships, women have, on the whole, experienced negative changes in this domain. What is crucial to the development of improved interpersonal relationships is the ability to disclose one's vulnerability to trusted individuals;[74] however, it appears that survivors prefer not to disclose and instead remain silent, perhaps reflecting the stigma surrounding survivors discussed in Chapter 1. This may be particularly the case for women because, as Burnet observes, emotion and loudness are discouraged among women in Rwandan society.[75] Obliterating interpersonal relationships was, moreover, an intended outcome of the genocide as *génocidaires* frequently forced friends and family members to kill one another. Female isolation and loneliness were also intended outcomes, as Burnet observes, many women report being told by the *génocidaires* who spared them that they would 'die from solitude'.[76] As a result of the overwhelming burdens that were placed on Rwanda's women after the genocide, however, their position in Rwandan society has changed rapidly and the post-conflict situation has paradoxically resulted in a situation not only of great challenges, but also of great opportunity.[77]

The Impact of the Genocide on Self-Perception: Agentic Growth

The social transformation of women's position in post-genocide society has largely taken place in three areas: (a) changing gender roles; (b) the women's movement in civil society; and (c) an increase in the number of women in political life.

---

[73] Newbury and Baldwin, *Aftermath*, pp. 3 and 8.
[74] Calhoun and Tedeschi, *Facilitating Posttraumatic Growth*, pp. 11–12.
[75] Burnet, *Genocide Lives in Us*, p. 44.
[76] Ibid., p. 67.
[77] Hamilton, 'Rwanda's Women', p. 14.

Changing Gender Roles

Gaining a sense of self-reliance or self-efficacy has frequently been cited as one of the ways in which survivors of trauma may experience a change in self-perception in other contexts. For example, studies on bereaved widows report that, because widows had to take on a wide array of new tasks which were previously considered their husbands' duties, these women gained a repertoire of new skills as well as a stronger self-image and an increased ability to cope.[78] Calhoun and Tedeschi suggest that if individuals are able to successfully tackle the challenges thrown at them in the wake of a crisis, this can greatly enhance the individual's sense of personal strength and competence.[79] This appears to be the case for many Rwandan women.

The devastation caused by the genocide made it impossible, particularly for women, to continue with traditional ways of life.[80] With their husbands either dead, in exile, or in prison, women were forced to think of themselves differently and develop skills that they would not otherwise have acquired. As a result of this disruption in gender relations, women were able to challenge customary notions of gender and women's roles in the family and even pursue careers or commercial activities.[81] These changes are directly reflected in the changes in self-perception observed in women's testimonies. Nikuze, for example, was previously reliant on her husband for economic support but became financially independent after the genocide by working to support her family. In the opening lines of her testimony where she describes life before the genocide, Nikuze anchors her identity around her role as a wife and mother.

I was born in 1967 and I got married in 1987. We had no child until 1990 when I gave birth to my first born. He was the only child we had. In 1990, my husband worked at Rwandex.

Besides the first clause about being born, all other clauses in this extract relate to marriage, children and her husband's profession (she makes no reference to her own professional activities). After the genocide, however, Nikuze talks at length about how she managed to find

---

[78] Calhoun and Tedeschi, *Facilitating Posttraumatic Growth*, p. 13; Tedeschi, Park and Calhoun, 'Posttraumatic Growth', p. 11.
[79] Calhoun and Tedeschi, *Facilitating Posttraumatic Growth*, p. 14.
[80] Burnet, 'Gender Balance', p. 384; Burnet, *Genocide Lives in Us*, p. 66.
[81] Burnet, 'Gender Balance', pp. 384–5.

work and a place to live in order to support her child. Her personal agency and independence is demonstrated in the following extract where Nikuze uses contrastive pairs, opposing active verbs in the first person (in italics) to statements which generally depict setbacks (underlined):

I changed my life by renting a house, I had a new life yet I still hadn't healed. *I kept on going for treatment.* My leg hadn't recovered because it still had bullets and fragments in it. *I continued going to King Fayçal hospital because we were treated for free. I went in for another operation once again* and my child was with me. *Later after getting my strength back, I looked for a house where I would live and I started to rent one.*

The fact that such difficulty is juxtaposed with assertive action highlights Nikuze's relentless pursuit of a solution to these challenges. Furthermore, her actions in seeking medical treatment or her search for a house culminate in success ('getting my strength back'; 'I started to rent one') suggesting that she manages to overcome the challenges posed by the genocide.

Losing a husband also changed Nakabonye's life, forcing her to take on new roles and responsibilities.

Life was bad. I felt like life was over. I couldn't picture my life without Kalisa [her husband]. I felt like I'd been left, I was worthless ... a widow. I didn't know who I was anymore. But today things seem to be better. It gives me hope.

The stigma of being a widow is clearly apparent in this extract. Translated as 'worthless', Nakabonye uses the Kinyarwanda word 'gusuzugurika' meaning 'to be discredited' (the same verb used by Kayisire to describe her position as an orphan in Chapter 1). However, despite feeling discredited or worthless, Nakabonye appears to have found a way to survive without her husband. As can be seen in the following extract, she seems not only to have survived but also to have gained hope and learnt to tackle life's challenges independently:

To see my kids growing up gives me hope. Raising my kids alone without Kalisa was inconceivable in the past. Raising them without a job ... But today, I have managed. And, I have hope for the future.

Similarly to Nikuze, in both of these extracts, Nakabonye contrasts setbacks with personal strength and agency as well as optimism for the future. This use of contrastive language, moving from setbacks to agency and hope demonstrates Nakabonye's ability to overcome the challenges of living without her husband. Moreover, she describes her situation as 'more positive than ever'. 'I think it's better now', she states, 'because I don't consider myself the same way I did before. Life changes for the better.' Thus, out of her loss, Nakabonye appears to have gained an enhanced sense of self-reliance.

Uwanyirigira also lost her husband during the genocide and, in the following passage, describes how it is the duty of widows to be strong for the sake of their children:

> Survivors shouldn't give up because life goes on. She must stand strong, the widow, she must know her responsibility to bring up children, to take care of them and make sure they get educated. She must strive for her life because life goes on.

Here Uwanyirigira switches from speaking about 'survivors' to 'widows', as if the two terms are interchangeable, perhaps indicating her recognition of the demographic reality that the majority of genocide survivors are women. The sense of duty is reinforced by Uwanyirigira's repetitive use of verbs of obligation ('gukwira' and 'kugomba', meaning 'must'). It could be said that there is a double meaning to the statement, 'She must stand strong' which is a translation of 'Agomba gushikama akaba umugabo'. This could more literally be translated as 'she must strive to be a man'. As we have seen, the Kinyarwanda word for 'man' is used synonymously with being 'strong'. And although Uwanyirigira undoubtedly means that widows must be strong, in many ways, widows also have had to be like men by carrying out traditionally male duties.

In addition to losing husbands and taking on traditionally male duties, many younger women and girls lost their parents and had to take on parental duties, becoming responsible for younger siblings. This was the case for Kayisire who enrolled in school and worked to support her younger siblings. Despite her young age (17 at the time of the genocide), and the stigma she faced as an orphan (see Chapter 1), Kayisire negotiated her way into a higher grade of school and 'never repeated a class'. Though she struggled without the support of her parents, she eventually reached university and managed to juggle her studies with work as well as parental responsibilities:

> I was working in the day time and going to university in the evening so that I could fulfil my duties of taking care of my siblings. Even though there

were other relatives who could play a role in helping them, I had to act like their parent showing them that I am responsible.

Kayisire's role as the oldest surviving member of her family has, it would seem, contributed to an enhanced sense of purpose and self-reliance.

Similarly, Uwimpuhwe was also the eldest surviving member of her family at just ten years of age at the time of the genocide. Despite living through extreme poverty, Uwimpuhwe's perceptions of her life begin to improve although she continues to suffer hardship in her post-genocide life. She is responsible for her only two remaining family members who are both younger than her but she does not possess the means to provide for them. In spite of this hardship, Uwimpuhwe appears to develop an increased optimism for the future as well as an understanding of the importance of her role as caregiver to her younger cousins:

As the oldest, the first thing to do is tell them that things won't stay like this. I promise them that our future will be much better, I tell them that after this life will come another one. Then I tell them that we will have a better future, even if there are no work opportunities, the fact that we study, we have a chance of succeeding. And if God does not abandon us and if we take care of ourselves, I think we will have a better future.

Uwimpuhwe's optimism is palpable and, despite her young age, she positions herself as a figure of authority by referring to herself as 'the oldest' who is able to advise and comfort her younger siblings.

While some girls and young women had to take on the role of caring for younger siblings, in other cases, women took on responsibility for orphaned children. Muteteri, for example, took on two orphans and explains how looking after them provides her with feelings of pride and accomplishment: 'When I see them in my home, I feel good. One is about to finish school in ISAI Busogo and the other one just completed secondary school.' Mukangoga also took orphans into her care after the genocide. At the time of the genocide, Mukangoga was an elderly woman whose husband had died years before due to illness. She did not have her own children, yet during the genocide Mukangoga protected many children in her home. She spent the three months looking after babies who would scream out with hunger. Mukangoga had nothing to feed them so would squeeze the water out of a banana stem into their mouths. Occasionally, a neighbour would bring food and Mukangoga would give it all to the babies. Mukangoga starved herself in order to feed the orphans. In the following extract, she describes how she eventually became responsible for thirteen children:

Life moved on, but later on I faced the challenges of having so many children to look after. I had eleven children with me, anybody who was helpless. People brought in babies, even all the way from Kibuye, newly born babies. Now the number has increased from eleven to thirteen, all under one roof. But looking at them today it's amazing.

Mukangoga later describes how she reached a crisis point in the aftermath of the genocide: with nothing to feed her children, she marched down to a ministry to demand help. She describes how the security guard tried to chase her off the premises but she held on to his belt, refusing to let go. 'I have eleven orphaned children at home. They are hungry and I am their only parent right now, my brothers are in exile,' she reports telling the man. 'If you don't help me, I will abandon them. Otherwise just give me assistance to throw them into the river.' Eventually, she was provided with a sack of beans and cooking oil as well as a car to return home. She explains how that day, 'I went and fed my children, my day was wonderful and I was the happiest woman alive.' It is unlikely that an elderly single woman would have been able to walk into a ministry demanding help before the genocide. However, like other women after the genocide, the urgency of her situation forced Mukangoga to seek action and get the minister to listen to her.[82] Moreover, by overcoming such significant challenges, it appears that many women have also become more self-reliant.

The Women's Movement and Civil Society

In addition to taking on new roles, women also organised themselves into development associations to address specific women's problems and interests.[83] Women's organisations stepped in to fill the void left by the genocide by providing services to meet women's basic needs such as food, clothing and shelter as well as other services such as counselling, social support, vocational training and assistance with economic activities.[84] The work of existing groups (such as

---

[82] Burnet, *Genocide Lives in Us*, p. 6.
[83] Ibid., p. 13; Hamilton, 'Rwanda's Women', p. 9.
[84] Burnet, 'Gender Balance', p. 372; Longman, 'Rwanda: Achieving Equality', p. 138.

Duterimbere, Haguruka and Réseau des Femmes) expanded while several new organisations were founded. One programme that directed its resources towards women's issues was known as Women in Transition (WIT), a partnership set up between the Rwandan government and United States Agency for International Development (USAID) in 1996 to provide assistance to women in the form of shelter, agricultural inputs, livestock and microcredit.[85] One of the best-known women's groups is AVEGA which helps provide genocide widows with greater power of advocacy and organises international humanitarian organisations to assist widows and their children.[86] Women's organisations organised themselves into a collective known as Pro-Femmes Twese Hamwe which works for 'the structural transformation of Rwandan society by putting in place the political, material, juridical, economic and moral conditions favourable to the rehabilitation of social justice and equal opportunity, to build a real, durable peace'.[87] Overall, the women's movement in Rwanda has been so successful that it has been described as 'the most vibrant sector of Rwandan civil society'[88] and 'nothing short of remarkable'.[89] The movement has become the backbone of contemporary Rwandan society, providing a wide range of essential services.

The work of women in civil society is directly implicated in the individual changes in self-perception observed in many of the women's testimonies. For example, AVEGA provided Nikuze with a house as well as emotional support, both of which are noted in her testimony as essential elements in her path to stability as they enabled her to rebuild her life:

AVEGA continued to help me; widows would visit me regularly and they would counsel me, some would talk about trauma and they would console me.

---

[85] Hamilton, 'Rwanda's Women', p. 9.

[86] Burnet, 'Gender Balance', p. 373.

[87] Pro-Femmes Triennial Action Plan 1998, cited in Hamilton, 'Rwanda's Women', p. 10.

[88] United States Agency for International Development (USAID) Office of Democracy and Governance, 'Rwanda Democracy and Governance Assessment', November 2002 . Retrieved from: http://pdf.usaid.gov/pdf_docs/PNACR569.pdf (accessed 4 December 2017), p. 37.

[89] Catharine Newbury and Hannah Baldwin, 'Confronting the Aftermath of Conflict: Women's Organisations in Post-Genocide Rwanda', in *Women and Civil War: Impact, Organisations, and Action*, ed. Krishna Kumar (Boulder, CO: Lynne Rienner Publishers, 2001), pp. 97–128 (p. 97).

They also offered me a house. Up to now, I am living in that house and life is going on.

Similarly, Mukamusoni explains how she also received a house from AVEGA which enabled her to continue with life:

After a while, AVEGA took responsibility for finding us American benefactors who took on the role of reconstructing the houses that had been destroyed ... Ours was rebuilt by the Americans. AVEGA looked after all homeless people, those with serious problems ... we were the first to be housed. Life has gone on now the children are in school.

While some women benefitted from the services offered by women's groups, others benefitted from active participation in the movement. Kayiraba, for example, describes how AVEGA trained her in trauma counselling and law:

I owe my life to AVEGA, because it trained me in trauma, it has provided me with confidence, I am now the representative of AVEGA in Rwamagana, and I enjoy helping others ... I always meet people, I am always solving other people's problems, I was trained in law, I was trained on GBV [gender-based violence] and I often advise people, direct them to the courts.

Clearly this training has enabled Kayiraba to gain a sense of agency and purpose. One of the primary achievements of the women's movement in civil society is its role in the expansion of women's representation in politics as it gave women the skills necessary for entering politics and promoted the legitimacy and importance of women holding office.[90]

Women in Politics

While the proliferation of women in Rwandan civil society may have been described as 'remarkable', the increased representation of women in the Rwandan parliament has been identified as 'revolutionary'.[91] In 2003, Rwanda made history by becoming the country with the highest number of women elected to parliament in the world, with 48.8 per cent

[90] Longman, 'Rwanda: Achieving Equality', pp. 138–9.
[91] Sarah Boseley, 'Rwanda: A Revolution in Rights for Women', *Guardian*, 28 May 2010. Retrieved from: www.guardian.co.uk/world/2010/may/28/womens-rights-rwanda (accessed 4 December 2017), para. 1 of 12.

of the seats in the lower house of parliament won by women.[92] This record was beaten again in the 2008 election in which women won 56 per cent of the seats and even again in the 2013 election in which women won 64 per cent of the seats.[93] In addition to the women's movement in civil society and changing gender roles, Elizabeth Powley cites the commitment of the RPF to women's inclusion as the principal reason behind the increased representation of women in Rwandan politics. The RPF was influenced by its exposure to gender equality issues in Uganda as well as the successes of women in South Africa's African National Congress (ANC).[94] As a result, it has made the inclusion of women a fundamental feature of its policy of unity and reconciliation.[95]

Even before the official introduction of quotas in government, the RPF consistently appointed women to nearly 50 per cent of the seats it controlled in parliament and, from 1994 to 2003, the transitional government saw women's representation rise to 25.7 per cent.[96] In 1998, nationwide elections were organised for representative leadership among women at all levels of government administration. These representatives became known as the Women's Councils and were responsible for advising local governance structures on women's issues and teaching women how to participate in politics.[97] In 1999, a significant government reshuffling saw the Ministry of Gender, Family and Social Affairs (MIGEFASO) split into two ministries: The Ministry of Family and Social Affairs and the Ministry of Gender and the Promotion of Women (MIGEPROFE). The role of the latter was to develop projects to reform all laws discriminating against women as well as projects to educate people about the concept of women's

[92] Elizabeth Powley, 'Case Study Rwanda: Women Hold Up Half the Parliament' in *Women in Parliament: Beyond Numbers*, eds. Julie Ballington and Azza Karam, rev. edn (Stockholm: The International Institute for Democracy and Electoral Assistance, 2005), pp. 154–63 (p. 154).

[93] Jane Dudman, 'Lessons from Rwanda's Female-Run Institutions', *The Guardian*, 1 July 2014. Retrieved from: www.theguardian.com/society/2014/jul/01/lessons-rwanda-female-run-institutions-mps (accessed 4 December 2017).

[94] Powley, 'Case Study Rwanda', p. 159.

[95] Ibid. The concept of post-conflict 'reconciliation' is discussed in greater detail in Chapters 2 and 4.

[96] Powley, 'Case Study Rwanda', p. 154; Elizabeth Powley, *Rwanda: The Impact of Women Legislators on Policy Outcomes Affecting Children and Families* (United Nations Children's Fund (UNICEF) Report, 2006), p. 4.

[97] Burnet, 'Gender Balance', p. 368.

rights and promote gender equality.[98] In 2000, when the transitional period was coming to an end, the drafting of a new constitution was set in motion. Of the twelve-member Constitutional Commission, three members were women, one of whom was considered a 'gender expert'. Judith Kanakuze had been a long-term leader in the women's movement and was appointed to liaise with women's groups and ensure the inclusion of gender sensitive clauses.[99] The women's movement coordinated efforts with MIGEPROFE to actively engage in the process of drawing up the constitution to ensure that gender equality would be a cornerstone of the new constitution.[100] This equality was partly ensured by granting women at least 30 per cent of the seats in both the Senate and the Chamber of Deputies.[101] In the Chamber of Deputies, the twenty-four seats (30 per cent) reserved for women are fought in women-only elections and voted for by women. However, as the parliamentary figures suggest, women have also been elected in the openly contested seats. The women in Rwanda's parliament have also formed a caucus known as the Forum of Women Parliamentarians whose members work together across party lines to address issues related to women and gender. The Forum reviews laws, introduces amendments, proposes new laws and liaises with the women's movement to sensitise the population about gender issues and advise on legal issues.[102]

While the number of women in power is not explicitly mentioned in the women's testimonies, the change undoubtedly provides individual women with important female role models. As Burnet observes, the process of normalisation of women in power has resulted in a greater acceptance of women as independent agents in public which has transformed women's 'identities, subjectivities and agencies'.[103] Moreover, since the genocide, there have been significant changes in law that have favoured women, such as the achievement of Category 1 status for rape or sexual torture in the post-genocide prosecution guidelines, a law extending the rights of pregnant and breastfeeding mothers in the workplace, a law on the protection of children from

---

[98] Ibid., pp. 367–8; Hamilton, 'Rwanda's Women', p. 11.
[99] Burnet, 'Gender Balance', p. 378; Powley, 'Case Study Rwanda', p. 155.
[100] Powley, 'Case Study Rwanda', p. 155.
[101] Ibid., p. 156.
[102] Ibid., p. 160.
[103] Burnet, 'Gender Balance', pp. 381, 386.

violence, the inheritance act guaranteeing that women have the same rights as men to inherit property and a law on the prevention, protection, and punishment of any gender-based violence.[104] It has also become illegal to discriminate against women, including discrimination on the basis of sex or HIV status.[105] Unfortunately, the changes in law do not necessarily reflect what happens in practice as many women survivors and their families continue to face stigmatisation and discrimination, making it difficult to assert their rights.[106]

These changes have nonetheless had a direct influence on the individual self-perception of some survivors. The political changes have allowed Nikuze, for example, to become an independent, property-owning head of household who is no longer dependent on her husband. Prior to the genocide, it would have been impossible for Nikuze to own her own house as all her property, including her children, would have belonged to her husband. This change is of great importance to Nikuze, who explains that before, 'Actually, my worries have reduced because my biggest concern was where to live. And now I have a house.' The expansion of women in politics has also affected Burizihiza. As mentioned in the Introduction, Burizihiza's achievements in the women's civil society movement (as co-founder of ABASA, an association of genocide widows), provided her with the skills and experience necessary for entering politics and she became the Elected Representative of Genocide Survivors in the Mukura Sector.[107] As noted earlier, both Nikuze and Burizihiza assert their intention to remain single women, a position which would not have been socially or economically tenable prior to the genocide. However, as a result of the legal and social changes, this is now the reality for a large number of women.

---

[104] Devlin and Elgie, 'The Effect of Increased Women's Representation in Parliament', p. 249.

[105] Chiseche Mibenge, 'Gender and Ethnicity in Rwanda: On Legal Remedies for Victims of Wartime Sexual Violence', in *Gender, Violent Conflict and Development*, ed. Dubravka Zarkov (New Delhi: Zubaan Books, 2008), p. 158.

[106] Amnesty International, *Rwanda*, p. 2.

[107] The transition of women from civil society to politics is a trend in Rwanda that has been noted by Burnet, 'Gender Balance', pp. 378–9; Burnet, *Genocide Lives in Us*, p. 186 and Longman, 'Rwanda: Achieving Equality', pp. 138–9.

Post-Traumatic Individualism

What Burnet refers to as 'a double burden of marginalisation' on women ('first as girls, wives or widows and second as ethnicised targets of violence'),[108] appears, paradoxically, to be the source of positive change in their self-perception while causing negative changes in their interpersonal lives. This pattern of change might be seen as a shift from a collectivist culture towards a culture of individualism in women. Another way of assessing the effect of the genocide on these women's culture is to take a more quantitative approach. Geert Hofstede argues that children from collectivist cultures learn to think of themselves in terms of 'we', while children from individualist cultures tend to think of themselves as 'I'.[109] Harry Triandis and Eunkook Suh also claim that during communication, people from collectivist cultures more frequently use 'we', while people from individualist cultures more frequently use 'I'.[110] In order to gain a quantitative insight into how the genocide has affected the way in which these Rwandan women relate to others, each testimony was divided into sections according to content matter. These sections included descriptions of pre-genocide life, descriptions of the genocide and of post-genocide life. Subsequently for the pre- and post-genocide life descriptions, the use of language was examined by tallying the total number of singular and plural first-person pronouns to calculate the proportion of plural first-person (we, us) relative to singular first-person (I, me).

As can be seen in Figure 3.1, the use of first-person plural (relative to first-person singular) among women reduces from an average of 44 per cent of the time in their pre-genocide life descriptions to an average of 23 per cent in their post-genocide life descriptions. A repeated measures *t*-test determined that this decrease is significant, echoing the shift towards individualism suggested by my qualitative analysis. This decrease in the use of 'we' relative to 'I' in post-genocide life descriptions appears also to be limited to the testimonies

---

[108] Burnet, *Genocide Lives in Us*, p. 194.

[109] Geert H. Hofstede, *Culture's Consequences: Comparing Values, Behaviours, Institutions, and Organisations across Nations*, 2nd edn (Thousand Oaks, CA: Sage Publications Inc., 2001), p. 236.

[110] Harry C. Triandis and Eunkook M. Suh, 'Cultural Influences on Personality', *Annual Review of Psychology*, 53 (2002), 133–60 (pp. 143–4).

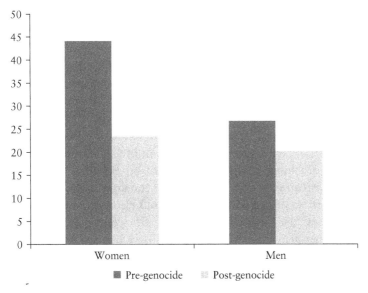

Figure 3.1 Proportion of plural to singular first-person pronoun use in men and women before and after the genocide

of women. The same analysis of men's testimonies shows a shift from just 26 per cent to 20 per cent which was not found to be statistically significant.[111]

Conclusion

In summary, both the qualitative and quantitative analyses suggest that the Rwandan genocide has resulted in a shift towards a more agentic culture among women: they no longer think of themselves in terms of 'we' but in terms of 'I'. While the changes in women's identities could be described as revolutionary, the situation should not be viewed too romantically. Firstly, the political situation in post-genocide Rwanda is not as favourable to women as it may initially appear. For example, many of the organisations that form Pro-Femmes as well as the women's councils lack the resources to maximise their impact which prevents them from providing a consistent

---

[111] For women, the probability of the difference being due to chance was less than 1 per cent ($p < 0.001$) while for men it was 35 per cent ($p = 0.35$).

level of service across the country.[112] The women's movement also remains reliant on a single political party, the RPF, which is less than democratic, and has become increasingly despotic. Such reliance places the movement in a precarious situation. While the trend to move from civil society into politics may benefit a small number of individual women, such as Burizihiza, Burnet suggests that this transition has created a vacuum of leadership in civil society.[113] She argues that more women in governance risks hindering the cooperation between women in civil society and women in office because, once in office, women no longer engage in activism on behalf of women's interests.[114] It is certainly true that many of the laws of great significance to women were passed before the 2003 elections and so were not a result of the high representation of women in political power.[115] Burnet also suggests that women may be used by political leaders to legitimise their agendas and achieve their own ends.[116] Overall, she describes the increased female representation as a paradox because while women's participation has increased, their ability to influence policy has decreased on account of the increasingly authoritarian nature of the regime.[117] Longman also criticises the role of women in government, arguing that the Rwandan government's conception of women's rights is highly constrained because it fails to tolerate the broader range of human rights.[118] According to Longman, because the government has become increasingly despotic and intolerant of independent expression, women in power may only challenge the authorities in limited ways and are thus only able to work on issues consistent with the regime's agenda.[119]

Secondly, the post-genocide climate may have facilitated post-traumatic growth in the domain of personal strength among Rwandan women. However, the disproportionate impact of the genocide on women combined with the stigmatisation of women survivors has had

---

[112] African Rights, *Rwanda: Broken Bodies*, p. 93; Powley, 'Case Study Rwanda', p. 157.
[113] Burnet, 'Gender Balance', pp. 378–9; Burnet, *Genocide Lives in Us*, p. 186
[114] Burnet, 'Gender Balance', p. 381.
[115] Devlin and Elgie, 'The Effect of Increased Women's Representation in Parliament', p. 249.
[116] Burnet, 'Gender Balance', pp. 380–1.
[117] Ibid., p. 363.
[118] Longman, 'Rwanda: Achieving Equality', pp. 146 and 149.
[119] Ibid., p. 149.

a catastrophic impact on their interpersonal lives. Evidence in other contexts suggests that the drives of both agency and communion are necessary for well-being. In her discussion of this subject, Vicki S. Helgeson warns that either drive, when taken to extremes, can have negative effects: 'The extreme form of communion', she notes, 'results in a lack of agency ... (i.e., a focus on others to the exclusion of self).'[120] In contrast, 'the extreme form of agency results in a lack of communion ... (i.e., a focus on self to the exclusion of others).'[121] Bakan and Helgeson agree that 'both agency and communion are required for optimal well-being'.[122] Thus, while the changes in women's roles, rights and positions may be seen as positive, women may still be suffering as a result of the negative impact on their interpersonal lives. In Chapter 4, gender differences in the ways men and women experience agency and communion are explored in more detail in a discussion of collective post-traumatic growth.

---

[120] Vicki S. Helgeson, 'Relation of Agency and Communion to Well-Being: Evidence and Potential Explanations', *Psychological Bulletin*, 116. 3 (1994), 412–28 (p. 425).

[121] Ibid.

[122] Ibid., p. 412.

4 *Communal Men and Agentic Women*
Post-Traumatic Growth at the Collective Level

Literature on post-traumatic growth in individuals abounds, but only a small number of authors have contemplated the idea of collective post-traumatic growth.[1] The scholars who have done so, tend to describe the actions that may result in positive social change, but say little about what is achieved by these actions.[2] When the outcomes of such actions have been discussed, those that are most commonly cited are positive emotions associated with enhanced social cohesion and group identity.[3] I have argued elsewhere that the 'positive emotions' identified by such authors as Carmelo Vázques, Pau Pérez-Sales and Gonzalo Hervás, may not be the same thing as post-traumatic growth, as similar observations of increased group cohesion and solidarity have been interpreted by some scholars as consistent with

---

[1] Sandra L. Bloom, 'By the Crowd They Have Been Broken, By the Crowd They Shall Be Healed: The Social Transformation of Trauma', in *Posttraumatic Growth: Positive Changes in the Aftermath of Crisis*, eds. Richard G. Tedeschi, Crystal L. Park and Lawrence G. Calhoun (Mahwah, NJ: Lawrence Erlbaum Associates, Inc. 1998), pp. 179–214 (pp. 182–207); Tedeschi, 'Violence Transformed', p. 331–2; Carmelo Vázquez, Pau Pérez-Sales and Gonzalo Hervás, 'Positive Effects of Terrorism and Posttraumatic Growth: An Individual and Community Perspective', in *Trauma, Recovery and Growth*, eds. Stephen Joseph and Alex Linley (Hoboken, NJ: John Wiley & Sons, Inc., 2008), pp. 63–91 (p. 64).

[2] For example, authors have highlighted factors thought to promote positive social transformation such as effective leadership, mutual self-help and sharing emotions, rescuing and altruism, political action as well as forms of self-expression such as art, humour and storytelling.

[3] Bloom, 'By the Crowd They Have Been Broken, By the Crowd They Shall Be Healed', p. 179; Darío Páez, Nekane Basabe, Silvia Ubillos and José Luis González-Castro, 'Social Sharing, Participation in Demonstrations, Emotional Climate, and Coping with Collective Violence after the March 11th Madrid Bombings', *Journal of Social Issues*, 63. 2 (2007), 232–7 (pp. 326 and 335); Vázquez, Pérez-Sales and Hervás, 'Positive Effects of Terrorism and Posttraumatic Growth', pp. 63–91.

typical responses to threat or fear.[4] Indeed a number of theories predict that situations of conflict, competition or threat may result in an increase in group cohesion but via processes of intergroup differentiation rather than post-traumatic growth.[5] Broadly speaking, intergroup differentiation encompasses processes of in-group enhancement and out-group derogation. In-group enhancement includes increased perceptions of the in-group in more favourable terms through processes of self-glorification while out-group derogation includes a narrowing of the boundaries of in-group inclusion as well as increased ethnocentrism and patriotism.[6] Thus many of the supposedly positive effects of trauma observed by scholars, could equally be understood as examples of ingroup enhancement rather than collective post-traumatic growth. Vázquez, Pérez-Sales and Hervás suggest that such positive outcomes may have 'collateral negative effects',[7] but this idea is not pursued in their chapter.

I have proposed that post-traumatic growth at the collective level, just as at the individual level, involves the realisation of a group's drives of agency and communion.[8] While in individuals this may

---

[4] Caroline Williamson, 'Towards a Theory of Collective Posttraumatic Growth in Rwanda: The Pursuit of Agency and Communion', *Traumatology: An International Journal*, 20. 2 (2014), 91–102 (p. 92); Cheryl R. Kaiser, S. Brooke Vick and Brenda Major, 'A Prospective Investigation of the Relationship between Just-World Beliefs and the Desire for Revenge after September 11, 2001', *Psychological Science*, 15. 7 (2004), 503–6 (p. 505).

[5] Theories such as: Realistic Group Conflict Theory, e.g., Muzafer Sherif, *In Common Predicament: Social Psychology of Intergroup Conflict and Cooperation* (Boston: Houghton Mifflin Company, 1966), p. 64; Social Identity Theory, e.g., Henri Tajfel and John C. Turner, 'An Integrative Theory of Intergroup Conflict', in *The Social Psychology of Intergroup Relations*, eds. William G. Austin and Stephen Worchel (Monterey, CA: Brooks/Cole, 1979), pp. 33–47 (p. 41); Terror Management Theory, e.g., Jeff Greenberg, Tom Pyszczynski and Sheldon Solomon, 'The Causes and Consequences of a Need for Self-Esteem: A Terror Management Theory', in *Public Self and Private Self*, ed. Roy F. Baumeister (New York: Springer, 1986), pp. 189–212 (p. 190); or Social Dominance Theory, e.g., Jim Sedanius and Felicia Pratto, *Social Dominance: An Intergroup Theory of Social Hierarchy and Oppression* (Cambridge: Cambridge University Press, 1999), p. 17.

[6] Gordon W. Allport, *The Nature of Prejudice* (Cambridge, MA: Addison-Wesley, 1954); Tajfel and Turner, 'An Integrative Theory of Intergroup Conflict', p. 42; Linda J. Skitka, Christopher W. Bauman and Elizabeth Mullen, 'Political Tolerance and Coming to Psychological Closure Following the September 11, 2001, Terrorist Attacks: An Integrative Approach', *Personality and Social Psychology Bulletin*, 30 (2004), 743–56 (p. 744–6).

[7] Ibid., p. 84.

[8] Williamson, 'Towards a Theory of Collective Posttraumatic Growth', p. 95.

manifest itself in areas such as self-perception and interpersonal relationships, collective growth may be expressed through increased freedom and autonomy of the group (agency) and improved relations with members from other groups (communion). The principal difference between individual and collective conceptualisations of post-traumatic growth is that while individual changes take place at the cognitive level, collective post-traumatic growth needs to take place at the ideological level; that is to say via the socially acquired beliefs, knowledge and other social representations that are shared by members of a given group. In the aftermath of trauma, Tedeschi suggests that social narratives serve a similar function to individual narratives.[9] While creating this narrative may bring about controversy over the historical record, such as who bears responsibility for the trauma and what is to be learnt from it, the creation of such a narrative may result in what Tedeschi refers to as 'the social equivalent to … schema change'.[10] Given that the production of a social narrative, just like a personal one, is likely to be effortful and time consuming, it seems probable that the immediate response of group cohesion and enhanced collective identity described by Vázquez and colleagues does not fit this conceptualisation of post-traumatic growth.

Because of its social nature, for collective growth to take place, members of non-dominant groups require access to the means of ideological production through public discourse, enabling them to challenge dominant ideologies and provide counter-narratives.[11] Giving their testimonies to the Genocide Archive of Rwanda enables survivors not only to work through their trauma by developing a personal narrative, but also to counter the official version of events in a public domain. This chapter presents an analysis of collective post-traumatic growth, taking gender differences into account.

Agency and Communion as Collective Post-Traumatic Growth

For Rwandan genocide survivors, the drive of communion may be achieved through reconciling with other groups. One of the most contested terms in peace-building and transitional justice debates, the precise meaning of reconciliation remains hazy. Phil Clark offers perhaps the most comprehensive understanding of this process. Through his

---

[9] Tedeschi, 'Violence Transformed', p. 333.
[10] Ibid.
[11] van Dijk, *Ideology*, p. 184.

study of Rwanda's Gacaca system, he discusses the court's profound objectives which include truth, peace, justice, healing, forgiveness and reconciliation; where reconciliation is the ultimate objective in which the other five are involved.[12] In its most ambitious form, Clark suggests that reconciliation involves 'the creation of a new dynamic between parties that generates a more meaningful engagement' between individuals, between individuals and groups or between groups.[13] As discussed in Chapter 2, the government tends to combine the goal of unity with that of reconciliation. The same chapter showed that many men in my corpus distinguish these terms, preferring the former. Although the women tend not to make this distinction, the goal of unity could be added to the profound objectives as a drive of communion at the collective level.

The drive of agency, on the other hand, involves the pursuit of such factors as freedom and autonomy. For Rwandan survivors, this may be seen in resistance to dominant ideologies which do not favour their group interests. As seen in Chapter 1, many aspects of the dominant ideology in Rwanda do not favour survivors and this includes the government's vision of reconciliation. According to Clark, in 'most government documents and pronouncements by state officials, reconciliation is described as a "national" process occurring between groups in society', thereby reinforcing the Hutu-perpetrator, Tutsi-victim dichotomy.[14] In contrast, survivors themselves tend to 'emphasise the importance of reconciliation between individuals'.[15] The only form of forgiveness represented in Rwandan law requires perpetrators to request forgiveness from a duly constituted bench, a judicial police officer or a public prosecutor, rather than from survivors themselves.[16] This has led some survivors to 'view forgiveness as a process driven more by the judges and leaders in charge of Gacaca, rather than by remorse from perpetrators or by survivors' willingness to forgive'.[17]

---

[12] Clark, *The Gacaca Courts, Post-Genocide Justice and Reconciliation in Rwanda*, p. 32.

[13] Ibid., p. 308.

[14] Ibid., 310.

[15] Ibid., 313.

[16] Ibid., p. 279.

[17] Ibid., p. 294. Gacaca offers reduced penalties to perpetrators who offer a full confession and request forgiveness. Critics include Klaas de Jonge (see Clark, *The Gacaca Courts, Post-Genocide Justice and Reconciliation in Rwanda*, p. 294) and Peter S. Uvin, *The Introduction of a Modernised Gacaca for Judging Suspects of Participation in the Genocide and the Massacres of 1994 in Rwanda* (Governance and Social Development Centre, 2000), p. 9.

This may be exacerbated by the more recent *Ndi Umunyarwanda* programme which, as discussed in Chapter 2, encouraged the Hutu population to apologise to the Tutsi in the name of the entire ethnic group
regardless of whether or not they were individually responsible for the
genocide, once again promoting the idea of collective Hutu guilt.
According to the former Executive Secretary of the National Summit on
Unity and Reconciliation (NURC), Aloysea Inyumba, reconciliation
requires that those who committed crimes ask for forgiveness but also
that survivors 'be courageous enough to forgive their offenders'.[18]
This is echoed by Rwandan President Paul Kagame who declared that
Gacaca should 'encourage' forgiveness, highlighting that those who
grant forgiveness will need to be 'courageous'.[19] Clark argues that
'the state does not appear to view forgiveness as survivors' duty';[20]
however, the government's emphasis on 'courage' undoubtedly has significant coercive powers. This is particularly the case for survivors who
wish to avoid the stigma associated with their survivorhood discussed
in Chapter 1. As Clark highlights, some critics have noted that the
burden to forgive may pressurise 'survivors to "move on" from their
pain and loss'.[21]

To satisfy their group drive of agency, then, survivors must pursue
autonomy and freedom by resisting this dominant ideology. As will
be seen in the analysis that follows, the main themes of collective
agency found in the testimonies include the rejection of such ideas as
government-led reconciliation, globalised Hutu guilt, reconciliation as
a group-to-group process, coerced forgiveness, and the idea of survivors as burdens or parasites. When such themes are present, survivors
tend also to adopt empowerment stigma management strategies.[22]
In Margaret Shih's view, 'stigmatised individuals who perceive that
the stigma has been unjustly forced on them may react to stigmatisation with righteous anger and be spurred into action to remove the
stigma'.[23] Empowered individuals are also more likely to identify

---

[18] National Unity and Reconciliation Commission (NURC), *Report on the
National Summit of Unity and Reconciliation*, 2000, p. 47. Cited in Clark,
The Gacaca Courts, Post-Genocide Justice and Reconciliation in Rwanda,
p. 279.
[19] Clark, *The Gacaca Courts, Post-Genocide Justice and Reconciliation in
Rwanda*, p. 281.
[20] Ibid.
[21] Ibid., pp. 42–3.
[22] Shih, pp. 180–1.
[23] Ibid., p. 181.

with other members of the same group, more likely to strive to maintain social status and more likely to reject the negative public images
of the stigmatised identity. The alternative to such a stigma management strategy, is to adopt what Shih describes as a 'coping strategy'
which involves avoiding the negative consequences of one's stigma; a
strategy which is ultimately draining and damaging to individuals.[24]
Survivors who adopt coping strategies tend not to pursue the drives
of agency noted above and instead support the dominant ideology,
which could be characterised as a form of 'false consciousness'. This
term refers to the phenomenon of a group accepting an ideology as
'natural' or 'common-sense' even though it runs counter to the interests of that group.[25] Examples of false consciousness might include
poor workers accepting the hegemony of the liberal market, black
people accepting racism or women accepting sexism. In the Rwandan
context, I use the term 'false consciousness' to describe the phenomenon of Tutsi survivors accepting the view that those who have not
'moved on' are somehow weak, parasitic or troublesome.

A Gendered Approach

In its analysis of these drives in Rwandan genocide survivors, this
chapter will also examine gender differences. Weiss and Berger highlight that gender – just as other social phenomena such as culture,
ethnicity and social class – is also likely to affect processes of post-
traumatic growth. As Chapters 2 and 3 of this book demonstrate, qualitative gender differences can be observed in Rwanda that are linked
to deeply embedded histories of social, cultural and gender identity
(such as the constructions of gender under Rwanda's militaristic
pre-colonial society and the impact of colonialism, neo-colonialism and
dictatorship on these constructions). In the broader literature on post-
traumatic growth, there has been only limited discussion of gender.
For example, studies in Somalia, Uganda and Ethiopia found more

[24] Ibid., p. 180.
[25] van Dijk, *Ideology*, p. 96; See also John T. Jost and Mahzarin R. Banaji, 'The
Role of Stereotyping in System-Justification and the Production of False
Consciousness', *British Journal of Social Psychology*, 33. 1 (1994), 1–27
(p. 1); Karl Mannheim, *Ideology and Utopia: An Introduction to the Sociology
of Knowledge* (New York: Harcourt, Brace and World, 1936); Karl Marx and
Friedrich Engels, *The German Ideology* (London: Arthur, 1974).

post-traumatic growth in men, while it was women who reported more growth in a study conducted in the Netherlands.[26] Other studies have found 'no gender differences'.[27] Tanya Vishnevsky and her colleagues conducted a meta-analysis of 70 studies 'to examine the direction and magnitude of gender differences in self-reported post-traumatic growth'.[28] Their analysis revealed 'a small to moderate gender difference, with women reporting more post-traumatic growth than men'.[29] The study does not discuss qualitative gender differences, however.

In the literature on drives of agency and communion more broadly, the picture is also mixed. Bakan himself argued that agency was 'prototypically masculine and communion was prototypically feminine'.[30] According to Vicki Helgeson, it is true that 'men typically score higher than women on measures of agency and women typically score higher than men on measures of communion, [but] men and women often possess features of both'.[31] In an investigation into the effects of sex segregation, Eleanor Maccoby found that in such a situation boys and men more 'frequently [engage] in behaviours to maintain dominance and position in the social hierarchy'.[32] Sex-segregated groups of girls and women, on the other hand, are more likely to engage 'in behaviours that reflect mutual reciprocity, such as acknowledging each other and expressing agreement'.[33] According to Maccoby, interactions in mixed-sex pairs may be less differentiated, as women may act more assertively with men than with women.[34] In Alice Eagly's view, gender differences in social behaviour are linked to

[26] Weiss and Berger, 'Posttraumatic Growth around the Globe', p. 192.
[27] Ibid.
[28] Tanya Vishnevsky, Arnie Cann, Lawrence G. Calhoun, Richard G. Tedeschi and George J. Demakis, 'Gender Differences in Self-Reported Posttraumatic Growth: A Meta-Analysis', *Psychology of Women Quarterly*, 34 (2010), 110–20 (p. 110).
[29] Vishnevsky and colleagues also discuss how women are more likely than men to meet the criteria for PTSD following a traumatic experience, Vishnevsky, Cann, Calhoun, Tedeschi and Demakis, 'Gender Differences in Self-Reported Posttraumatic Growth', p. 111.
[30] D. S. Moskowitz, Eun Jung Suh and Julie Desaulniers, 'Situational Influences on Gender Differences in Agency and Communion', *Journal of Personality and Social Psychology*, 66. 4 (1994), 753–61 (p. 753).
[31] Helgeson, 'Relation of Agency and Communion to Well-Being', p. 425.
[32] Eleanor E. Maccoby, 'Gender and Relationships: A Developmental Account', *American Psychologist*, 45. 4 (1990), 513–20 (p. 519).
[33] Ibid.
[34] Ibid., p. 513.

social role rather than sex.[35] D. S. Moskowitz and colleagues investigated this theory by observing drives of agency and communion in the workplace. They found that it was indeed the prescriptions of a social role and not gender that influenced agentic behaviour.[36] However, gender role and not social role influenced communal behaviours in their participants.[37]

Given the paucity of research into collective psychological responses to trauma, there is unsurprisingly little written on gender. There is, however, considerable focus on gender in peace (and war) studies. For example, in his book, *War and Gender*, demographer Joshua Goldstein discusses the arguments of 'difference feminism', which suggest than 'men and women think differently about their separateness or connection with other people'.[38] In particular, Goldstein discusses Carol Gilligan's 'separation-versus-connection' theory of gender according to which 'men tend to fear connection and women tend to fear competition'.[39] While men view social relations as a hierarchy, hoping to reach the top and fearing falling to the bottom, women perceive social relations as a web and seek to be at the centre, fearing the periphery. According to Goldstein, some theorists have applied these ideas to war, 'arguing that women have a distinctive perspective on war based on "maternal thinking"' making them more predisposed to peace than men.[40] In his extensive review of gender roles in wartime, however, Goldstein suggests that this common view of women as more peaceful and men as more warlike may be unfounded because 'many women actively support wars' even if they do not always engage in combat.[41] Nonetheless, Goldstein does show that 'a sizeable number of women in many societies – generally somewhat more women than men, and often women acting in the name of their gender – do oppose wars and work

---

[35] Eagly, *Sex Differences in Social Behaviour*, p. 42.
[36] The term 'agentic', derives from 'agency' and is used by Bakan to refer to someone or something that demonstrates assertiveness, competitiveness, independence, courageousness and mastery. Bakan, *Duality of Human Existence*, pp. 39, 140, 152 and 195.
[37] Moskowitz, Suh and Desaulniers, 'Situational Influences on Gender Differences in Agency and Communion', pp. 758–9.
[38] Joshua S. Goldstein, *War and Gender: How Gender Shapes the War System and Vice Versa* (New York: Cambridge University Press, 2001), p. 46.
[39] Ibid.
[40] Ibid.
[41] Ibid., p. 322.

Table 4.1. *Number of women and men who fall into each response type*

	Type I	Type II	Type III	Type IV	Insufficient evidence	Total
Women	4	5	5	6	3	23
Men	1	5	5	8	0	19

for peace'.[42] Furthermore, he argues that 'women have shown a modest propensity to vote for peace more than men do, on average'.[43]

In the analysis of their testimonies that follows, it can be seen that survivors' descriptions demonstrate four different patterns of belief or ideological positions about the nature of their group (i.e., Tutsi survivors) and how it interacts with other groups (i.e., whether or not it seeks to re-establish its drives of agency and communion). These four patterns include: (1) Those who, in the context of their group identity, do not pursue agency or communion; (2) those who pursue communion, but not agency; (3) those who do not pursue communion, but pursue agency; and (4) those who pursue both communion and agency. Of the twenty-three women and nineteen men, four of the women's and one of the men's responses fall into the first category (response type I), five women and five men fall into the second category (response type II), five women and five men fall into the third (response type III) and six women and eight men fall into the last category (response type IV). Three of the women do not discuss their perceptions of post-genocide society to provide sufficient evidence for analysis (see Table 4.1). As the analysis that follows reveals, the ways in which men and women pursue agency and communion differ, with women tending to pursue more agentic themes overall, and men tending to pursue more communal themes overall.

Type I: Neither Communion nor Agency

The first response type observed in the testimonies includes four women and one man who have neither communal nor agentic motivations satisfied in the context of their group identity as genocide

---

[42] Ibid.
[43] Ibid., p. 329.

survivors. These women and men express uncertainty towards all the profound objectives discussed above. In his discussion of the perpetrators, Ruhurambuga, for example, notes that:

Most of the time when they plead guilty, they know who was killed on such a date, and in such an attack, but they say simply that they fell in with the mob but did not personally take part in any massacres. They only talk politics but don't show what they really did.

Robert Rotberg argues that 'if societies are to prevent recurrence of past atrocities and to cleanse themselves of the corrosive enduring effects of massive injuries to individuals and whole groups, societies must understand – at the deepest possible levels – what occurred and why?'[44] But many of the survivors in this group believe that the perpetrators will never reveal the full truth.

Survivors whose testimonies fall into this category also tend to think that justice is not possible (e.g., Nikuze: 'How can you punish them?'). Those who do believe it is possible prefer retributive justice, that is, punishing the perpetrators in a manner that is commensurate with their crime (e.g., Umulisa: 'personally I would suggest they kill them').[45] Forgiveness is another step survivors in this group feel unable to take because, as Niyongira puts it, 'those people had intended the Genocide and it did not surprise them', therefore she does not 'think [she] can forgive them'. Moreover, she fears that 'if you forgive them they will repeat what they did'.

The ability to forgive the perpetrators is also linked to the survivors personal healing, another of the profound objectives. It is impossible to overstate the extent of the trauma caused by genocide and healing is an extremely complex process. Clark defines it as 'rehumanising

---

[44] Robert Rotberg, 'Truth Commissions and the Provision of Truth, Justice and Reconciliation', in *Truth V. Justice: The Morality of Truth Commissions*, eds. Robert I. Rotberg and Dennis Thompson (Princeton, NJ: Princeton University Press, 2000), pp. 3–21 (p. 3).

[45] In his book on Gacaca, Clark identifies three types of justice: retributive justice aims to punish perpetrators in a manner that is commensurate with their crime so as to give them what they 'deserve'; deterrent justice aims to punish perpetrators in a way that will dissuade them and others from committing further crimes so as to avoid further punishment; and finally restorative justice holds that while punishment may be necessary, it should be facilitated in ways that allow perpetrators and survivors to rebuild relationships and renew the social fabric. Clark, *The Gacaca Courts, Post-Genocide Justice and Reconciliation in Rwanda*, pp. 38 and 238.

survivors and perpetrators to overcome the negative identities that they assumed during conflict.'[46] Niyongira links her inability to forgive to the psychological consequences caused by the killers' actions: 'I feel I can't manage living with them, it is beyond my imagination. You cannot forgive someone who really tortured you, with all the side effects it had on me.'

Ultimately, survivors in this group feel unable to reconcile with their killers or with the Hutu in general. Although, as Clark highlights, reconciliation is both a process and an end point, at the time of giving their testimonies, survivors in this group tend to see reconciliation as impossible (e.g., Ruhurambuga states: 'I don't think reconciliation is possible'). In its most ambitious form, reconciliation 'entails much more than peaceful coexistence', it requires the 'reshaping of parties' relationships, to lay the foundation for future engagement between them'.[47] Yet even a peaceful cooperation may be impossible for this group, at least at the time their testimonies were recorded. As Nikuze puts it, 'I have no reasons to communicate with the killers. Nothing at all'.

Survivors whose responses fall into this category also tend to support the dominant ideology in Rwanda which collectivises Hutu guilt and stigmatises survivors and, therefore, do not have their collective drive for agency met either. These survivors may accept, for example, that processes of reconciliation should be state imposed. In her discussion of justice and reconciliation, Umulisa M states, for example: 'It's not my place to say, it is the role of the law, and I don't have that right.' This sentiment is echoed in the following citation from the testimony of Muteteri:

For me, Hutu are ruthless animals. They still have that wickedness in their hearts. They are still hurting me, and that makes it hard for me to forgive them. Honestly, when three or four people decide to defecate on top of a grave, tear to pieces every photo that I lay on the grave, it means they cannot change. They teach them about unity and reconciliation but their hearts can never change. They are animals. I have no names for that kind. They are animals. Even animals are better; they let us hide in the bushes next to them. We lived with lions, leopards ... they would let you run away without eating you. But them ... I still fear them. If they had the opportunity ... If they were given a chance, they would hack us again with the same machetes.

---

[46] Ibid., p. 42
[47] Ibid., p. 43.

It would seem that Muteteri agrees with the government and believes that it is the Hutu who 'cannot change'. The statement also suggests that she agrees with the collectivisation of Hutu guilt and that reconciliation, therefore, is a group-to-group process. Given that within the framework of the dominant ideology, Tutsi survivors are also stigmatised, it could be argued that Muteteri is operating under false consciousness as it would appear that her internalisation of the government's ideological stance leads her to alienate other survivors. This is evidenced in other sections of her testimony in which she criticises survivors who turn to alcohol or prostitution, labelling them 'a target for mockery' and encouraging them to 'deal with the pain and endure it' because 'that's the Rwandese way'. She continues her message to other survivors saying, 'preserve your dignity, as we are being taught' because 'there are survivors who are out of control'. I would argue that responses like this provide survivors with neither communion by relating with other groups, nor agency by liberating them from the dominant ideology.

Type II: Communion but Not Agency

Women and men who have their communal but not agentic motivations satisfied comprise the second type of response observed. These five men and five women show a willingness to achieve some of the profound objectives identified by Clark, albeit in a manner that is consistent with the official understanding of 'unity and reconciliation'. Sebasoni explains, for example, that 'justice is needed'. She agrees that finding 'the appropriate punishment' is a challenge, but of the various possibilities, she prefers restorative rehabilitation over retributive or deterrent justice: 'Death is not a punishment, neither is imprisonment. To be honest, I think people should be sensitised'. For Kayiraba, the Gacaca system has not only provided her with justice but also enabled her in the process of healing as she has found 'a place where [she] can express [her]self'.

Other survivors in this group demonstrate a willingness to forgive which is often hinged on receiving the truth. As Harerimana puts it, 'Why not forgive. For me, forgiveness should be given to a person who admits the bad things.' For others, truth is not a prerequisite to forgiveness, as Sebasoni's testimony shows: 'Even though no one has asked me for forgiveness, I have forgiven all those who participated in the killing.' Mukangoga obtained neither truth nor justice but nonetheless expresses a willingness to forgive:

I even filed a case in the Gacaca court, but it's so unfortunate that he bribed them to destroy the evidence ... As a Christian, I will forgive them with no regrets ... There is no way the dead can come back to life. If I knew that killing would bring back the person I lost, I wouldn't hesitate to do it. But I prefer to give out my forgiveness in order to save my soul.

Kabalisa has also been dissatisfied by the justice system stating that it 'was not done fairly' because 'sometimes the sentence did not match the crime committed'. Like Mukangoga, however, he is willing to forgive because of his Christian faith:

When you have been attacked by fellow humans, by neighbours of yours, it is a very demanding sacrifice for you to forgive. But thanks to God we have that power, and the government has helped and we ... I believe in it because it is what builds a country.

A number of survivors in this group also demonstrate an ability to engage in reconciliation, such as Kayiraba who states the following: 'When they [the killers] were released they came home and now we live in harmony. They invite us to theirs and we give them our daughters' hands: in brief we live in harmony.' Kayisire also failed to obtain justice and ended up abandoning her case. She does, however, demonstrate her intention to reconcile:

Reconciliation is important because no man is an island. It is impossible that one ethnic group can occupy the country, a Tutsi needs a Hutu and vice versa. I can take an example of this from school. Without children from different ethnic groups I could lose my job because the vacancy I occupy wouldn't exist. In remote areas, they need agriculturalists, so without all categories of people no one can live better. People need each other in life. I support the unity and reconciliation policy but anxiety of genocide ideology is still there and those who committed the crimes are angrier than us. For us, we are ready to play our role in reconciliation.

Although Kayisire mentions the word 'unity' here, the women in this group do not, in general, distinguish between unity and reconciliation in the same way that men do. As discussed in Chapter 2, a number of the men make this distinction and, in this response type, there are two men who underscore unity as a specific goal, including Nshimiyimana who states that 'Rwandans should unite and put their hands together in the development of their country.' Similarly, Harerimana discusses

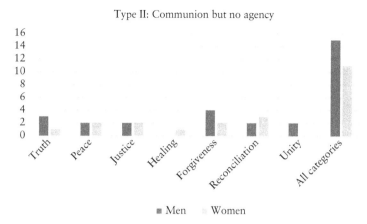

Figure 4.1 Number of men and women who pursue each of the profound objectives (communion)

the need for people to 'live together because they are one people'. In contrast, the women in this category do not discuss unity as a separate goal but rather talk about 'unity and reconciliation' more generally. The other difference between men and women is that, despite the similar numbers who seek communion overall (e.g., five men and five women) the men and women do not always pursue the same communion goals. As Figure 4.1 presents, men appear more concerned with truth, more willing to forgive and more inclined to view reconstruction in terms of unity. Women, in contrast, appear slightly more inclined to reconcile but generally have equal or lower numbers than men. Men pursue more communion goals overall.

Although survivors whose testimonies fall into this category express the desire to restore drives of communion via the profound aims discussed above, these survivors do so in a manner that is consistent with the dominant ideology in Rwanda. Indeed, survivors in this group tend to see the process of reconciliation as largely top–down. Bugirimfura, for example, states that the government should be 'the ones who will explain [reconciliation] so that we understand it'. Similarly, Harerimana suggests that there should be a 'centre in charge of teaching Rwandans to live together'. Many of the survivors in this category could also be said to follow the government line when it comes to forgiveness. This may be the case for Nshimiyimana who advises other survivors to 'overlook what happened and go on with life'. Similarly, Sebasoni's blanket approach to forgiving 'all those who participated in the killing' echoes the government's emphasis on a group-to-group process rather than interpersonal one.[48]

Forgiveness is controversial not only because of government pressure, but also because it is 'so readily connected with religious perspectives'.[49] Religious forgiving can, as Ken Pargament and colleagues suggest, help to shift the anger, hurt and fear associated with a traumatic experience to peace and facilitate life transformation.[50] It is clear that the religious component of Mukangoga's ability to forgive is central as it is not as a human being, a Tutsi, or as a woman, but *nk'umukirisitu* (as a Christian) that she may forgive. Similarly, Kabalisa notes his 'thanks to God' for giving survivors *imbaraga* (the power) to forgive. However, this emphasis on forgiving as a Christian or thanks to God could also be problematic. As Clark observes, 'some survivors argue that they must forgive perpetrators, regardless of the latter's motivations for requesting forgiveness, because their Christian faith requires them to forgive out of gratitude for God's mercy.'[51] Clark suggests that the 'interpretation of a biblical commandment to forgive unconditionally amounts to a damaging level of coercion'.[52] Mukangoga's emphasis on saving her soul (*nzarokora roho yanjye*) could be seen to reflect this coercive sense of duty.

In many cases, survivors in this group also follow the government's ideology through their globalisation of Hutu guilt. As can be seen in the above citation from Kayisire's testimony, implicit intergroup differentiation is carried out, with 'us' being portrayed as 'survivors' who are 'ready to play our role' while 'Hutu' are all 'agriculturalists' who 'committed the crimes' and who still subscribe to the genocide ideology. Thus, despite her attempts to improve horizontal social relations via reconciliation, Kayisire submits to the ideology of Tutsi being synonymous with victim and Hutu being synonymous with perpetrator, echoing the government's stance of collective Hutu guilt.

---

[48] Ibid., p. 313.
[49] Ibid., p. 42.
[50] Harold G. Koenig, Kenneth I. Pargament and Julie Nielsen, 'Religious Coping and Health Status in Medically Ill Hospitalised Older Adults', *Journal of Nervous and Mental Disease*, 186 (1998), 513–21.
[51] Clark, *The Gacaca Courts, Post-Genocide Justice and Reconciliation in Rwanda*, p. 302.
[52] Ibid., pp. 302–3.

Like survivors in the first category, survivors in this category also tend to adopt coping strategies to manage social stigma. As seen in Chapter 1, Kayisire avoids revealing her survivor identity by telling people that her scar is a birthmark. In general, these survivors also follow the government line in encouraging survivors to 'move on'. Kabalisa believes, for example, that survivors 'have to move forward' while Nshimiyimana suggests that survivors 'who don't want to move forward and make that step are fools'. Overall, despite having their shared need for communion satisfied, by following the dominant ideology, survivors in this category do not pursue agency.

Type III: Agency but Not Communion

The third type of response observed in the testimonies includes five men and five women who, like in type I, do not have their communal motivations satisfied but do fulfil agentic motivations. Women and men who respond in this way candidly refuse to forge improved horizontal relationships by rejecting the notion of reconciliation and related objectives, thereby defying the government's ideology and, thus, gaining a sense of liberty.

Many survivors who respond in this way believe in retributive justice and are critical of the way the authorities handle the justice system. Twagirashema, for example, explains that 'unfortunately, the present judiciary system doesn't accept [the death penalty]' and states that 'the judiciary system isn't doing its best'. Similarly, Mukamusoni believes that killers should be punished in 'an exemplary way so that others will learn a lesson'. She also thinks that reconciliation is impossible and asks, 'how can you reconcile with someone who is angrier than you yet it was he who tried to kill you?' Mukamusoni is also critical of the judicial system, particularly the notion of forced apologies:

I've heard that in Gacaca, if they ask for forgiveness then they get released. But who are they asking? Is it the government? Or is it those who they killed? How can it work? This is the question we ask ... Maybe the government has a plan that we don't know, one that uses Rwandan tradition, but Gacaca for crimes of genocide? ... I don't know. It's beyond me!

Similarly, Rutagarama, who sees the killers as his 'enemies', does not believe that justice will 'relieve the pain from losing [his] loved ones'.

In his view, 'laws are not very consistent' and perpetrators are 'easily released'. When the interviewer asks Rutagarama about the government's policy of calling 'upon people to ask for forgiveness' and whether he would forgive if asked genuinely, his reply demonstrates the complexity of this process (and the impossibility of the government's demands):

If they told me the truth ... and said, 'I killed so and so ... I killed them and put them here or there.' That would soothe me slowly. That would be good. At least they would be demonstrating the will to be forgiven. The next thing would be telling you the whereabouts of your family members so you could at least bury them ... But I don't believe that you would be granting total forgiveness. There will always be something. Genocide is quite something. Killing your family members ... it's really hard to forgive. It is very hard to forgive someone who committed genocide. How do you forgive them? Maybe if they resurrect my people. Maybe that's the only thing that would make me forgive them 100% otherwise it is impossible.

Nakabonye also sees Hutu as her enemy and has a similar view to Rutagarama.

– What do you think of Hutus?
– As my enemy, as an enemy of peace. They ask us to reconcile and we reconcile. But you can only reconcile with someone when their cows eat from your field [i.e., over trivial matters]. In the past, people used to move from this hill to go and kill one another over there and there would be a war. Now, just because the Government says, 'Reconcile,' then we reconcile because there's no choice. What would you do? Nothing. If they say, 'Let's unite', we unite. But it's not real. You reconcile with someone in circumstances where their animal damaged your land. You reconcile with someone after fighting because you were drunk. You do not reconcile with someone after they killed your family. That's how it was in the past but for me ... I don't want to reconcile with them at all. But maybe with a Hutu who did not kill, a Hutu with whom I have no problem related to Gacaca and the killing of my family. Those others with whom we don't have problems, it's fine. But that doesn't mean that I live freely and openly with them. But we have to live together because it is our country all together, there's no other way of moving forward. But I won't feel any sympathy towards them ... none. I saw how they changed overnight.

Although in this extract Nakabonye clearly states her reluctance to improve horizontal relations via reconciliation, she does negotiate more favourable vertical relations. She refuses to accept the stigma surrounding survivors by unashamedly defying the government's call for survivors to show 'courage' by forgiving perpetrators. Her ironic tone mocks the government's authoritarian style, as she clearly implies the superficiality of this compliance ('it's not real'). Despite stating her outright refusal to reconcile, Nakabonye does not, however, globalise guilt onto the entire Hutu population as she demonstrates a willingness to reconcile with Hutu who were not involved in the killing of her family. Moreover, in her defiance of government authority, her use of the plural first person actually unites her with other Hutu in their collective resistance against the government, as her use of 'us' and 'them' actually refers to 'us' (Tutsi and Hutu) versus 'them' (the government), in contrast to survivors discussed earlier who voice their willingness to reconcile, but speak in terms of 'us' (Tutsi) versus 'them' (Hutu).

Rather than avoiding the stigma that surrounds survivors who have not 'moved on', survivors in this group appear more critical of the government for not meeting survivors' needs, adopting an empowerment strategy. Rutayisire criticises the government because 'the security of genocide survivors is insufficient' while, in his view, too much money is spent on perpetrators: 'You find the government is spending a lot on [perpetrators] while there are old women ... who have nothing to eat, nowhere to live.' Indeed, contrary to the responses in types I and II, rather than criticising survivors with ongoing problems, Rutayisire is critical of the government for not doing enough:

[The government] should take care of weak people, wounded people, raped people and old women ... they have already forgotten our people. They say that the Genocide came to an end but you find it is still there, so we don't understand. Among our leaders there are some who committed crimes during the genocide.

Similarly, Bukumura criticises the government for not doing enough for survivors and says that it is the perpetrators who 'are the ones who are catered for. The survivors are not remembered, no one talks for them'. Contrary to Kayisire who hides her scar because it marks her as a genocide survivor, Bukumura was offered the opportunity to

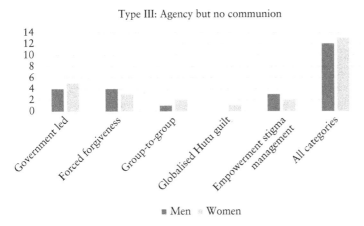

Figure 4.2 Number of men and women in type III who pursue agentic objectives on behalf of their group

have his scar removed but refuses on the grounds that he explicitly wants 'a souvenir of the genocide' so that people will 'never forget what happened'.

Like those in type II, there are similar numbers who seek agency overall (e.g. five men and five women), however, the men and women do not always pursue the same agentic goals. As Figure 4.2 presents, men are slightly more against forced forgiveness and more readily adopt stigma empowerment strategies, while women are more outraged at the idea of reconciliation being a government-led, group-to-group process which globalises guilt. Although the difference is small, women pursue slightly more themes of agency than men in this group.

Type IV: Agency and Communion

The final type of response observed includes six women and eight men who seek to satisfy both communal and agentic motivations in the context of their group identity. The following examples come from the testimonies of women who pursue both improved horizontal relations via the objectives identified by Clark, but who do so independently of the government's ideological framework and, thus, also pursue freedom and autonomy.

Bampiriye is critical of the justice system for allowing cases to 'just disappear' and also for creating a climate in which 'some survivors today fear to accuse killers'. On the other hand, she recognises the enormity of the process of justice in post-genocide Rwanda:

I cannot fail to acknowledge the role of the judiciary system ... What I can credit Gacaca for is that it was better than nothing, having it instilled us with a sense of trust. There are people in prison serving time, and those who are doing TIG[53] who also admitted to have wronged. That is one fact about Gacaca, to some, it was a blessing because it made them repent.

Bampiriye is also sensitive not to globalise guilt to the entire Hutu population as she recognises that '[n]ot everyone was killing'. Kavubi is also critical of the government's implementation of justice. In his view, community service is not helpful to survivors because it 'is not for rebuilding [survivors'] houses, it is not even for giving them back what was looted from their houses'. Instead, he points out that the work is for building roads but, he notes, he pays 'taxes to build those roads' so it has 'nothing to do with justice'. Kavubi shares Bampiriye's view that the atmosphere at the Gacaca trials can be particularly difficult for survivors:

Families of people who killed will be there and preside over the trials yet survivors are represented by only one person who was a child during the genocide, or a traumatised person and who will be mocked by those *Inyangamugayo*[54] and the accused families.

In Kavubi's view, the government is actually preventing personal healing for survivors like him:

I still have nightmares and I still feel so much sorrow and the genocide for me is still taking place because there has been political oriented justice but not absolute justice.

What he means by this is that the killers 'only asked for forgiveness from the government, they didn't ask for forgiveness from those they harmed' and because of this, their sentences were reduced. This criticism does not mean that he is unwilling to engage in reconciliation. Indeed, in Kavubi's view, reconciliation is 'an easy process': 'The one who did wrong comes and apologises [saying] "Forgive me for what I did, I have recognised that I was wrong".' Alluding to the sort of

---

[53] TIG or *Travail d'Intérêt Général* refers to the community service that many perpetrators were obliged to carry out.

[54] *Inyangamugayo* is the Kinyarwanda word for a Gacaca judge. This literally means a trustworthy, reliable person – usually a respected elder on a hill.

official form of apology encouraged by the state, he complains, 'but you can't be in prison and say things and then I hear it from the radio and you expect me to forgive you'.

In a similar vein, the testimony of Mukabyagaju also demonstrates remarkable progress in several of the profound Gacaca objectives identified by Clark while also disagreeing with the government's version of this process:

If a person acknowledges his fault, he admits his sin genuinely and from the heart, then he is already being punished. It will always affect him and there is no greater punishment than the guilt in someone's heart. If it comes from the heart when a person says to me, 'Forgive me, I was involved in the killing of your sibling, your parent ...' I would understand. I would forgive him because the burden he carries in his heart is enough of a punishment. But forgiving in general without a request to be forgiven ... that is very hard for me. I find it so hard. That's like forcing them to receive forgiveness. That's like forcing them to be forgiven when the person doesn't care enough about forgiveness to ask for it from the heart. Forgiveness is about one person seeking it and another one granting it. The person forgiving shouldn't forgive before the seeker asks for it. People should seek to be forgiven genuinely and then be granted forgiveness.

As can be seen in this extract, Mukabyagaju is willing to forgo retributive and deterrent justice by agreeing to accept an apology and acknowledging that genuine guilt is punishment enough. The objectives of forgiveness and reconciliation are also present in this extract. Unlike the blanket approaches to forgiveness discussed earlier in this chapter, Mukabyagaju clearly opposes the government's pressure on survivors to forgive. Instead, Mukabyagaju, like Kavubi, demonstrates an understanding of what forgiveness must entail by emphasising its interpersonal nature. Mukabyagaju continually refers to the perpetrators of genocide in the singular third person[55] and to herself in the singular first person, highlighting the interpersonal nature of this process. Mukabyagaju's resistance to governmental pressure is apparent in the statement 'forgiving in general', which alludes to the government's demands for collective forgiveness and reconciliation. By emphasising the interpersonal nature of reconciliation, Mukabyagaju counteracts the government's interpretation of reconciliation as a 'group-to-group'

---

[55] Although translated as 'he' and 'him', Mukabyagaju uses the gender-neutral word for 'person' (*umuntu*); she does not specify a gender.

process and its tendency to generalise guilt to the entire Hutu population, simultaneously pursuing improved horizontal and vertical relations. Similarly, Gatare is willing to forgive but does so by openly
criticising the government's approach to reconciliation as a group-to-
group process. For example, he states:

About forgiveness ... Personally, I may forgive the man who wounded me
on the head if he asks me to forgive him. But when it comes to collective
forgiveness ... you cannot forgive in the name of someone else.

Murebwayire is also willing to forgive on an individual level but
refers to state-led, group-to-group forgiveness as 'forgiveness out of
hypocrisy'. She explains that, 'someone coming and saying that I am
asking forgiveness from every Rwandan, I don't have that forgiveness. I don't forgive those ones because I see that they are just saying
it, it's like a slogan.' Murengezi highlights the difficulty shared by
many survivors of needing 'to know who you're forgiving'. 'You cannot forgive if no one asks you to forgive him or her,' he says.
Speaking against the globalisation of Hutu guilt, he continues, 'The
question is who to forgive ... Who is it? Not all Hutus killed, therefore you cannot say that you're forgiving the Hutus.'

Indeed, many of the survivors in this category understand that the
line between victim and perpetrator is not as clear as the dualism of
Hutu-perpetrator–Tutsi-victim. Mukabyagaju expresses this view:

Those who did not die in the genocide, died in exile.[56] Whether Hutu, Tutsi
or even Twa, none of us was spared. Some were perpetrators, others were
victims ... But all of us were in trouble, even if it was not to the same extent.

At the same time, her inclusion of Hutu, Tutsi and Twa in the collective 'we' demonstrates significant steps towards a more inclusive
understanding of society. Ruyenzi's testimony also demonstrates this
empathy with the killers: 'Even though we have scars and they know
it ... I know it affects them as it affects us'. He recognises that the
lives of perpetrators are also far from easy: 'they have more problems
than most people. Unlike survivors, they might not have financial

---

[56] Some two million Hutu, perpetrators and others, fled to neighbouring Zaire in
the immediate aftermath of the genocide. Dorethea Hilhorst and Mathijs van
Leeuwen, 'Emergency and Development: The Case of Imidugudu, Villagisation
in Rwanda', *Journal of Refugee Studies*, 13. 3 (2000), 264–80 (p. 266).

problems but they certainly have moral ones'. Ruyenzi also thinks that reconciliation is possible:

Reconciliation will be achieved because when we give testimonies and we feel relieved because we say things that were difficult for us to say in front of people, I think reconciliation will be achieved.

As seen in Chapter 2, a number of the men choose to speak about unity as a separate goal to reconciliation (and even if they say they believe in 'unity and reconciliation', they are often really speaking about unity). Karenzi is one of these who prefers 'to talk about unity because reconciliation is hard'. Similarly, Mutanguha finds forgiveness 'difficult' and has not 'gone down that road yet', but he is in favour of the concept of unity: 'all people in the country should put their energy together and develop the country'.

Like responses in type III, responses in type IV also reveal the pursuit of agency through empowerment strategies for dealing with stigma. For example, rather than avoiding other survivors Ruyenzi gains strength in sharing with them to gain solidarity and inclusion:

In the AERG association [*Association des Etudiants et Elèves Rescapés du Genocide* or Genocide Survivors Students' Association], we interact as we are all survivors. We tell each other what happened to us and it changes something in our lives, it makes us feel integrated in society.

Burizihiza also adopts an empowerment stigma management strategy by confronting truths that are impossible for many Rwandans to articulate. In particular, she speaks out about her experiences of rape and sexual violence:

When they had killed my brothers, that is when he started to use me for sex. He told me, he would go and sit there ... I'd like to demonstrate because he would ... He would do very bad things. He would say ... He would go and sit somewhere like there. He would sit and take off his clothes. He would take off his pistol and place it on the floor with his sword. And he would tell me to take off my clothes and come crawling to him. I remember I showed it in the Gacaca courts, when he was seated in front of me. The judges were shocked. Even he himself was shocked as he didn't think that I would repeat those acts.

Burizihiza's Gacaca testimony against a perpetrator of rape led to this man's imprisonment, enabling her to gain justice. She also confronts the stigma surrounding survivors of sexual violence. What is particularly

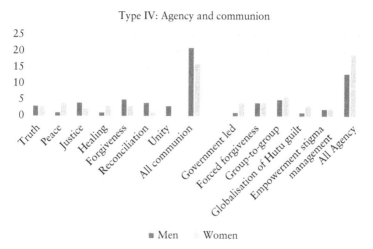

Figure 4.3 Number of men and women in type VI who pursue agentic and communal objectives on behalf of their group

shocking about Burizihiza's testimony, is not only that she volunteers an account of what happened to her, but that she performed a re-enactment of what her rapist forced her to do. More shocking still, is the fact that she did this in front of the Gacaca judges, the local community and the man who raped her. Gacaca judges are among the most prestigious people in a community so having the audacity to confront the very man who raped her, given that he himself was a powerful man in Rwandan politics, clearly surprised everyone present.

In contrast to the coping and avoidance strategies employed by survivors in other categories, Burizihiza clearly adopts the empowerment model and actively encourages the women in ABASA to follow her lead by speaking out. Despite putting her life in danger, Burizihiza's commitment to truth contributes significantly to a more open and honest social narrative of the events of 1994, rather than relying on the monolithic official narrative, and her emphasis on individual, named perpetrators defies the government's tendency to collectivise Hutu guilt.

Overall, it would seem that women and men in this group, who seek to satisfy their group's motivations of agency and communion, produce the most socially constructive response to the genocide which is most likely to generate positive change and collective post-traumatic growth. In a similar pattern observed in types II and III, women in type IV appear to adopt more agentic and fewer communal goals relative to men (see Figure 4.3). Figure 4.4 shows the mean number of

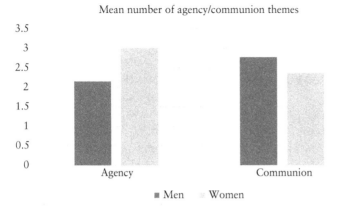

Figure 4.4 Mean numbers of agency and communion themes pursued by men and women

agentic and communal goals pursued by men and women across all groups, demonstrating that this is a trend across the corpus.[57]

Communal Men and Agentic Women

The trend of higher levels of agentic growth in women and higher levels of communal growth in men is perhaps surprising in the face of theories such as Bakan's prototypical agentic men and communal women; or Gilligan's separated men and connected women.[58] The modestly higher levels of communion in men is consistent with the discussion of individual growth in Chapter 2 where I argue that post-genocide masculinity draws heavily on pre-colonial military values such as patriotism, dignity, unity and a shared culture known as *Ndi Umunyarwanda* which, although linked to a warrior identity, are all based on a form of collectivism. While the concept of *Rwandicity* is undoubtedly important for women too, it was not such a salient theme in their testimonies. This may be on account of the militaristic way in which it is experienced by men.

On the other hand, the relatively higher levels of agentic growth in women is consistent with Chapter 3's discussion, which argues that

---

[57] Women were significantly more agentic than men, with the probability of the difference being due to chance at just 3 per cent (p = 0.031). The difference for communion was 44 per cent (p = 0.44) which is not considered statistically significant.

[58] Gilligan, *In a Different Voice*, pp. 234–5.

there has been a shift towards individualism among Rwanda's women linked to broader social transformations in women's roles in society since the genocide. Overall, the results discussed in this chapter would appear to offer support for Alice Eagly's view that situational factors play a role, possibly to a greater extent than gender differences do, in determining social behaviour.[59] The fact that women pursue significantly more agentic goals at the collective level than men also supports Elissa Helms' warning against essentialist constructions of women (as 'nurturers, peacemakers, and anti-nationalists') because they risk 'closing off women's potential for influence in the formal (male) political sphere'.[60] Ann Tickner agrees that, 'in the context of a male-dominated society, the association of men with war and women with peace also reinforces gender hierarchies and false dichotomies that contribute to the devaluation of both women and peace'.[61]

In their book on women and peacebuilding, Albrecht Schnabel and Anara Tabyshalieva note that conflict and violence tend to have disproportionate effects on women but that women are also often marginalised from peacebuilding activities.[62] However, they argue that, '[T]he post-conflict moment offers a window of opportunity to rewrite many rules that previously governed – and misgoverned! – the society. Among these are the rules that determine the relations between men and women, and between women and society at large.'[63] On the other hand, the authors highlight that one of greatest flaws in peacebuilding both in terms of design and application is 'the general tendency to underestimate, underutilise and purposefully marginalise women's roles in peacebuilding activities at local, national and international levels'.[64] In Rwanda, women have been able to seize the opportunity

---

[59] Eagly, *Sex Differences in Social Behaviour*, p. 140.
[60] Elissa Helms, 'Women as Agents of Ethnic Reconciliation? Women's NGOs and International Intervention in Postwar Bosnia–Herzegovina', *Women's Studies International Forum*, 26. 1 (2003), 15–33 (p. 15).
[61] J. Ann Tickner, *Gendering World Politics: Issues and Approaches in the Post-Cold War Era* (New York: Columbia University Press, 2001), p. 59.
[62] Albrecht Schnabel and Anara Tabyshalieva, 'Forgone Opportunities: The Marginalisation of Women's Contributions to Post-Conflict Peacekeeping', in *Defying Victimhood: Women and Post-Conflict Peacebuilding* (New York: United Nations University Press, 2012), p. 3.
[63] Ibid., p. 12.
[64] Ibid., p. 8.

for change through changing gender roles, the women's movement in civil society and through an increased number of women in political life. Having said that, the women's movement continues to face significant challenges primarily because positive changes in women's rights are constrained by failures of the Rwandan government to tolerate the broader range of human rights.[65] However, it would appear that women are leading the way in terms of holding the government to account.

What does need to be addressed still in Rwanda, for both men and women, but particularly for women, is the ways in which agency and communion can be pursued together. Although there has not been any research into the impact of collective agency and communion on societal well-being, as noted in Chapter 3, evidence in individuals suggests that both drives are necessary to promote individual well-being. In light of this, I would argue that there is a need to take these fundamental human drives into consideration when defining what we mean by 'peace-building' or 'post-conflict reconstruction', particularly given that more men than women are experiencing both drives and more women than men are experiencing neither.

Joseph and P. Alex Linley argue that human beings are intrinsically motivated towards post-traumatic growth as part of their innate tendency toward self-actualisation, however, circumstances and environments 'may restrict, impede or distort this intrinsic motivation'.[66] As Ronnie Janoff-Bulman maintains, the 'restorative efforts of survivors to rebuild a valid and comfortable assumptive world are always embedded within the larger context of social relationships'.[67] This is equally relevant to post-traumatic growth processes at the collective level. One of the challenges that groups face when it comes to achieving positive change and post-traumatic growth is that ideological change requires communication between group members. Given that elites tend to have control over the means of ideological production, their social representations about society are hugely influential and tend to favour the ruling class.[68] Elites often apply a number of manipulation strategies in order to maintain ideological control, such as dividing non-dominant groups, preventing in-group solidarity, or

---

[65] Longman, 'Rwanda: Achieving Equality', pp. 146 and 149.
[66] Joseph and Linley, 'Positive Psychological Perspectives', p. 15.
[67] Janoff-Bulman, *Shattered Assumptions*, p. 143.
[68] van Dijk, *Ideology*, pp. 97, 233.

preventing or limiting access to public discourse.[69] As we have seen, the Rwandan government uses a number of these strategies, such as dividing the population and preventing free speech, making the development of counter ideologies far from straight forward. In order to produce and reproduce ideologies, access to public discourse is essential.[70]

Organisations like the Genocide Archive of Rwanda which collected these testimonies play a fundamental role in facilitating collective post-traumatic growth by providing survivors with access to public discourse. Giving their testimonies enables survivors to tell their stories without coercion or contestation. With such an opportunity, even in the aftermath of such devastating horror and under the restrictive environment of an authoritarian regime, some survivors demonstrate that people, whether as group members or as individuals, are capable of developing positive outcomes. Yet although there are some outlets from which the unhindered voices of ordinary Rwandans can emerge, undoubtedly more are needed. As Chapter 5 will reveal, this is also the case for outlets that allow survivors to communicate with the world beyond Rwanda. Although the archive provides a helpful outlet for survivors at the national level, Chapter 5 will argue that the effectiveness of the translated testimonies published by the Aegis Trust is more questionable.

---

[69] In his book on ideology, van Dijk underscores the importance of having access to 'public discourse' in order to either propagate or challenge dominant ideologies. In this respect, 'public discourse' refers to various forms of media through which 'knowledge and opinions may be expressed and widely circulated'. van Dijk, *Ideology*, pp. 162 and 184.

[70] Even in a restrictive setting; however, Thomson has observed tacit forms of resistance against the dominant ideology in Rwanda. Thomson, 'Whispering Truth to Power', pp. 449–54.

5 | *What Is Really Unspeakable?*
Gender and Post-Traumatic Growth at the International Level

As the previous chapter argued, post-traumatic growth at the collective level involves the realisation of a group's drives of agency and communion.[1] Because post-traumatic growth at this level involves changes to shared beliefs, or ideologies, it requires the development of social stories in order for the drives of agency and communion to be satisfied. It is possible to facilitate post-traumatic growth at the collective level by providing members of non-dominant groups with the means of ideological production through access to public discourse, enabling group members to challenge dominant ideologies and provide a counter narrative.[2] Giving their testimonies to the Genocide Archive of Rwanda not only enables survivors to work through their trauma by developing a personal narrative, but also enables them to counter the official version of events in a public domain.

As we have seen in Chapter 1, giving one's testimony is an 'aggressive act'[3] with the potential to challenge the status quo (agency) while gaining acknowledgement for survivors' pain and histories (communion).[4] Clark discusses this communal aspect of testimony – 'healing as belonging' – in the context of the local community, but survivors also attempt through their testimonies to have their histories acknowledged and recognised by the international community, overcoming feelings of social dislocation and estrangement at a global level.[5] As the testimonies collected by the Genocide Archive of Rwanda are translated and

---

[1] Bakan, *Duality of Human Existence*, pp. 14–15; McAdams, *The Stories We Live By*, p. 71.

[2] van Dijk, *Ideology*, p. 184; Williamson, 'Towards a Theory of Collective Posttraumatic Growth', p. 100.

[3] Tal, *Worlds of Hurt*, p. 7.

[4] Clark, *The Gacaca Courts, Post-Genocide Justice and Reconciliation in Rwanda*, pp. 272–3; Dauge-Roth, 'Fostering a Listening Community', para. 10 of 23.

[5] Clark, *The Gacaca Courts, Post-Genocide Justice and Reconciliation in Rwanda*, p. 262.

made accessible in international exhibitions,[6] survivors who give their testimonies have an opportunity to communicate with, and contest the dominant perceptions of, the world beyond Rwanda. Some of the testimonies also appear in a collection that has been published as a book in English by the Aegis Trust, entitled *We Survived: Genocide in Rwanda*, edited by Wendy Whitworth, publishing manager at the Aegis Trust.[7] While such a text might be considered an important platform for survivors to gain a voice with transformative power, this chapter will argue that this is in fact not the case.

In Rwanda, the international community is (justifiably) considered to have been influential in causing the genocide. For example, colonialism is thought to be responsible for racialising Rwandan social divisions[8] and it is widely recognised that the international community failed to prevent the genocide despite being aware of government plans to exterminate the Tutsi population.[9] As President Paul Kagame writes, the international community 'refused to intervene' during the genocide and simply 'turned its back on Rwanda in its hour of greatest need'.[10] Despite the role played by numerous international stakeholders, there nonetheless remains to this day a failure to acknowledge guilt.[11] Indeed, in the West, the genocide is frequently portrayed as 'an inevitable and primitive process that had no rational explanation and could not be stopped by negotiation or force'.[12] Although, in their testimonies, Rwandan survivors contest such an ideology by speaking out and highlighting the failures of the international community, this chapter will demonstrate that interventions made by the editor of *We Survived* in fact have the effect of bolstering it.

---

[6] Some are exhibited by a project called 'Witness for Humanity', developed by the Shoah Foundation at the University of Southern California (https://sfi.usc. edu/), others are made available on the Genocide Archive of Rwanda's own digital archive (www.genocidearchiverwanda.org.rw).

[7] Whitworth, *We Survived*.

[8] Eltringham, *Accounting for Horror*, pp. 19–27.

[9] Melvern, *A People Betrayed*, p. 229.

[10] Paul Kagame, 'Preface' in *After Genocide: Transitional Justice, Post-Conflict Reconstruction and Reconciliation in Rwanda and Beyond*, eds. Phil Clark and Zachary D. Kaufman (London: Hurst and Co., 2008), pp. xxi–vi (p. xxi).

[11] Melvern, *A People Betrayed*, pp. 172–80.

[12] Richard Dowden, 'The Media's Failure: A Reflection on the Rwanda Genocide', in *The Media and the Rwanda Genocide*, ed. Allan Thompson (London: Pluto Press, 2007), pp. 248–55 (p. 252).

Ethics and Representation in Genocide Literature

We Survived is one example among a large body of literature that has been produced about the Rwanda genocide including works of fiction, historical, political and sociological texts, as well as testimonial accounts. All of these works attempt to tell the story of the genocide to a readership that reaches beyond Rwanda, however, their relationship with reality is not always clear. As Paul Kerstens notes, 'often, history and fiction merge'.[13] 'Contrary to literary fiction', Kerstens writes, 'journalistic discourse aims at objectivity, at empirical verification. A journalist observes and reports, but he [or she] does not invent or create.'[14] However, in so-called 'New Journalism', 'the distinction between fiction and non-fiction has lost much of its importance' as such works in this genre 'extend to what one can suppose or imagine, such as individual emotions, unexpressed ideals or goals, and unknown conditions and circumstances'.[15] In contrast, in her book *Rwanda Genocide Stories: Fiction after 1994*, Nicki Hitchcott concludes that authors of fictional texts about the genocide 'share a preoccupation with grounding their texts in historical fact'.[16] She asserts that authors have a 'political agenda to educate readers on the subject of the truth about the genocide'.[17] According to Kerstens, all texts about the genocide attempt in some way 'to grasp the horrific reality and its origins' and that all manifest 'the particular relationship between the writer as a human being and reality'.[18]

Trauma theory's preoccupation with the (un)representability of trauma is pertinent to a discussion of Rwandan genocide literature, as many works have been criticised for their representational practices. Gil Courtemanche's novel *Un Dimanche à la piscine à Kigali* (A Sunday at the Pool in Kigali)[19] and Terry George's movie *Hotel Rwanda*,[20]

---

[13] Paul Kerstens, '"Voice and Give Voice": Dialectics between Fiction and History in Narratives on the Rwandan Genocide', *International Journal of Francophone Studies*, 9. 1 (2006), 93–110 (p. 93)

[14] Ibid., p. 96.

[15] Ibid.

[16] Nicki Hitchcott, *Rwanda Genocide Stories: Fiction after 1994* (Liverpool: Liverpool University Press, 2015), p. 192

[17] Ibid., p. 193.

[18] Kerstens, 'Voice and Give Voice', p. 95.

[19] Gil Courtemanche, *Un Dimanche à la piscine à Kigali* (Montréal: Editions du Boréal, 2000).

[20] *Hotel Rwanda*, dir. Terry George (Metro Goldwyn Mayer, 2004).

for example, have been criticised 'for being too entertaining'.[21] For different reasons, Gilbert Gatore's *Le passé devant soi* (The Past Ahead)[22] has also provoked negative commentary. Hitchcott discusses how critics have condemned the text for 'generat[ing] empathy for a fictional perpetrator and suggest[ing] that perpetrators as well as victims have important stories to tell'.[23] According to Hitchcott, some critics have gone so far as to accuse Gatore 'of using fiction as literary revisionism'.[24] Meanwhile, in a discussion of media representations of the genocide, Vidal highlights the excessive use of images depicting corpses accompanied by graphic descriptions which she believes amounts to voyeurism.[25] Another ethical question that arises when representing the genocide in literature concerns some authors' 'anxiety about speaking for survivors',[26] which Hitchcott contrasts with Dauge-Roth's observation that not doing so 'runs the risk of feeding discourses that profit from survivors' silence and translate their social silence into denial'.[27] While these myriad ethical questions might be considered as corroboration of trauma theory's contention that trauma is ultimately unrepresentable, I remind readers of Bisschoff and Van de Peer's argument (see Chapter 1), that representing trauma in Africa is necessary if we are to move beyond the simplistic and one-dimensional narratives of the continent that tend to prevail.[28] As Nicki Hitchcott insists, 'it is only by reading all the stories together that anything resembling the truth can begin to emerge' and, therefore, multiple stories and representations are necessary.[29] Nonetheless, there is one ethical concern which remains at the

---

[21] Kerstens, 'Voice and Give Voice', p. 95.

[22] Gilbert Gatore, *Le passé devant soi* (Paris: Phébus, 2008).

[23] Nicki Hitchcott, 'Between Remembering and Forgetting: (In)Visible Rwanda in Gilbert Gatore's *Le Passé devant soi*', *Research in African Literatures*, 44. 2 (2013), 86.

[24] Ibid., p. 86.

[25] Claudine Vidal, 'La commémoration du génocide au Rwanda: Violence symbolique, mémorisation forcée et histoire officielle', *Cahiers d'études africaines*, 175 (2004), 575–92.

[26] Hitchcott, *Rwanda Genocide Stories*, p. 133.

[27] Dauge-Roth, *Writing and Filming the Genocide*, p. 118. Cited in Hitchcott, *Rwanda Genocide Stories*, p. 133.

[28] Bisschoff and van de Peer, 'Representing the Unrepresentable', p. 5.

[29] Hitchcott, *Rwanda Genocide Stories*, p. 195.

heart of most genocide literature: the question of *who* is telling the story and it is pertinent to all genres of genocide literature. As Hitchcott observes:

Rwanda's story has for too long been told by outsiders: colonisers, missionaries, journalists, researchers, humanitarian organisations and non-indigenous writers of fiction. Even Rwandan survivor testimonies are, for the most part, written in collaboration with a Western interpreter or co-author.[30]

Who Is Telling the Story?

Hitchcott's book aims to redress this trend by offering 'a more Rwanda-centred perspective on the genocide'.[31] As she notes, 'studies of literary responses to the genocide focus almost exclusively on the works produced by [the Fest'Africa] project,' *Ecrire par devoir de mémoire* (Rwanda: Writing with a Duty to Remember).[32] The project resulted in nine texts, published in 2000 yet, among the authors involved, only two were Rwandan.[33] In Hitchcott's view, there has been 'an overemphasis on this particular group of texts, resulting in the marginalisation of the growing corpus of fictional works by authors born in Rwanda' with some authors being 'completely overlooked'.[34] 'Such selective research', Hitchcott argues, 'risks reducing genocide fiction to a small number of texts written only by outsiders'.[35] The work of Rwandan authors also seems to go unnoticed when it comes to literary prizes.[36]

Alongside the fictional works about the genocide, another genre that has proliferated since 1994 is the literary testimony. In contrast to fictional accounts, texts in this genre are necessarily authored by

---

[30] Ibid., p. 12.
[31] Ibid., p. 11.
[32] Ibid., p. 9.
[33] The other seven were from Burkina Faso, Senegal, Guinea, Cote d'Ivoire, Djibouti, Chad and Kenya. See Nicki Hitchcott, 'A Global African Commemoration – Rwanda: Ecrire par Devoir de Mémoire', *Forum for Modern Language Studies*, 45. 2 (2009), 151–61.
[34] Hitchcott, *Rwanda Genocide Stories*, p. 9.
[35] Ibid.
[36] Ibid., p. 11.

Rwandans, however, the vast majority are written with a Western collaborator.[37] Catherine Gilbert discusses these collaborations and concludes that, although they provide Rwandan survivors with 'access to the Western publishing industry and readership', the relationship between survivor and collaborator may also be 'fraught with hidden tensions and underlying struggles'.[38] In Gilbert's view:

The use of a Western collaborator immediately introduces a power dynamic which potentially places the survivor-witness in a vulnerable position. An imbalance of power between the two contributors creates the potential for abuse: there is a risk of appropriating the survivor's story, or even displacing the survivor's voice in favour of a narrative more familiar to a western audience.[39]

'The collaborator-writer exerts an imaginative authority over the narrative', she continues, 'which leads us to question whether the survivor's voice has been displaced, or even fictionalised.'[40] According to Gilbert, the 'danger of manipulation' is particularly observable in Kayitare's *Tu leur diras que tu es hutue!* (You will tell them you are Hutu), where the collaborator Patrick May 'is described as having *enhanced* her original narrative'.[41] Similarly, Kerstens writes that Mukagasana, also working with May, 'confirms that some specific "literary knowledge" was needed in order to tell her story'.[42] Thomas Couser warns that:

[W]hen mediation is ignored, the resulting text may be (mis)taken for a transparent lens through which we have direct access to its subject (rather

---

[37] Some famous examples of testimonies written with a collaborator include: Immaculée Ilibagiza [with Steve Erwin], *Left to Tell* (London: Hay House Ltd., 2006); Pauline Kayitare [avec Patrick May], *Tu leur diras que tu es Hutue!* (Bruxelles: André Versaille, 2011); Yolande Mukagasana [avec Patrick May], *La Mort ne veut pas de moi* (Paris: Fixot, 1997); Esther Mujawayo [avec Souâd Belhaddad], *SurVivantes* (Paris: Editions de l'Aube, 2004).

[38] Catherine Gilbert, 'Making the Impossible Possible?: Collaboration in Rwandan Women's Testimonial Literature in *The Unspeakable: Representations of Trauma in Francophone Literature and Art*, eds. Névine El Nossery and Amy L. Hubbell (Newcastle: Cambridge Scholars Publishing, 2013), pp. 115–36 (p. 131).

[39] Ibid., p. 118.

[40] Ibid., p. 131.

[41] Ibid., p. 131. (My emphasis)

[42] Kerstens, 'Voice and Give Voice', p. 101.

than to its author) ... The problem is that the monological prose belies the very labour-intensive dialogical process by which it was produced.[43]

This is certainly true of these Rwandan collaborative works.

A third genre common to Rwandan genocide literature is the collection of edited testimonies to which *We Survived* belongs. The most well-known examples of this genre are the three, award-winning books comprised in Jean Hatzfeld's trilogy: *Dans le nu de la vie* (Into the Quick of Life), *Une saison de machettes* (Machete Season) and *La strategie des antilopes* (The Strategy of Antelopes).[44] Respectively, these volumes present the testimonies of survivors, the testimonies of perpetrators and, in the last volume, the testimonies of both groups after the perpetrators have returned to their homes following their release from prison. All testimonies are based on interviews conducted by the French journalist himself. The three texts consist in chapters of testimonies interspersed with chapters authored by Hatzfeld, which mostly describe life in present-day Rwanda, although in the second volume, Hatzfeld's comments also include his reflections on responsibility, guilt and morality. Despite the success of these books among both French

---

[43] Gil Thomas Couser, 'Making, Taking, and Faking Lives: Ethical Problems in Collaborative Life Writing', in *Mapping the Ethical Turn: A Reader in Ethics, Culture, and Literary Theory*, eds. Todd F. Davis and Kenneth Womack (Charlottesville, VA: Virginia University Press, 2001), pp. 209–26 (p. 213). Cited in Gilbert, 'Making the Impossible Possible?', p. 131.

[44] Hatzfeld, *Dans le nu de la vie*, Jean Hatzfeld, *Une Saison de machettes* (Paris: Éditions du Seuil, 2003), Jean Hatzfeld, *La Stratégie des antilopes: Rwanda après le génocide* (Paris: Éditions du Seuil, 2007). The UK English translations are as follows: Jean Hatzfeld, *Into the Quick of life: The Rwandan Genocide – The Survivors Speak*, trans. Gerry Feehily (London: Serpent's Tail, 2005); Jean Hatzfeld, *A Time for Machetes: The Rwandan Genocide: The Killers Speak*, trans. Linda Coverdale, preface by Susan Sontag (London: Serpent's Tail, 2005); Jean Hatzfeld, *The Strategy of Antelopes: Rwanda after the Genocide*, trans. Linda Coverdale (London: Serpent's Tail, 2009). The US English translations are as follows; Jean Hatzfeld, *Life Laid Bare: The Survivors in Rwanda Speak*, trans. Linda Coverdale (New York: Farrar, Straus & Giroux, 2005); Jean Hatzfeld, *Machete Season: The Killers in Rwanda Speak. A Report by Jean Hatzfeld*, trans. Linda Coverdale, preface by Susan Sontag (New York: Farrar, Straus & Giroux, 2005); Jean Hatzfeld, *The Antelope's Strategy: Living in Rwanda after the Genocide*, trans. Linda Coverdale (New York: Farrar, Straus & Giroux, 2009).

and English-speakers, Hatzfeld has also come under criticism for his work.[45]

Scholars have highlighted, for example, the ambiguity of this trilogy. The original French subtitle in the first two volumes includes the term, *Récits*, which, as noted by a number of commentators, is 'an ambiguous term' sometimes used to 'denominate texts of fiction that are neither novels ("romans") nor short stories ("nouvelles")', but can also be used 'for journalist texts, meaning "account" or "report"'.[46] Narelle Fletcher equates the term to the English word 'story' which is similarly vague.[47] Fletcher also observes that most of the appreciation of Hatzfeld's project has 'stemmed from readers' appreciation of the stylistic and "literary" qualities of his writing'.[48] The texts were all published in France by the 'well known literary publishing house' Seuil as part of the series *Fiction & cie* (Fiction & Company), yet, according to Kerstens, 'by the cover of the book, one does not know if it is fiction or non-fiction'.[49] Examining the English translations of *Machete Season*, both Fletcher and Anneleen Spiessens observe how the ambiguity in the original text is largely absent from the translated versions.[50] Both the English and American publications bear the subtitle 'The Killers Speak' and the American version even identifies the text on the cover as 'A Report by Jean Hatzfeld'.[51] According to Hron, the book is indeed often cited or referenced

---

[45] Each of the three books won a prestigious literary prize following publication: *Dans le nu de la vie* was awarded the France Culture Prize in 2001; *Une Saison de machettes* won the Femina Essai Prize in 2003 and *La Stratégie des antilopes* won the Médicis Prize in 2007. Linda Coverdale also won the Scott Moncrieff prize in 2006 for her translation of *Une Saison de machettes*.

[46] Kerstens, 'Voice and Give Voice', p. 102.

[47] Narelle Fletcher, '(Re)Telling the Story of the 1994 Tutsi Genocide in Rwanda: *Une Saison de machettes* (*Machete Season*) by Jean Hatzfeld', in *Storytelling: Critical and Creative Approaches*, eds. J. Shaw, P. Kelly and L. Semler (Basingstoke, UK: Palgrave Macmillan, 2013), pp. 66–79. Cited from www.academia.edu/7566816/_Re_Telling_the_story_of_the_1994_Tutsi_genocide_in_Rwanda_Une_Saison_de_machettes_Machete_Season_by_Jean_Hatzfeld (accessed 4 December 2017), pp. 1–12. See also Anneleen Spiessens, 'Voicing the Perpetrator's Perspective: Translation and Mediation in Jean Hatzfeld's *Une Saison de machettes*', *The Translator*, 16. 2 (2010), pp. 315–36.

[48] Fletcher, '(Re)Telling the Story of the 1994 Tutsi Genocide in Rwanda', p. 2.

[49] Ibid., p. 102.

[50] Ibid., p. 2; Spiessens, 'Voicing the Perpetrator's Perspective', p. 329.

[51] See Fletcher, '(Re)Telling the Story of the 1994 Tutsi Genocide in Rwanda', p. 2; Spiessens, 'Voicing the Perpetrator's Perspective', p. 321.

'without questioning or situating its context, genre, or form, as if the text were an accurate historical document or research report'.[52] Even the original French text employs a number of techniques 'to enhance [the] authority or authenticity' of Hatzfeld's work.[53] For example, he is said to adopt the 'anthropologists' tradition', according to which a writer must emphasise that 'he [or she] "has been there" for a more-or-less extended period'.[54] According to Kerstens, such 'verisimilitude is enforced by mentioning name, age, profession and place of residence of the witnesses, as well as by including a photograph of each witness in his or her "natural surroundings"'.[55]

Scholars have also identified Hatzfeld's use of language as misleading. In the parts of *Une saison de machettes* written by him, Fletcher comments on his 'highly poetic language, including instances of alliteration and assonance, while the deliberate inclusion of a term in Kinyarwanda, written in italics, reinforces both the authenticity and the "otherness" of the setting'.[56] She shows how Hatzfeld creates a relationship between 'author and reader through their shared status as "foreigner"', a relationship which thus necessitates a '"translator" of the material to ensure that the French readers are given an accurate representation of the killers' perspective'.[57] Yet, according to Spiessens, Hatzfeld 'questions the moral acceptability' of his own project and 'feels the need to distance himself from his interviewees and to show "which side he is on"'.[58] He thus 'actively frame[s] the killers' testimony' while 'simultaneously offer[ing] a counter discourse'.[59] Spiessens thus challenges Hatzfeld's 'illusion of an authentic text in which the reader can "hear the voice" of the perpetrator'.[60] She argues that, 'as author-narrator, Hatzfeld not only contextualises the killers' testimonies but evaluates their stories, explicitly presenting them as suspect, deceptive or even plainly false'.[61]

---

[52] Hron, '*Gukora* and *Itsembatsemba*', p. 126.
[53] Kerstens, 'Voice and Give Voice', p. 102.
[54] Ibid., p. 103.
[55] Ibid.
[56] Fletcher, '(Re)Telling the Story of the 1994 Tutsi Genocide in Rwanda', p. 4.
[57] Ibid., pp. 2 and 3.
[58] Spiessens, 'Voicing the Perpetrator's Perspective', p. 333.
[59] Ibid., p. 334.
[60] Ibid., p, 319.
[61] Ibid., p. 322.

The language employed in the Rwandan testimonies is even more intriguing. In *Dans le nu de la vie*, Hatzfeld explains that there are three languages in play: Kinyarwanda, ('langue des cultivatrices' [the language of the women farmers], Rwandan French, 'langue des autres personnes et des traducteurs' [the language of other people and of the translators], and Hexagonal French.[62] Yet, as a few commentators have pointed out, we do not know which testimonies were expressed in Kinyarwanda and which were expressed in so-called Rwandan French.[63] In her discussion of *Une saison de machettes*, Madelaine Hron draws attention to Hatzfeld's translator, Innocent Rwililiza, an educated teacher who was among the survivors of the same region. Although Hatzfeld refers to his translator as a 'neutral witness', Hron is sceptical of the veracity of the killers' statements given Rwililiza's subject position as a genocide survivor from the same region. Spiessens concurs that Hatzfeld 'mismanages certain linguistic aspects of his project, including his unquestioned belief in Innocent's "faithful" translations and his lack of transparency in indicating which parts of his text were translated and which were not'.[64] Moreover, Spiessens suggests that the opposition of Hatzfeld's '"Hexagonal" French to the killers' Rwandan French, ultimately creates the false illusion that the author's voice and that of the killer can remain neatly distinguishable in the text'.[65] What Spiessens is alluding to here, is the fact that not only were the testimonies orally translated by Rwililiza, but they were also adapted from spoken to written word by Hatzfeld. Fletcher argues that Hatzfeld 'is very much aware that his material must be engaging and evocative'.[66] The problem, however, is that 'anyone who has had occasion to read transcriptions of testimonies or unedited interviews would be very much aware that they can be repetitive and long-winded'.[67] She argues that 'in order to capture and retain the reader's attention, Hatzfeld has imbued not only the opening pages, but also his transcriptions of the killers' words with rhythm, imagery, stylistic effects such as alliteration and

---

[62] Hatzfeld, *Dans le nu de la vie*, p. 13.
[63] Kerstens, 'Voice and Give Voice', p. 103, Spiessens, 'Voicing the Perpetrator's Perspective', p. 334.
[64] Spiessens, 'Voicing the Perpetrator's Perspective', p. 334.
[65] Ibid.
[66] Fletcher, '(Re)Telling the Story of the 1994 Tutsi Genocide in Rwanda', p. 6.
[67] Ibid.

repetition of sentence structure'.[68] As Kerstens concludes, the first-person narration adopted in the testimonies 'is misleading, as it is not a transcription of the testimony, but a reworked and re-written version of it'.[69] Furthermore, in Hron's discussion, she highlights the fact that Hatzfeld censored the killers by asking them to rephrase if they used heroic, military vocabulary to refer to the killing while allowing them to use agricultural terms.[70] In Hron's view, omission of past episodes of violence leads readers to perceive the killers as ordinary and ignorant when in fact farming vocabulary has been used in past anti-Tutsi campaigns. By omitting historical context, readers are left to assume that the killers in *Machete Season* are uneducated when a historically informed reading would suggest otherwise.[71] Overall, Hron concludes that the editorial and translational interventions portray the killers as '"ordinary" before 1994' and suggest 'that this "primitive" African ethnic group is not as culturally or psychologically complex as … a single Western serial killer'.[72] This, Hron intimates, 'reflects popular Western stereotypes about the "savage", "dark continent" of Africa, while also positing the genocide in Rwanda as an exceptional, unpredictable catastrophe'.[73]

Like Hatzfeld's texts, the testimonies included in *We Survived* were also edited by a Westerner, Wendy Whitworth, publishing manager at the Aegis Trust. Thus, *We Survived* would appear to support Hron's conclusions that 'in current cultural production, Rwandans … rarely speak for themselves.'[74] Because it is based on testimonies housed at the Genocide Archive of Rwanda, however, *We Survived* does offer researchers a window into the production processes involved in a published collection of testimonies because, unlike with the Hatzfeld texts, we can carry out a direct comparison between the original testimonies and the published versions. In the paragraphs that follow, this chapter offers such an analysis and the findings are quite striking.

---

[68] Ibid.
[69] Kerstens, 'Voice and Give Voice', p. 103.
[70] Hron, '*Gukora* and *Itsembatsemba*', p. 133.
[71] Ibid., p. 136.
[72] Ibid., pp. 139 and 141.
[73] Ibid., p. 136.
[74] Ibid., p. 133.

A Gendered Approach

We Survived is comprised of twenty-eight testimonies (fifteen women and thirteen men), all from the Genocide Archive of Rwanda. These were, therefore, recorded orally in Kinyarwanda, transcribed, translated into English and/or French by the archive before being subsequently edited by Whitworth (who, incidentally, speaks neither French nor Kinyarwanda). I have elsewhere examined the archive translations of testimonies and found a significant amount of ideologically driven skewing involved in the process.[75] Thus, having already been through the 'violence of translation',[76] the testimonies in *We Survived* have been subsequently modified by an editor with no specialist knowledge of the source language. This chapter compares the published edited versions of twenty testimonies (ten men and ten women)[77] with the archival translations to examine how the voices of survivors have been shaped for a Western audience. Where relevant, I comment on differences between the original Kinyarwanda versions and the archive translations although my focus is to analyse Whitworth's editorial strategy rather than the archive translations.

The main editorial tendencies include: the general domestication of the texts, the removal of orality, the correction (and sometimes insertion) of errors, the linearisation of the narrative and the reduction in length by means of cutting text describing life before and after the genocide, the portrayal of survivors as 'nicer' than the original versions, the removal of gendered dimensions of the genocide and the censoring of criticisms of outsiders. I demonstrate that, while the words of both men and women are altered in the published text, criticisms of the international community are censored to a greater extent in the testimonies of women than those of men. This chapter discusses the implications of these findings and how they might influence our interpretations of other testimonial texts available in the West. In the concluding remarks, I refer back to trauma theory's insistence on the unrepresentability of trauma discussed in Chapter 1 and highlight once again how damaging such a concept can be in a context where survivors, particularly women, have to fight to be heard.

[75] Williamson, 'Posttraumatic Growth at the International Level', p. 41.
[76] Lawrence Venuti, 'Translation as Cultural Politics: Regimes of Domestication in English', in *Critical Readings in Translation Studies*, ed. Mona Baker (London: Routledge, 2010), pp. 67–79 (p. 68).
[77] These include all the testimonies published in *We Survived* with transcripts available.

Domestication

One of the most consistent editorial tendencies in *We Survived* is the overall domestication of the testimonies included therein, which serves to enhance the fluency of reading, giving the appearance that the testimonies are not translations but 'original' texts.[78] This includes, among other things, the domestication of foreign sounding language, the removal of specific cultural references, the conventiona-lisation of names, and the removal of names of people and places.

Language domestication can be found throughout the text but Ruyenzi's testimony provides a good example. In reference to the RPF being able to save the survivors who were forced to walk from the ETO (École Technique Officielle) to Nyanza after being abandoned by UNAMIR soldiers, Ruyenzi states 'nta bundi buryo bari bafite bwo kutugeraho'. This is rendered in the unedited archive translation as 'they had no way to reach us' but as 'they didn't have any means of get-ting to us' in *We Survived*.[79] The verb 'to reach' is a direct translation of the Kinyarwanda verb *kugera* ('kutugeraho'), but Whitworth's use of the phrasal verb ('getting to us') sounds more like the choice of a native English-speaker. Although this domestication strategy is not alto-gether consistent, there are many other examples of this type.

Another form of domestication in *We Survived* is the removal of cultural references. For example, in Mukamusoni's testimony, she makes the following statement when describing an *Interahamwe* who came after her while she was hiding at the district office in Nyarugenge, Kigali: 'They were *Interahamwe* from Bikindi's place, he was a Gisenyi man from their place'.[80] Simon Bikini was a Rwandan singer from Gisenyi, famous for singing anti-Tutsi songs on *Radio Rwanda*. He was later charged by the ICTR for, among other things, direct and public incitement to commit genocide. This reference is

---

[78] This is not unsurprising as fluent, domesticated translations are usually those favoured in the British and American Publishing industries. Laurence Venuti, *The Translator's Invisibility: A History of Translation* (London: Routledge, 2004), pp. 1–6.

[79] Whitworth, *We Survived*, p. 189.

[80] Unlike elsewhere in this book, all quotes in English in this chapter use the unedited archival translations. If there are discrepancies between the archive translation and the Kinyarwanda version, this is highlighted. Throughout this chapter, I also give the original Kinyarwanda version of quotes in the notes. For this statement, the original words are as follows: 'Zari za Nterahamwe zo kwa Bikindi. Yari umunyagisenyi yari uwo iwabo.'

removed from *We Survived*, and the man is described simply as: 'a notorious killer from Gisenyi'.[81] Similarly, in the same testimony, when explaining why the *Interahamwe* did not kill her on that occasion, Mukamusoni explains that they were ordered to attend Habyarimana's funeral, stating: 'Our parent [father], we must go and bury him. Who will cover him otherwise? Let these women go, we can come back for them'.[82] The term 'umubyeyi' meaning 'parent' or 'father' was frequently used to refer to former President Juvénal Habyarimana, who was known as 'Umubyeyi w'Igihugu'/'the Father of the Nation'. This reference is removed in *We Survived*, where the sentence is rendered as follows: 'We must first escort Habyarimana on the day of his burial. I order you now, don't kill these women'.[83]

Kinyarwanda names are also domesticated in *We Survived*. In Rwanda, every child is given a European Christian name as well as a unique Kinyarwanda name. By convention, the Kinyarwanda name comes first and is followed by the Christian name. In dialogue with people from Western countries, however, Rwandans themselves tend to reverse the order to meet European conventions. This is not done in the archive translations of the testimonies, e.g., in Niyongira's testimony she states: 'My father was called Butare Charles; my mother was called Mukamunana Agnes'. In *We Survived* the names are reversed: 'My father's name was Charles Butare and my mother's Agnes Mukamunana'.[84] In some cases, the Kinyarwanda name is dispensed with altogether. Ruyenzi, for example, introduces himself in the usual Kinyarwanda way, 'Nitwa Ruyenzi Olivier' which is rendered word for word in the archive translation ('I am called Ruyenzi Olivier') but the Christian name only is given in *We Survived*: 'My name is Olivier'.[85] On other occasions, the names of people are entirely removed as can be seen in the following extract from Twagirashema's testimony:

Gasana Bihehe again tried to save me due to the friendship we shared before. But he told me, Jane and Munyankindi, a daughter of Nyankindi Athanase who were also hiding with us: 'First of all, you are going to sign

---

[81] Whitworth, *We Survived*, p. 96.
[82] In Kinyarwanda: 'Ngo umubyeyi wacu ni tumushyingura tuzamworosa iki? Ngo: ndavuze ngo nimureke abo bagore ... ngo nimubasubizeyo.'
[83] Whitworth, *We Survived*, p. 96.
[84] Ibid., p. 148.
[85] Ibid., p. 188.

for me that you're giving me all your properties as a sign of gratitude for what I will have done for you'.[86]

The *We Survived* version of this text reads as follows:

Gasana again tried to save me because of our previous friendship. But he told me (and the others hiding with us), 'First of all, you're going to sign to say that you're giving me all your properties out of gratitude for what I'm doing for you'.[87]

Clearly Gasana Bihehe's name is simplified to 'Gasana' while the names of those hiding with Twagirashema are removed altogether. This anonymisation of people (and places) can be observed throughout *We Survived*.

Removal of Orality

Another editorial tendency in *We Survived* is the removal of signs of orality. This can be observed in a number of ways. One way is the reduction of dialogue embedded within the narrative. When stories are told orally in Kinyarwanda, the teller will usually report speech directly, adopting the voice of the person speaking, as can be seen in the archival translation of Kavubi's testimony:[88]

I found people sharpening machetes there. When they saw me, they said, 'Halt. Where are you going?'

– 'I was going to drink water,' I lied.
– 'Come here,' they ordered. 'Drink and come here'. I drank once and then they said, 'Bring your papers'. I gave them to them. When they saw them, one read that I was a Tutsi; he then took my ID and kept it. 'Where were you going?' he asked me.

---

[86] In Kinyarwanda: 'Byongeye muri icyo gihe ehh uwo Gasana bihehe yabaga nkaho arwanyeho bitewe n'ubushuti twari dufitanye mbere niho yambwiraga ati n'ubwo bimeze gutyo mwebwe abazasigara mbere na mbere nuko umutungo wanyu ugizwe n'amasambu y'uko mwansinyira nkazayagumana akaba ariyo ngororano y'ineza naba nabagiriye. Ibyo yabibwiye uwitwa Jeanne na Munyankindi mwene Munyankindi Atanase nawe yari ahishe kimwe nanjye.'
[87] Whitworth, *We Survived*, p. 208.
[88] Direct quotations can be made in one of two ways in Kinyarwanda. First, by using the word *ngo* ('that') and second, with the verb stem '-ti'. '-Ti' can be used as the main verb or in conjunction with the verb *kuvuga* ('to speak' or 'say'). As can be seen in the following note, Kavubi uses a mixture of these ways.

- 'I was going to drink water,' I said.
- 'Where are you from?' he asked.
- 'From Karugira,' I responded.
- 'Can someone come from Karugira to drink water here?' he continued asking.
- 'No. I was coming to look for something to feed my children because things are tough, markets are closed.'
- 'Does anyone here know you?' he asked again.
- 'Yes. That church watchman knows me. You can even ask him, I am not an Inyenzi,' I said.
- 'Let's go and ask him,' he said. When we arrived there, he was sitting on a stool.
- 'Do you know this man?' they asked.
- 'Yes,' he said.
- 'How do you know him?' they asked again,
- 'We are brethren and he lives at Karugira,' he said.
- 'What is his name?'
- 'Kavubi Pierre,' he said.
- 'What is his ethnic group?' he asked.
- 'I don't know about the ethnic group but he is an ordinary man and we all know him,' he said.
- 'Give him back his ID, and let's go,' said the other man
- 'Do you want me to give him his ID back even though he is a Tutsi?' He asked him.
- 'Is he a Tutsi?' asked the other man. They tied me up and put me in front. The first one beat me with a big wooden stick.
- 'Before killing me, go and ask people if I am Inyenzi,' I pleaded them. After a few steps, they started beating me.[89]

---

[89] In Kinyarwanda: 'Nsanga abantu bariho baratyaza imihoro ahongaho. Bambonye ngo: "hagarara". Ngo: "urajya hehe". Nti: "nari nje kunywa amazi". Ndababeshya ngo nari nje kunywa amazi. Bati: "ngwino hano". Ndaza. Bati: "nywa amazi, uze tukubwire". Nyora amazi rimwe ngize ubwa kabiri numva birananiye, ngo: "zana ibyangombwa". Ndabizana. Barebye umwe asanga handitsemo ko ari umututsi, idantite [indangamutu] arayifata arayibika. Ngo: "wari ugiye hehe?" Nti: "Nari nje kunywa amazi". Ngo: "Uje kunywa amazi uva hehe?" Nti: "Mvuye ruguru iriya ahantu bita ku Karugira". Ngo: "Se" ngo: "Umuntu ava ku Karugira, akaza kunywa amazi hano?" Nti: "Oya", nti: "Ntabwo aricyo kinzanye, nari nje gushaka utwo kurya, kuko ibintu byacitse ahantu hose amasoko yafunze, nari nje ngirango ndebe utwo kurya nishyirire abana". Bati: "Ino ahangaha hari umuntu ukuzi?" Nti: "Baranzi". Ngo: "Ukuzi ni nde?" Nti: "Uriya umuntu urarira ku rusengero hirya hariya aranzi, bishobotse mwagenda mukajya kumubaza njyewe rwose ntabwo ndi inyenzi". Ngo: "Noneho niba ari ibyongibyo ngwino tugende".

This is rendered as follows in *We Survived*:

'I found some people there sharpening their machetes. They stopped me and asked, 'Where are you going?' I told them I'd come for some water. They asked for my ID card and one of them realised that it said Tutsi on it. They asked me where I came from and where I was going. 'I'm not an Inyenzi,' I said. But the man with my ID card told them it said Tutsi. They tied me up and started beating me.[90]

Of course, the *We Survived* version differs here in a number of ways, most notably in its length but also in its anonymisation of people and places (e.g. references to 'Karugira' and to Kavubi himself are removed). In the parts of this text which are rendered, the speech is often reported indirectly rather than directly as it is in the original (e.g. 'I told them I'd come for some water' instead of '"I was going to drink water," I lied'). This omission of internal dialogue makes the testimony considerably less animated and dialogic than the original and could also be considered a form of domestication as, in English, indirectly reported speech would be the norm.

Orality is also removed in *We Survived* through omissions of dialogue that takes place between the survivor and the interviewer. This can be seen most clearly in the testimony of Bugirimfura:

– Could you tell us your background, your name, and your profession?
– About my background? I am 28 years old; I was born in Kamegeri in the cell of Kirehe.
– Speak louder please.
– I was born in Kamegeri in the cell of Kirehe.

Turagenda tugeze imbere ye, yari yicaye ku "gataburete", baramubaza ngo: "niko ngo: uyu mugabo uramuzi?" Undi aravuga ati: "Ndamuzi". Ngo: "Umuzi ute?" Ngo: "Uyu mugabo ndamuzi rwose, turasengana hano ku rusengero", ngo: "Kandi atuye ruguru iriya ku karugira". Ngo: "Yitwa nde?" Undi ati: "yitwa Kavubi Pierre". Ngo: "Umwanya umuzi … wawundi ufite ibya ngombwa byanjye ahita amubwira", ngo: "Umwanya umuzi, ni bwoko ki?" Undi aramubwira ati: "Njyewe uby'ubwoko simbizi", ati: "Gusa icyo nzi cyo ni uko atuye ruguru iriya akaba ari umuntu usanzwe tuzi". Ngo noneho … undi mugabo aravuga ngo: "Sha" ngo: "Musubize idantite ye" ngo: "Yigendere". Umh, ngo: "Musubize identite ye, kandi ari umututsi?" Eh! Ngo: "Mbese burya bwose ni umututsi?" Ngo: "Yee". Ako kanya baba baramfashe, baba baramboshye bashyira imbere. Uwa mbere aba ankubise umuhini hano mu bitugu, ndababwira nti: "ariko rero mube muretse kunyica", nti "kubera yuko n'ubwo mujya no kunyica, mubanze mugende mujye kubaza n'abantu ko naba ndi inyenzi". Turagenda tugeze imbere, bamaze kunkubita ibintu by'ibikoni bari bafite.'

[90] Whitworth, *We Survived*, p. 64.

– What is your name?
– My name is Bugirimfura Athanase.
– How old were you during the Genocide?
– During the Genocide, apart from this of recent ehh, anyway I was
  born in 1976 so I was ahh …
– You were 18 years old.
– Yes.[91]

All traces of dialogue are removed in *We Survived*, where the extract is
rendered as follows: 'My name is Athanase and I was eighteen years old
during the genocide. I was born in 1976 in Kamegeri, in Kirehe cell'.[92]

Correction (and Insertion) of Errors

As part of the tendency to remove orality, the editor corrects historical and other errors made by survivors in the course of speech.
Nibagwire, for example, states that the plane carrying Habyarimana
was shot down on 7 April 1994 but this is corrected by Whitworth
('the death of President Habyarimana on 6 April 1994'[93]). At times,
Whitworth also adds explanations not present in the original testimony, presumably to clarify meaning. For example, in another
section of Nibagwire's testimony, where she describes leaving the
man who took her from her family, there is an additional line of
description in *We Survived* that is not present in the original: 'I was
with Hutu people who were scared of the Inkotanyi'.[94] While such

---

[91] In Kinyarwanda:

  – 'Watubwira umwirondora wawe, amazina yawe, n'icyo ukora ubungubu?'
  – 'Njyewe umwirondoro wanjye, mfite imyaka 28, nkaba mvukira
    kamegeri sellure kirehe'.
  – 'Vuga cyane'.
  – 'Nkaba mvukira Kamegeri, sellule Kirehe'.
  – 'Ubundi witwa nde?'
  – 'Nitwa Bugirimfura Athanase'.
  – 'Mugihe cya génocide wari ufite nk'imyaka ingahe?'
  – 'Mu gihe cya génocide? mbega jyewe ubundi navutse mu w'i 1975.ubwo
    rero … nari mfite nka cumi n'ingahe …'
  – 'Ndikumva yari nka cumi n'umunani ahari'.
  – 'Yego'.

[92] Whitworth, *We Survived*, p. 26.
[93] Ibid., p. 128. In Kinyarwanda: 'Mu mwaka w'i 1994 mu kwa kane, ku itariki
    zirindwi.'
[94] Ibid., p. 129.

modifications may add some clarification for readers, the editor some-times adds mistakes to the testimonies. Some of these mistakes appear unmotivated and do not significantly affect the narrative (e.g., Ruyenzi describes how his sister was 'the hit in the head with a ham-mer' which is rendered as 'hit in the head with a club')[95]. At other times, changes made by the editor add incoherence to the story, such as in Kavubi's case where he states: 'They hacked me, I fell forward. They hacked my back as they had hacked my head and blood was flowing. That is how they didn't notice that they hadn't hacked my neck, that is how I survived.'[96] This is rendered in *We Survived* as 'Blood was flowing from the back of the neck and they didn't know they hadn't finished me off'.[97]

Some of the inaccuracies even add a surplus racial dimension to the narrative that is not present in the original. When being helped by some watchmen (after having already been hacked), Kavubi explains that 'someone came and knocked on the door. He [one of the watchmen] went to open it thinking that it was one of his colleagues but then we saw someone with a CDR [Coalition for the Defence of the Republic] hat'.[98] This is rendered, somewhat oddly, in *We Survived*, as: 'we heard someone knock at the door. He opened it, thinking it was one of the white men, but it was a black guy wearing a CDR cap'.[99] This addition of racial categories is hard to interpret. Perhaps the editor misread the term 'watchman' and saw 'white man'. This error, perhaps an uncon-scious one, appears to automatically associate positive values with the supposed 'white guy', and also to add, unnecessarily, 'blackness' to the threatening person wearing the extremist hat.

---

[95] In Kinyarwanda: 'Baramukubise inyundo mu mutwe noneho.'
[96] In Kinyarwanda: 'Ubwo kuko bamaze kuntema, nitura hasi nubamye. Noneho bajya mu mugongo baratema uko bashatse, barangije … Icyokora kuko bari batemye mu mutwe, amaraso ashokera hano hose [mu irugu] ntibamenya ko batatemye ijosi. Ubwo niyo mahirwe yatumye mbese kugeza uyu munsi wa none nkiriho.'
[97] Whitworth, *We Survived*, p. 65.
[98] In Kinyarwanda: 'Akomanze agiye gukingura agira ngo ni abazamu bagenzi be, tubona umuntu wambaye ingofero ya CDR.' The Coalition pour la Défense de la République, was a radical Hutu racist, staunchly anti-Tutsi party, working on the right of the National Revolutionary Movement for Development (MRND). Prunier, *The Rwanda Crisis*, p. 128.
[99] Whitworth, *We Survived*, pp. 66–7.

Linearisation of Narrative, Reduction in Length and Depoliticisation

In all cases, the testimonies have been edited to adhere to chronological linearity, with the addition of the sub-headings: 'Before the Genocide', 'The Genocide' and 'After the Genocide'. Many include other subheadings (such as 'The Future' or 'Today') but all are structured in terms of before, during and after the genocide, which is not strictly the case in the original versions. The reorganisation serves to remove the feeling of orality by making the texts seem more carefully planned and also renders the testimonies more understandable to a Western reader (by following conventions of western narratives). The testimonies are also all reduced in length from the original versions.

As Table 5.1 shows, the original men's testimonies are, on average, slightly longer than the women's but have been cut to a greater extent, occupying, on average, fewer pages in *We Survived*. The final column in Table 5.1 presents an estimation of the average final word count of the testimonies (based on an average number of 500 words per page). Although men started out by saying more words but end up with a lower average total, none of these differences between the men and women's figures are statistically significant and, as will be seen, women are still censored more than men when it concerns comments about the international community. What is important for the testimonies of both men and women, is that the cutting of words tends to occur in the 'Before the Genocide' and 'After the Genocide' sections of their testimonies, leaving their stories of survival more or less intact in most cases.

While this editing strategy is in line with the title and theme of the book (i.e., surviving genocide), it means that what gets removed is, very often, discussions of history and politics, making the testimonies sound less political than the original versions. One of the most

Table 5.1. *Average total word length of testimonies, the average number of pages in* We Survived *and the estimated average number of words in the testimonies appearing in* We Survived

	Average total number of words	Average total number of pages	Estimated final average word count
Women	5,647.6	7.95	3,975
Men	5,887.7	7.4	3,700
Overall	5,767.65	7.675	3,837.5

striking examples of this is in the testimony of Kavubi. The length of his original Kinyarwanda transcript is 15,282 words but is reduced to 9.5 pages.[100] There are lots of sections where he discusses the politics of the 1990s, as well as post-genocide politics of justice and reconciliation that have been omitted (as well as many distortions in his discussions of the international community). The same can be said for Mudahogora, whose original Kinyarwanda transcript has a word count of 6,087 (above the average, even for men) yet a page count of 6.5 (below the average).[101] Among the omitted details are descriptions of history, several early predictions of the genocide, and early acts of resistance. Moreover, in the *We Survived* version Mudahogora's testimony ends as follows:

I stayed with my aunt until she died in 2000. I lived there with a few of my cousins who had also survived. When I found my aunt, she thought no one had survived. She was surprised to see me and although she saw how much I had changed, she was happy that I was at least still alive.[102]

This abrupt and somewhat happy ending leads, in the original testimony, to an almost 2,000-word discussion of post-genocide family life, hospital treatments, her return to school, as well as post-genocide politics of justice and reconciliation, all of which is redacted from *We Survived*. While not all political comments are omitted or removed from the text, Whitworth's editing approach leads to an overall impression of survivors as significantly less political than their original testimonies suggest and also makes the genocide appear as an unpredictable event with no causes or consequences. Thus, in *We Survived* the genocide appears as if it were a sudden eruption of tribal violence, much like it was portrayed in the international media at the time.[103]

Portrayals of Survivors as 'Nicer'

Combined with this editorial approach which makes survivors appear less political, there is also a tendency to make them appear 'nicer' by altering statements about acts of self-preservation, selfishness or

---

[100] Going by my estimation of 500 words per page, this means that the *We Survived* version has around 4,750 words, almost a third of the original.
[101] Going by my estimation of 500 words per page, this means that the *We Survived* version has around 3,250 words, almost halving the original.
[102] Whitworth, *We Survived*, p. 80.
[103] Allan Thompson, ed., *The Media and the Rwanda Genocide* (London: Pluto Press, 2007).

acts that could be considered culturally controversial in the West. Acts of self-preservation are described in Mudahogora's description of life during the genocide in the Bugesera district where she notes that, by the 10 April 1994, 'everyone was fighting for his or her own life' which is rendered in *We Survived* as follows: 'we were all carrying on life as usual'.[104] After a second attack in which she herself was hacked, she notes how 'a certain person came and said, "Oh no, Mudahogora has been hacked look at how she is hurt!"' but 'at that time everyone was running for his or her own life'. The second part of this statement is removed from the *We Survived* version.[105]

Survivors also appear nicer when discussing post-genocide politics. For example, the *We Survived* version of Mukamusoni's testimony reports her saying that: 'The most important thing is to set up a culture of punishing those who harassed and killed others. They should be punished accordingly and in public, for others to see and learn a lesson.'[106] In the original Kinyarwanda version, however, Mukamusoni also states her support for public executions: 'the prisoners from Gikongoro who have been condemned to the death penalty will be publically executed; I think this will serve as a lesson to the people of Gikongoro'.[107] This does not appear in *We Survived*. Kamuronsi similarly wants retributive justice, stating that 'killing them would do them some good. Even if they killed them, they would kill them "nicely" compared to the way they killed my parents'.[108] This statement should appear on page 57 in *We Survived* but has been redacted.

Sometimes survivors report doing things which might be considered culturally controversial or taboo in Western culture. Kavubi, for

---

[104] Whitworth, *We Survived*, p. 76. In Kinyarwanda: 'Umuntu wese yari asigaye yirwariza, yirwanaho.'

[105] In Kinyarwanda: 'Sinzi umuntu umwe wahaciye aravuga, ngo: "yewe we!" Ngo Mudahogora bamutemye disi, ngo reba ukuntu yabaye. Noneho aho kugira ngo undi ... icyo gihe abaturage nabo babaga basigaye, babaga bameze nk'abahahamutse nyine buri wese yi ... aramira amagara ye.' Rendered in *We Survived* as: 'And then someone came and said, "Oh no, Mudahogora has been hacked. Look how badly she's hurt!"' Whitworth, *We Survived*, p. 77.

[106] Ibid., p. 98.

[107] In Kinyarwanda: 'Nka bariya bantu bo ku Gikongoro nk'uko bavuze ko babakatiye urwo gupfa, kandi bazabarasa kumugaragaro, ibyo ... buriya nibakora biriya ntabwo ku buriya nibakora biriya ntabwo ku Gikongoro ... ndizera ko bitakongera.'

[108] In Kinyarwanda: 'Kuko kumwica ni ukumugirira neza yaba apfuye kandi n'uwamwica yamwica neza ntabwo yamwica nk'uko yishe ababyeyi banjye.'

example, was reunited with his son in hospital after both of them had survived being hacked by the killers. Once the genocide was over, Kavubi explains that he 'left [his] son there and went to see where we used to live'.[109] Even the translation presents Kavubi as less self-centred as in the Kinyarwanda version, he actually says 'went to see where *I* used to live'. This act of leaving the son is omitted altogether in *We Survived*. Kavubi also describes how he met the wife of his brother who died in the genocide but she 'survived with her children'.[110] The archive translation explains how he 'married her and now we live together' which is not a completely accurate translation of his Kinyarwanda words: 'Nashoboye rero ku mufata ubu ngubu niwe Mudamu tubana' which might more literally be rendered as 'I was able to take her and now this woman and I live together'. The whole sentence is removed from the paragraph in which it would have appeared in *We Survived*.[111]

Removal of Gendered Dimensions

Another editorial intervention tendency in *We Survived* is the removal from the testimonies of gendered aspects of the genocide. In Kavubi's original testimony, he describes a scene where he and other patients were being moved to King Faisal hospital. He explains how 'the men went in the trailer and the women went in the lorry in front'.[112] This separation of men and women is absent in the *We Survived* version which reports the event as 'we got in the lorry'.[113] Similarly, Mudahogora describes running away from the killers, explaining that 'They [the killers] were already coming near us. First they hacked the men, meanwhile we ran to the sector offices at the Ntarama church'.[114] As discussed in Chapter 2, it was often men and boys who were first targeted in the genocide, but this gendered dimension is absent in *We Survived* where the same section is rendered as

---

[109] In Kinyarwanda: 'Ndagenda wa mwana wanjye musiga ahongaho, njya kureba aho nari ntuye.'

[110] In Kinyarwanda: 'Washoboye kurokoka, arokokana n'utwana.'

[111] Whitworth, *We Survived*, p. 70.

[112] In Kinyarwanda: 'Ab'abagabo babashyira muri remoruke [igice cy'inyuma cya rukururana] abagore babashyira mu'ikamyo imbere.'

[113] Whitworth, *We Survived*, p 69.

[114] In Kinyarwanda: 'N'ubundi badusatiriye. Ubwo bahugira mu gutema abagabo tuba turirukatse, tugiye kuri secteur ... ku kiriziya cy'i Ntarama.'

follows: 'the attackers were coming close. Then we ran to the sector offices at Ntarama church'.[115] Later in her testimony, Mudahogora describes how people began committing suicide to avoid being hacked. She comments how 'more people committed suicide than were hacked' and, in response, other people said, 'Let us die like men. Committing suicide is a sin' while another said, 'let's go and hide'.[116] The gendered component of dying 'like men' is absent from this section in *We Survived* and suicide is portrayed as a much easier option, as people's objections to suicide are omitted and in their place are the words: 'They dived into the water and were carried away.'[117]

Censoring Criticisms of Outsiders

Perhaps the most surprising aspect of *We Survived* is the way the editor handles comments made by survivors about the role of outsiders in the genocide. There are three main ways in which survivors address this role: (a) by depicting the actions of the international community; (b) by describing the behaviour of individual foreign people; and (c) by directly addressing the international community.

Depictions of the International Community

The first way is by portraying the actions of members of the International community (e.g., the role of the United Nations or of France). None of the women whose testimonies appear in *We Survived* depicts the international community in this way and, of the ten men, five of them offer a negative portrayal. Three of the five are censored to a greater or lesser extent. One of the most extreme cases of censoring can be observed in the testimony of Twagirashema who devotes 506 Kinyarwanda words to a description of French involvement in Murambi. It could be argued that these words were cut as part of the general editing process which requires a reduction in length in the testimonies. Twagirashema's Kinyarwanda testimony is 3,128 words long and in *We Survived* it occupies 4.5 pages (approximately 2,250 words)

---

[115] Whitworth, *We Survived*, p. 76.
[116] In Kinyarwanda: 'Reka dupfe kigabo, nta kwiyahura, kwiyahura ni icyaha'. Ukavuga uti: "reka njye kwihisha".'
[117] Whitworth, *We Survived*, p. 77.

so, as a proportion of the overall number of words cut (approximately 878 words) it makes up a significant portion (just under 60 per cent). But the editing goes beyond the removal of information as it changes the nature of Twagirashema's portrayal of the French, suggesting that the editorial intervention is ideological rather than the 'neutral' cutting of material. The first paragraph of his discussion of the French, for example, is rendered in *We Survived*. It appears as follows:

> After some time, French troops came to Murambi – although to me it seemed as if they came to help the perpetrators. But the *Interahamwe* had already been defeated by the RPF troops and had started to flee. The French troops then started looking for Tutsis who had been in hiding. They gathered survivors from their hiding places after collecting all the dead bodies into a nearby mass grave.[118]

This paragraph is rendered more or less accurately from the original Kinyarwanda transcript. Admittedly, it does include Twagirashema's criticism that the French had come only 'to help the perpetrators'.[119] However, it also portrays the French as somewhat apolitical as when they see that the perpetrators 'had already been defeated', they decided to help in whatever way they could – i.e., by burying the dead and gathering together the remaining survivors. It also cuts out the last sentence of the paragraph where he states: 'After they had gathered all of the survivors, strong men were nowhere to be seen'.[120] This sentence is made clear later in the archive version but, in *We Survived*, the story about French involvement in Murambi ends here. There are another 426 words covering the topic in the original version and the following is a section of what he goes on to say:

> Allow me to go back to what I was telling you about the French. After they found the perpetrators defeated, they went into the villages asking people where the Tutsis were. That's the way they managed to gather the Tutsi from here and there, but the strong men who had survived could not be found. Wherever we were hiding, we would always know who was dead and who was still alive. Somebody you knew or people could come and say, 'So and so is still alive'. Nevertheless, when the French came, they

---

[118] Ibid., p. 209.
[119] This should be rendered as: 'help the Interhamwe' as in the original: 'Baje mu buryo bwo gufasha Interahamwe.'
[120] In Kinyarwanda: 'Abari abagabo bafite imbaraga ntabwo bagaragaye.'

isolated them and left only very old men and women who were helpless and young children. Those are the people we found in Murambi where we were hiding. The only help we got from the French was the biscuits they brought us. We lived there with them while they were pretending to be guarding us but really, they didn't help us at all. For example, there were some *Interahamwe* who could come following girls they had abducted during the genocide and take in as their 'wives' [they would force them to live with them and rape them for days]. We would report them to the French and the latter would lie to us saying that they were going to punish them. They [the French] would take them [the *Interahamwe*] away and they would come back telling us that they had put them in aeroplanes, which were at S.O.S Gikongoro, and thrown them in Nyungwe forest. They would even add that their bodies would never be found. However, after a while we would see them again. This clearly shows that they were working hand in hand with the *Interahamwe*.[121]

Thus, rather than simply helping out in whatever way they could, Twagirashema accuses the French of a much more political agenda and of playing a duplicitous role which involved isolating vulnerable genocide survivors, pretending to murder Hutu perpetrators, and lying to survivors about it. Twagirashema makes other accusations throughout this section that the French were working with the genocidal government (e.g., 'They tried to work with the members of the

---

[121] In Kinyarwanda: 'Hanyuma aho nari ngereje hariya hajyanye n'iby'abafaransa mu gihe bazaga bitwa ko baje gufasha Interahamwe basanze zacitse intege ubwo niko kujya mu Biturage bakabaza abantu ahantu haba hari abatutsi. Ubwo ni muri urwo rwego babashije kuba kusikanya hirya no hino barababona ariko ab'Abagabo bari bararokotse icyo gihe ntabwo bongeye kuboneka kandi Abafaransa bamaze kuza kuko aho twabaga turi twumvaga ngo kanaka ariho kanaka ariho kanaka ariho tukumva nk'umuntu wari uzi kanaka ariho ariko nyuma Abafaransa bakabarobanura basiga udukecuru tudafite shinge na rugero, basiga utwana, basiga udusaza, abo nibo twasanze ahangaha i Murambi mu gihe natwe twari twihishe. Tugeze hano ubwo turahaba ikintu babashije kutumarira ni twa biswi baduhaga, tuba aho ngaho twitwa ngo baraturinze ariko wareba ugasanga nta kintu batumariye nk'urugero hari nk'Interahamwe zahadusangaga zari zarabohoje abakobwa bamwe na bamwe zikaza zibakurikiye, zikaza zibakurikiye hanyuma tukazereka ku bafaransa, Abafaransa bati tugiye kubahana, bakabashyira mu modoka baka bakagaruka batubwira ngo baburije Indege iyo indege zabaga ziri hariya ku kigo cya SOS i Gikongoro kiri ubwo bakaza bakatubwira ngo baburije indege ngo bageze mu Nyungwe ngo bararekura ngo za Mayiti yabo ngo ntabwo yaboneka. Mu kanya gato tukongera tukababona bigaragara ko bari bafatanyije n'interahamwe nk'uko twabibonye ni uko nguko byabaga bimeze.'

then Government in exile.'[122]) and repeats on several occasions that the French 'were working with the *Interahamwe*'. None of these accusations are rendered.

Depictions of Individual Foreign People

The second method for addressing the role of outsiders in the genocide is describing the behaviour of individual foreign people. Of all testimonies analysed, one man and two women offer negative portrayals about individual foreigners: All three are censored. The two most extreme cases, which involve more than just the cutting of words, can be found in the testimonies of Kavubi and Mupenzi.

In Kavubi's testimony he describes a scene arriving at the Red Cross after having been hacked by the killers. It is portrayed in *We Survived* as follows:

I had to get past two Habyarimana soldiers who were on guard and another person on the door who didn't like Tutsis ... He refused to open the door for me and I pleaded ... suddenly a white guy appeared and ordered him to open up very quickly. That's how I got to the Red Cross. The white guy asked me what had happened and I told them the truth.[123]

The interventions in this citation enhance the power of the white doctor while reducing Kavubi's own agency. For example, the words 'suddenly', 'appeared' and 'ordered' do not feature in the original. The *We Survived* version also misses a section which takes place between the white man arriving and his request for the door to be opened. The full section is rendered in the archive translation as follows:

A white man was coming from the operating room. He saw me and asked 'what is happening'. The other man [watchman] spoke to him in French, saying 'This man wants to come in here but he has no papers.' But I understood and told them, 'I have been hacked and those who did it are looking for me. They'll kill me if you don't open the gate.'

---

[122] In Kinyarwanda: 'Hanyuma bagerageje gufatanya n'ubutegetse bwariho bucyura igihe bariho bahunga bushakisha ukuntu hari hano I Murambi muri ya Salle koza amagufwa baraa koza amaraso barapatana bahemba za Mayibobo, bahemba Abatwa bafata amazi kugirango bazimanganye amaraso y'abantu bahaguye.'

[123] Whitworth, *We Survived*, p. 68.

– 'Quickly, open it,' The white man said. Then the watchman opened and I entered.[124]

The *We Survived* version masks the fact that the white doctor might not be able to speak Kinyarwanda and removes Kavubi's knowledge of European cultural codes. The last part of the *We Survived* version is also a misrepresentation as where it says, 'and I told them the truth', Kavubi actually states: 'I started lying about the bomb but they said, "Tell us the truth, we can see that you have been hacked".'[125] Other instances of Rwandans lying to white people are also removed from Kavubi's testimony (e.g., the following sentence is omitted: 'They used to lie to those white people saying that those people were taken to 'Etat major'[126]). Overall, the representation of the same story in *We Survived* makes the doctor appear more powerful, more in control and more benevolent than the original version.

Even more extreme editorial interventions are found in Mupenzi's testimony. In the original version, Mupenzi describes how a Swiss charity named *Sentinelles* takes her to Switzerland after the genocide for medical treatment. Mupenzi explains how, after numerous operations, she is told by the charity to return to Rwanda: the high level of anaesthesia in her body precludes any further treatment. Although reluctant to return to Rwanda, she is reassured that the charity will pay for her to come back to Switzerland later. Mupenzi goes on to describe how other Rwandans present at the time encourage her to follow this advice:

Then some Rwandans came to say to me, 'Don't disrespect the people who are helping you. You see all the things they are doing for you; if you

---

[124] In Kinyarwanda: 'Umuzungu wari uvuye muri salle y'aho abagiraga abantu arambona. Ambonye arabaza ngo: "byagenze bite?" Undi amubwira mu gifaransa, ngo: "uyu muntu", ngo: arimo arashaka kwinjira hano, ngo kandi nta byangombwa afite. Noneho avuze gutyo mu gifaransa nanjye mba nabyumvise. Ndavuga nti: oya. Nti: ikibazo mfite, natemwe none n'abantu bantemye bari hano inyuma, niba mutandetse ngo ninjire ndaba mfuye. Undi ngo: "kingura vuba vuba, ngo kingura vuba vuba" "Arakingura, akinguye ninjira muri Croix-Rouge".'

[125] In Kinyarwanda: 'Ngezemo ndababwira nti: umva rwose bombe, mbabwira ibya bombe. Aho bigeze noneho barambwira ngo: "umva, tubwize ukuri biragaragara ko watemwe, utubwize ukuri."'

[126] In Kinyarwanda: 'Ubwo rero twamenye yuko … twaje kumenya nyuma yuko, ngo "umuzungu" yavuganye na Etat major' [ubuyobozi bw'ingabo] yo kwa Habyarimana. Arababwira ngo: 'abantu tujyanye, tubajyanye tugiye kubavura none ngo bagiye kubica'.

disrespect them they will never give you another operation. If you refuse to go home, then they will stop helping you and this will ruin your chances'.[127]

This passage from Mupenzi's testimony shows the precariousness of her situation demonstrated by her apparent duty to follow the instructions set by these foreigners or risk their refusal of further help. Mupenzi's belief that the Europeans will cut off medical assistance unless she complies suggests that she perceives them as somewhat punitive. In the Kinyarwanda version of the text, Mupenzi uses the verb *gusuzugura* ('to disobey'); however, this verb is translated as *refuser* in the French archival translation ('je ne devais pas refuser' (I shouldn't refuse)), and as *disrespect* in the English one ('If you disrespect them'). Both translated versions, thus, soften the Europeans' authoritarian portrayal by making Mupenzi's return to Rwanda more a request than an order. Furthermore, neither of the translations includes her original words 'abazungu ntabwo bakunda abantu babasuzugura nyine' ('White people do not like people who disobey them'), thereby further mitigating Mupenzi's depiction of whites as authoritarian. At least the translated versions remain somewhat close to Mupenzi's words, however. In the edited version of her testimony that appears in *We Survived*, this entire paragraph is omitted.

In a later passage, Mupenzi discusses how, after returning to Rwanda, she receives help from an uncle who is a doctor. The uncle writes to *Sentinelles* to explain Mupenzi's condition and in the following extract, Mupenzi describes the response they receive:

After just a month, they replied to him [my uncle]. They replied saying that they were surprised that he had never cared for me at the time and that only now was he remembering to speak up. 'We have done things for you. Your own country will have to do the rest. We did a lot of work for you, there is not much left to do'. That is how *Sentinelles* immediately refused, they stopped helping me.[128]

---

[127] In Kinyarwanda: 'Ubwo abanyarwanda baraza barambwira bati: "Koko wisuzugura abantu bakugiriye neza urabona ibintu bagukoreye wibasuzugura na ubasuzugura izindi operation ntabwo bazazikora kandi Abazungu ntabwo bakunda abantu babasuzugura nyine. Ubwo nyine Niwanga gutaha nabo barareka kugufasha, usange byose birapfuye wiyicire amahirwe".'

[128] In Kinyarwanda: 'Ubwo nko mu kwezi nyine nabo bari bamusubije. baramusubiza baramubwira ngo batangazwa n'ukuntu utigeze unyitaho mbere y'igihe ngo none ubu ngo niho wibutse kuvuga, ngo "Ibyo twakoze twarabikoze ngo igihugu ngo cy'iwanyu ngo kizabikore ngo kandi ngo rwose ngo twakoze akazi kenshi ibisigaye nibyo bike". N'uko nyine centinelle ihita ihakana ko itazongera kumfasha.'

It would appear that the charity is angry at Mupenzi's uncle for not helping her earlier. They downplay the severity of Mupenzi's injuries and stop their support. Given that Mupenzi's condition was gravely deteriorating, this decision left her in a desperate situation. The extract is modified significantly in *We Survived*:

> They replied that the difficult operations had already been done in Switzerland and the rest could now be done elsewhere. *Sentinelles* had done so much for me, but now it was up to my own country.[129]

This edited version of Mupenzi's words paints a very different picture of the Swiss charity, suggesting that Mupenzi is grateful. Moreover, it implies that it was her country's choice to help her rather than the result of the charity's abandonment that left Mupenzi with no choice but to try and find treatment in Rwanda. Overall, the book portrays Mupenzi as a passive and grateful recipient of benevolent Western charity when, in reality, Mupenzi presents a much more critical depiction of this organisation. Moreover, at the end of Mupenzi's testimony in *We Survived*, two entirely new paragraphs appear under the subheading 'Amazing news', in which Mupenzi apparently describes 'how an Aegis staff member came to visit me in the evening and told me something I've been dreaming of for years'.[130] This staff member explains how the 'Aegis Trust and some other people in the UK have managed to gather together the money for me to have another operation'.[131] Mupenzi goes on to 'thank all the people who have contributed towards raising the money for further surgery. I am so happy to know that some people think and care about me'.[132] None of this information is present in the original version of Mupenzi's testimony, suggesting that this text may have been added later.[133]

Directly Addressing the International Community

There are also times when survivors directly and explicitly address the international community, calling for it to acknowledge the genocide and its role in the latter. In the twenty testimonies studied for this

---

[129] Whitworth, *We Survived*, p. 108.
[130] Ibid., p. 111.
[131] Ibid.
[132] Ibid., p. 112.
[133] It is possible that the additional content in Mupenzi's testimony (and the distortions observed in other testimonies in *We Survived*) came from subsequent interviews, but there is no acknowledgement that this is the case.

chapter, four women and five men make this type of comment: all four of the women are censored and so are three of the men.[134] In all but one case, the section where the international community is addressed is simply redacted from the text. In Mukamusoni's testimony, however, her words are not removed but manipulated. In the following extract, translated from the original version of her testimony, Mukamusoni describes how pleased she is when the international community accepts that genocide took place in Rwanda:

What made us happy, what made me happy, was to see the international community admit that it [the genocide] took place. This makes me very happy. Preserving our history is what makes me strong.[135]

Above all, this paragraph demonstrates how important it is to Mukamusoni that the international community acknowledges the genocide. The following passage is what appears in place of this statement in *We Survived*:

One of the things that keeps me strong is commemorating the genocide. That's why the history of these killings should never be forgotten. Not only my testimony, but everyone's. The events must be written down in books so our grandchildren will be able to read about it and know what happened. All future generations should learn that there was genocide here. We must keep remembering our loved ones who were killed – and what happened to them.[136]

---

[134] It must be noted that the two men who were not censored are employees of the Aegis Trust: Freddy Mutanguha and Yves Kamuronsi. Moreover, Kamuronsi makes comments in the context of his work for Aegis, stating:

I've been working with Aegis Trust to establish the Kigali Memorial Centre because it's ours; we need to be the ones doing it. If I don't do it, who else will? Not everyone is capable of doing it. It's very sad spending all your time looking into the lives of people who were killed and looking at their pictures. But I do it – and I do it with all my strength because it needs to be done – so that even the people who want them to be forgotten will have failed. When the project is completed, I think it will have a lot of impact. It is very helpful even for us. When you want to remember your friends and family, you will be able to go there. That's why I give myself fully to that project because it will be a great help. It will even show the international community that the genocide actually happened. Whitworth, *We Survived*, p. 58.

[135] In Kinyarwanda: 'None rero ikintu Kidu … gishimishije rwose, ikintu cyanshimishije ni uko amahanga yarangije kwemera ko no kubibona, ko byabaye koko. Ibyo bintu birashimishije cyane. Guhora iteka tubyibuka. Nabyo mu binyubaka, biranyubaka.'

[136] Whitworth, *We Survived*, p. 99.

Clearly this paragraph is a distortion of Mukamusoni's words. Not only does the replacement text omit Mukamusoni's attempt to highlight the importance of the international community's acknowledgement, but also it could be interpreted as an attempt to promote the (invaluable) work of documenting and recording the genocide carried out by the Aegis Trust.

In total, there are eleven negative comments about the role of outsiders made by men, seven of which are censored (64 per cent), and six such comments made by women, all of which are censored (100 per cent). Thus, while the testimonies of men are cut to a greater extent (albeit not statistically significantly so), there appears to be a greater interference in the testimonies of women when it comes to the editing of these types of comments.

Overall, the presentation of the testimonies in *We Survived* does not appear solely to give a voice to survivors. Credited in the acknowledgements for having 'shaped and edited' the testimonies, Whitworth, it seems, has made specific choices to present a certain image of Rwandans; one that is more passive, less critical and less gendered than the original texts. While the words of both men and women are altered in this way, criticisms of the international community are censored to a greater extent in the testimonies of women than of men. The fact that a Western audience can accept criticism is illustrated by the introduction written by James Smith, Aegis Trust CEO, which includes a short summary of the role played by the international community in the genocide.[137] Nonetheless, it seems that an international (Western) audience cannot tolerate the idea of being challenged by those it perceives as victims (or, at least, that the editor believes a Western audience cannot tolerate such an idea). It appears preferable to portray Rwandan survivors, particularly women, as passive, defenceless recipients of Western good will.

What Is Really Unspeakable?

Similarly to the tendency to portray perpetrators in accordance with Western stereotypes of the 'savage' continent of Africa, there appears to be a tendency to perpetuate the culturally acceptable view of survivors as passive, genderless victims. Such reductionist dichotomizations

[137] Ibid., pp. 9–10.

of those involved provides the international audience with a sense of immunity to the possibility of genocide. If killers can be perceived as politically and historically informed actors, and survivors as agents with the ability to contest, criticise or reinterpret, this would humanise them and threaten this perceived immunity. Much like popular media images at the time of the genocide, *We Survived* perpetuates the comforting stereotypes of Western heroes saving poor, helpless African victims by omitting survivors' criticisms of the West.

Of course, without the role played by the Aegis Trust, the voices of survivors would not be heard at all. And as we have seen in the discussion of genocide literature above, most texts tend towards a Western rather than a Rwandan reading of the genocide. If *We Survived* were to go against this tendency by including subversive portrayals of survivors that went against Western expectations, it is possible that this would impact on the book's commercial viability or discourage interest and consequent monetary donations to the Aegis Trust. Given that the book is sold to support the Trust's work, it is in the interest of the charity to make the testimonies as appealing as possible. Nevertheless, the distorted versions obstruct survivors' attempts to take control of the interpretation of their trauma, imposing conformity to the dominant culture which labels them powerless victims.

Conclusion

As discussed above, ideological change is necessary for post-traumatic growth at the collective level to take place. By developing social stories through access to public discourse, group members are able to challenge dominant ideologies and provide a counter-narrative through which they may fulfil their collective needs of agency and communion. The interventions made by the editor of *We Survived* may, however, remove any chance of genuine engagement or dialogue with an international audience and hinder survivors' attempts to gain acknowledgement and overcome feelings of estrangement from the world beyond Rwanda.

The findings presented in this chapter should prompt critical reflection among scholars and others interested in Rwandan genocide literature. Ironically, Western society is often regarded as a place where free speech prevails while many Western scholars and others have been exceptionally vocal in their criticism of the Rwandan government, particularly for its control over the genocide narrative.[138] The existence of such extensive ideological modifications in a book of Rwandan testimonies prepared for a Western audience suggests that scholars and other readers of genocide texts should also consider that the West, too, can be dogmatic in its depiction of the events of 1994. An awareness of dominant Western views on Rwanda combined with a consideration of such factors as the identity of the author, the location and ideology of the publishing house, and the presence and identity of any collaborators/editors are all essential for interpreting books published on Rwanda.

The findings discussed in this chapter also have theoretical implications. As discussed in Chapter 1, it would seem that survivors, particularly women, are fighting to have their voices heard both within Rwandan society and at the international level. The recourse to a theory which insists on trauma's unrepresentability seems particularly inappropriate for such a context.

---

[138] See, for example, the work of Filip Reyntjens, Susan Thomson, Timothy Longman, and Lars Wardorf, among others.

Conclusion

This book has offered a reading of trauma texts that draws on a theory that, even within the psychological sciences, is marginal.[1] It has demonstrated that post-traumatic growth theory is not without limitations. As discussed in Chapter 2, scholars usually investigate the phenomenon using quantitative, self-report scales which are unable to detect the specificities of a cultural and historical context and are also blind to long-term, chronic or structural forms of trauma. Adopting a text-based application of the theory has allowed me to address some of these limitations by drawing on historical and cultural knowledge and listening to survivors' own understandings of the ways in which their lives have been affected by trauma.

Another drawback to post-traumatic growth theory is that it has been too individualistic and unable to account for social or political change. Chapter 4 demonstrated how previous attempts to label certain collective changes following trauma as 'growth' in other contexts may have been misguided. The chapter proposed a new model of collective post-traumatic growth and, within this framework, Chapters 4 and 5 showed how such a model can be drawn on to investigate social change at the national and international levels.

Despite revealing some of its limitations, the book has also highlighted the advantages of post-traumatic growth above other dominant theories such as trauma theory in the humanities and the medical

---

[1] While research into PTSD abounds, there are only two research centres dedicated to post-traumatic growth: The Posttraumatic Growth Research Group at The University of North Carolina at Charlotte, in the United States, run by Lawrence Calhoun and Richard Tedeschi (https://ptgi.uncc.edu/) and the Centre for Trauma, Resilience and Growth in Nottingham, UK, co-convened by Stephen Joseph and Steve Regel. The Growth Initiative Lab (www .nottinghamshirehealthcare.nhs.uk/centre-for-trauma-resilience-growth) at Wake Forest University in the United States has a research centre which is generally focused on personality growth, but there is also a subsection on post-traumatic growth (see http://growthinitiative.org/research/).

model in the psychological sciences. Chapter 1 identified the drawbacks of these theories, namely their narrow understanding of what constitutes 'traumatic', their Eurocentrism, and, in the case of trauma theory, its shaky empirical foundations and its prescriptivism in terms of how trauma should be represented. While this is not the first time such criticisms have been levelled against these theories, Chapter 1 showed how they may be particularly damaging in a post-colonial, post-genocide context like Rwanda. Post-traumatic growth theory, in contrast, is founded on empirical evidence and, via a textual application, it can enable trauma scholars to move beyond the Eurocentrism of traditional trauma theory and its focus on events, belatedness and unrepresentability and beyond the medical model and its pathologisation of distress. I hope that the book has demonstrated that focussing on strengths, interests and hopes as opposed to deficit and dysfunction does not mean taking an uncritical, romantic approach. Moreover, an openness to negative and positive change, combined with historical and cultural knowledge and close reading of texts, can lead to new theories, understandings and conclusions. One of the main advantages of this study is that by gaining an understanding of post-traumatic growth in the Rwandan context, it can provide insights into how such positive change might be facilitated in a culturally and politically sensitive way. Following a general overview of approaches to facilitating post-traumatic growth as well as a discussion of existing therapy paradigms in Rwanda, the remainder of this Conclusion will provide advice as to how growth might be promoted in Rwanda, reconciling the theory with data-driven insights from the testimonies.

Facilitating Post-Traumatic Growth in a Clinical Setting: A General Overview

As discussed in the Introduction, psychologists have in the past attended primarily to the distressing emotional, cognitive, behavioural and physical symptoms that occur in the aftermath of a traumatic experience. As a result of this medicalised orientation, clinical assessments of individuals suffering the effects of trauma have tended to focus on identifying these 'symptoms' by applying 'a deficit- or problem-focussed approach'.[2] This medical model may be misplaced in cross-cultural

---

[2] Tedeschi and Kilmer, 'Assessing Strengths, Resilience, and Growth to Guide Clinical Intervention', p. 230.

situations, however, as the diagnosis of psychological dysfunction may be culturally alien in some contexts.[3] Tedeschi and Kilmer suggest that the deficit-approach is insufficient and instead propose a strength-based assessment, 'attending to and assessing positive factors and pursuing means to facilitate their development or enhancement'.[4] As Calhoun and Tedeschi observe, '[T]he exclusive focus on the need to identify and address the negative consequences of trauma may lead clinicians to overlook the possibility that some, and perhaps many, individuals can experience positive change in the wake of tragedy and loss.'[5]

On the other hand, the notion of post-traumatic growth may also seem alien to some survivors, and thus, before the idea of growth is introduced, the initial focus of therapy in any context should be to help the individual to manage their psychological distress.[6] This involves a process of desensitisation by re-exposing the individual to the trauma through detailed descriptions or thinking about the experience(s) in a safe, therapeutic atmosphere. A second aim of this process is to support individuals during the rumination process so that they may create a narrative which will enable them to gain a model of the experience to refer to in therapy.[7] Indeed as Calhoun and Tedeschi suggest, therapy is 'a continual process of narrative development, where events and experiences are revisited and retold many times, with new details included in each version, and different perspectives are taken on the same events'.[8] Finally, before the notion of growth is introduced, trauma treatment should also help the individual recreate a worldview that encompasses what happened. According to Calhoun and Tedeschi, 'this aspect of trauma treatment is involved in the construction of the narrative that describes the trauma and provides some understanding of it'.[9]

Tedeschi and Kilmer propose that a strength assessment may be made via informal qualitative methods, such as listening to the client's

---

[3] Irene Rizzini and Andrew Dawes, 'Editorial: On Cultural Diversity and Childhood Adversity', *Childhood*, 8 (2001), 315–21 (p. 316).

[4] Tedeschi and Kilmer, 'Assessing Strengths, Resilience, and Growth to Guide Clinical Intervention', p. 235.

[5] Calhoun and Tedeschi, *Facilitating Posttraumatic Growth*, p. 54.

[6] Ibid., p. 58.

[7] Because traumas are often poorly encoded in memory, the generation of a narrative enables individuals to link together elements of their traumatic memories. Calhoun and Tedeschi, *Facilitating Posttraumatic Growth*, p. 60.

[8] Ibid.

[9] Ibid., p. 53.

narrative for evidence of strengths. The authors suggest using a growth scale such as the Post-Traumatic Growth Inventory or the Stress-Related Growth Scale to serve as a template for discussions with trauma survivors.[10] Tedeschi and Kilmer advise that the clinician should make the decision as to when to introduce the notion of growth and subsequently focus questioning on positive changes. It is clear that clinicians cannot produce growth for the individual nor should they try to push the individual into a conversation about growth too soon. However, labelling growth when it is apparent and discussing positive changes with an empathic understanding of the individual's worldview can, according to Tedeschi and Kilmer, 'encourage further development of the cognitive processing of trauma into growth'.[11] Overall, Tedeschi and Kilmer conclude that efforts to harness and promote post-traumatic growth may 'not only enhance the health and well-being of clients in the context of their current presenting concerns but potentially reduce their need for formal mental health services in the future'.[12]

Existing Therapy Paradigms in Rwanda

As in other contexts, most studies of trauma and its consequences in Rwanda have also focused on the negative consequences of psychological trauma. For example, several studies have attempted to quantify distress levels among the Rwandan population through 'epidemiological investigations'.[13] Similarly, most published reports on therapy evaluate

---

[10] Tedeschi and Calhoun, 'The Posttraumatic Growth Inventory', p. 460; Park, Cohen and Murch, 'Assessment and Prediction of Stress-Related Growth', p. 78.

[11] Tedeschi and Kilmer, 'Assessing Strengths, Resilience, and Growth to Guide Clinical Intervention', p. 234.

[12] Ibid., p. 235.

[13] For example, the National Trauma Recovery Centre carried out a National Trauma Survey in 1995 which was analysed by Richard Neugebauer, Prudence W. Fisher, J Blake Turner, et al., 'Post-Traumatic Stress Reactions among Rwandan Children and Adolescents in the Early Aftermath of Genocide', *International Journal of Epidemiology*, 38. 4 (2009), 1033–45 (p. 1043). The authors found that among Rwandans aged between eight and nineteen, 54%–62% exhibited 'probable PTSD'. In a similar study, researchers interviewed children and adolescents about a year after the genocide and concluded that 79 per cent of the survivors showed moderate to severe PTSD. Atle Dyregrov, Leila Gupta, Rolf Gjestad and Eugenie Mukanoheli, 'Trauma Exposure and Psychological Reactions to Genocide among Rwandan Children', *Journal of Traumatic Stress*, 13. 1 (2000), 3–21. See also Susanne Schaal and Thomas Elbert, 'Ten Years after the Genocide: Trauma Confrontation and Posttraumatic Stress in Rwandan Adolescents', *Journal of Traumatic Stress*, 19. 1 (2006), 95–105.

the effectiveness of an intervention on its ability to reduce levels of distress and PTSD symptoms.[14]

Psychosocial trauma and recovery programmes are implemented by various actors in Rwanda including clinicians working at Rwanda's Psychosocial Consultation Centre or at the National Trauma Recovery Centre at Ndera Neuropsychiatric Hospital, Western trauma specialists, as well as various local and international non-governmental organisations (NGOs). Besides Muganga Rutangarwamaboko's Rwandan Cultural Psychotherapy, most therapy programmes are dominated by variations of the Western medical model. Indeed, according the Marie-Odile Godard, traditional doctors do not recognise cases of severe trauma (known in Kinyarwanda as *ihahamuka*) and instead send them to hospitals or churches.[15] Godard suggests that this is because both trauma and genocide are seen as somehow 'extracultural' and therefore untreatable by cultural methods.[16] Such a view is similar to Rutangarwamaboko's understanding, who sees the genocide as an extreme taboo – i.e., a violation of culture which is linked to the long-term destruction of indigenous culture. Unlike the traditional practitioners discussed in Godard's book, Rutangarwamaboko does treat trauma patients and, as discussed in Chapter 1, his approach is to reconnect patients with tradition. The most frequent method for treating cases of *ihahamuka* in Rwanda is, however, the Western medical model.

As Favila reports, 'the genocide destroyed infrastructure necessary for effective treatment of trauma and PTSD'.[17] The only psychiatric hospital, Ndera, had become non-operational as most of its patients and staff had been killed in the genocide.[18] Professor Naasson Munyadamutsa, the only psychiatrist left in Rwanda after 1994, played

---

[14] Darious Gishoma, Jean-Luc Brackelaire, Naason Munyandamutsa, et al., 'Supportive-Expressive Group Therapy for People Experiencing Collective Traumatic Crisis during the Genocide Commemoration Period in Rwanda: Impact and Implications', *Journal of Social and Political Psychology*, 2. 1 (2014), 469–88; Valerie Chu, 'Within the Box: Cross-Cultural Art Therapy with Survivors of the Rwanda Genocide', *Art Therapy: Journal of the American Art Therapy Association*, 27. 1 (2010), 4–10.

[15] Marie-Odile Godard, *Rêves et traumatismes: Ou la longue nuit des rescapés* (Paris: Éditions Érès, 2003), p. 59.

[16] Ibid.

[17] Favila, 'Treatment of Post-Traumatic Stress Disorder in Post-Genocide Rwanda', p. 2.

[18] Ibid.

a major role in developing mental health services in the aftermath of the genocide.[19] With support from UNICEF and the Swiss government, he established Rwanda's National Trauma Recovery Centre at Ndera hospital in 1995 and later collaborated with the Ministry of Health to develop the Psychosocial Consultation Centre which provides outpatient counselling for genocide survivors. In collaboration with a team of experts at the University of Rwanda, Professor Munyandamutsa developed a four-year Masters of Medicine (MMED) degree in Psychiatry which is offered in the College of Medicine and Health Sciences. Munyandamutsa's achievements in mental health are obviously remarkable, but the methods adopted by him and his colleagues are very much embedded within the Western medical model which, as Rutangarwamaboko argues, does not fully capture the traumatic experiences of Rwandans.

For example, in one of Munyandamutsa's published studies, the effectiveness of a trauma intervention using group therapy was measured via a series of Western self-report scales (including the Differential Emotions Scale, the UCLA [University of California, Los Angeles] Loneliness Scale, the Centre for Epidemiological Studies Short Depression Scale, the Impact of Events Scale-Revised and a resilience scale) before and after the intervention.[20] While the scales were translated into Kinyarwanda, they replicate the Western quantitative method of assessing various psychological states which, as noted elsewhere, may be unable to detect the specificities of a cultural and historical context. Moreover, besides one scale measuring resilience, the others measured negative emotions and states and the effectiveness of the intervention was based, primarily, on the reduction of 'symptoms'.[21] The study, thus, demonstrates a deficit-focused, symptom-focused approach to therapy and, as noted in the Introduction, the

---

[19] Professor Munyandamutsa sadly died in 2016. The Belgian Embassy in Kigali wrote a short obituary on its Facebook page where further bibliographical information about him can be found. See www.facebook .com/permalink.php?story_fbid=496125003908613&id=108988062622311 (accessed 4 December 2017).

[20] Gishoma, Brackelaire, Munyandamutsa, Mujawayezu, Mohand and Kayiteshonga, 'Supportive-Expressive Group Therapy for People Experiencing Collective Traumatic Crisis during the Genocide Commemoration Period in Rwanda', pp. 474–6.

[21] Ibid., p. 482.

psychiatric infrastructure continues to lack the resources necessary to meet mental health needs in Rwanda.[22]

Alongside Rwandan-authored studies of trauma, there are also a number of published studies of therapeutic interventions conducted by Western trauma specialists. In addition to focusing on deficit, many of these interventions also fail to adequately recognise the cultural context of Rwanda. For example, French psychologist, Godard offers a psychoanalytical study of the traumatic dreams of genocide survivors in Rwanda.[23] In her book, *Rêves et traumatismes* (Dreams and Trauma/s), Godard draws on Freudian psychoanalysis, particularly the ideas laid out in *Beyond the Pleasure Principle*.[24] For her, as for Freud, the repetitive return to the scene of horror that characterises traumatic dreams may be seen as an attempt to master or manage the state of arousal caused by the traumatic experience from which the subject was unable to protect themselves. The survivor thus reproduces the scene in the dream to try and find the event once again in order to gain a sense of mastery over it. This return is driven by the desire, inherent to all organisms, to return to an original, inanimate state. As Freud writes, '[T]he most universal endeavour of all living substance – [is] to return to the quiescence of the inorganic world.'[25] In Godard's view, the compulsion to repeat sets the survivor on a journey towards death in a way that is somehow under the control of the survivor. In other words, '*C'est un: mourir comme je le veux*' (It is to die in the way I choose).[26]

Despite being heavily influenced by Freudian theory, Godard takes a culturally sensitive approach with survivors in Rwanda, making an

---

[22] Favila, 'Treatment of Post-Traumatic Stress Disorder in Post-Genocide Rwanda', p. 2.

[23] Godard also examines the dreams of *Engagés de guère* (Enlisted soldiers) in Algeria and Holocaust survivors. Godard's work in Rwanda included several trips where she provided psychological support to genocide survivors, working also with the non-profit organisations *Secours populaire français* and *Fondation de France*, as well as with two smaller Rwandese charities: *Benimpuhwe* ('those with compassion'), a Kigali-based women's organisation and Rwanda Sustainable Families (RSF), an NGO providing micro-loans for impoverished families to start small businesses. Godard, *Rêves et traumatismes*, p. 3.

[24] Sigmund Freud, *Beyond the Pleasure Principle*, trans. James Stachey (New York: Dover Publications, 2015).

[25] Ibid., p. 55.

[26] Godard, *Rêves et traumatismes*, p. 27.

active attempt to understand their culture. As she puts it: 'J'ai écouté, engrangé, je me suis laissé imprégner de cette culture et de ces événements' (I listened, took it all in, allowed myself to soak up this culture and these events).[27] Interestingly, Godard found that many survivors look for cultural explanations of their troubles (in contrast to the traditional practitioners she discusses). By listening to their interpretations of dreams, she learns that her Rwandan patients understood their nightmares and traumatic dreams as messages from the *abazimu*. According to traditional Rwandese cosmology, the *abazimu* are the spirits of dead ancestors who can either protect or bring misfortune and require regular supplication to prevent them from bringing about punishments such as disease or other hardships.[28] For genocide survivors, the *abazimu* are their family members who died in the genocide and who force them to relive their persecution.[29] Godard attempts to balance Freudian therapeutic methods with an understanding of the patient's desire to 'amadouer les Abazimu' (appease the *Abazimu*) which involves 'identifier et expliquer minutieusement leur survenue' (identifying and meticulously explaining their presence).[30] For Godard, therapy thus requires a certain 'va-et-vient entre le nouveau et l'ancien qui doit se faire, entre ces deux cultures dont sont pétris les Rwandais' (back and forth between the new and the old which must be done between these two cultures which have shaped Rwandans).[31]

Godard nonetheless experiences some cultural barriers in her work with Rwandans. For example, she was unable to communicate with survivors in Kinyarwanda and, therefore, took recourse to an interpreter.[32] She also takes a somewhat limited cultural-historical view, seeing the source of survivors' difficulties through an event-based lens, focusing on the genocide alone rather than on the longer-term historical process which led to it.[33] Moreover, the Rwandans' interpretation

---

[27] Ibid., p. 20.

[28] Timothy Longman, *Christianity and Genocide in Rwanda* (Cambridge: Cambridge University Press, 2010), p. 36.

[29] Godard, *Rêves et traumatismes*, p. 52. Similar ideas are evoked in literature on the genocide, e.g., Véronique Tadjo, *L'Ombre d'Imana* (Paris: Actes Sud, 2005), pp. 51–8.

[30] Godard, *Rêves et traumatismes*, p. 133.

[31] Ibid.

[32] Ibid., p. 20.

[33] For example, in Godard's view, traumatic dreams are a return to 'l'événement traumatique' (the traumatic event). Godard, *Rêves et traumatismes*, p. 26.

of their dreams does not deter her from returning more generally to a Freudian understanding of traumatic dreams, which she sees as 'signes d'une bataille acharnée de la pulsion de vie au service de la pulsion de mort' (signs of an unremitting battle between the life drive at the service of the death drive).[34] Moreover, the ultimate aim of therapy, in Godard's view, is to 'soulager les patients' (alleviate patients) from their traumatic dreams, rather than look for evidence of strengths.[35] In other words, she takes an event-based, deficit-focused approach.

Perhaps the most unsettling aspect of Godard's work, however, is its resemblance to what Erik Linstrum refers to as the 'dream-collectors' of the early twentieth century.[36] In his book, *Ruling Minds: Psychology in the British Empire*, Linstrum describes the work of 'agents', mostly anthropologists and psychoanalysts, who were sent by the imperial government to Britain's colonies in Africa and Asia to collect and interpret dreams through psychoanalysis in an attempt to better understand and ultimately control their colonial subjects.[37] While I'm not suggesting that Godard had any intention other than to help survivors, she also does not problematise her methodology despite its historical use as a mechanism of control in the European colonisation of Africa. Also absent from Godard's discussion is a recognition that the very same colonial anthropologists largely failed to find universal validity for Freudian psychoanalysis among African people.[38]

In a third type of intervention, New York-based art therapist, Valerie Chu, describes an intervention with Rwandan genocide survivors using art therapy.[39] Chu designed and implemented a series of art therapy projects working in conjunction with a faith-based community development organisation working with children and adults affected by HIV/AIDS and people orphaned or widowed as result of the genocide. Recognising that art therapy is 'a product of the West', Chu designed a creative box-making project, arguing that the box metaphor had 'functional equivalence in Rwandan culture'.[40]

---

[34] Ibid., p. 217.
[35] Ibid., p. 105.
[36] Erik Linstrum, *Ruling Minds: Psychology in the British Empire* (Cambridge, MA: Harvard University Press, 2016), p. 53.
[37] Ibid., pp. 53 and 138.
[38] Ibid., p. 56.
[39] Chu, 'Within the Box', p. 4.
[40] Ibid., pp. 4 and 5.

She argues that the box could be compared with Rwandan traditional basket metaphors and proverbs which refer to the body as a container, but could also be seen as having a pragmatic value for storage of important items and even as an object with a 'memorialising and preserving function'.[41] In her article, Chu describes the art projects of three Rwandans: Margaret, Noah and Rosa (pseudonyms) and the impact of the therapy on them.

Much like the interventions advocated by post-traumatic growth theorists, Chu's approach aims to enable survivors to 'reintegrate their experiences into their life narratives'.[42] On the other hand, like others, Chu focuses on the alleviation of trauma 'symptoms', arguing that art therapy can help 'counter the repetitive nature of [the] trauma response' and combat 'feelings of helplessness and loss of control'.[43] Most of her discussion of trauma in Rwanda refers to the epidemiological studies of PTSD mentioned above, suggesting her agreement with the medical model. Despite this focus on symptoms, Chu notes that the survivors may have 'found empowerment in having their stories and lives shared with others' and suggests that the box art form 'provided them with a sense of control and safety'.[44] Whether Chu discussed such post-traumatic growth themes with the survivors themselves is, however, unclear. Moreover, like Godard, Chu relied on an interpreter to conduct her therapy sessions and, despite the supposed cultural equivalence of the box concept, she notes that the art materials used in her classes would have been ordinarily inaccessible to the survivors. In addition, the images provided by Chu seem inappropriate to be used in a therapeutic intervention for expressing identity as they exclusively depict white people (or at least those selected by the survivors do). These images include one chosen by Noah 'to represent himself' and another, selected by Margaret, because it was 'reminiscent' of her.[45] The only words written on the projects appear on Rosa's box and are in English rather than in Kinyarwanda, which Chu interprets as demonstrating 'the importance of memory for Rosa'.[46] However, it might also be considered an attempt to create the box for the art therapist rather than for

---

[41] Ibid., p. 6.
[42] Ibid., p. 5.
[43] Ibid., p. 5.
[44] Ibid., pp. 9 and 10.
[45] Ibid., pp. 8 and 9.
[46] Ibid., p. 9.

herself, given the language choice. Of course, without asking Rosa, it is not possible to know for sure.

It can be seen from these examples that most therapy interventions in Rwanda apply a deficit-focused approach, rather than listening for strengths.[47] Moreover, those administered by Western therapists include elements which are arguably culturally inappropriate. While I would not discount the contribution made by Western therapists in Rwanda, the colonial history of Rwanda combined with global patterns of racism and inequality are likely to create a power imbalance between therapist and survivor that may prove inappropriate or even counter-productive. I wound not suggest that problems of historical inequality are insurmountable, but any Westerner conducting therapy should show sensitivity to historical and cultural factors which could form part of the trauma experienced by Rwandans. Moreover, given the challenges involved in translation noted in Chapter 5,[48] I would advocate that therapists and clinicians engage with survivors in Kinyarwanda, particularly given the link between Western languages and colonisation. Something that all the different interventions share is their emphasis on narrative development, also advocated by Calhoun and Tedeschi.[49] They could, therefore, incorporate the post-traumatic growth paradigm into their therapy by attending to strengths and other positive changes. Of course, this must be done in a culturally informed way.

Facilitating Post-Traumatic Growth in Rwanda: A Culturally Informed Approach

A similar approach to that outlined above could be adopted by those engaged in psychosocial work in Rwanda which, in addition to the

---

[47] One exception is Ervin Staub, Laurie Anne Pearlman, Alexandra Gubin and Athanase Hagengimana, 'Healing, Reconciliation, Forgiving and the Prevention of Violence after Genocide or Mass Killing: An Intervention and Its Experimental Evaluation in Rwanda', *Journal of Social and Clinical Psychology*, 24. 3 (2005), 297–334. In this study, the researchers used a theory-based intervention involving psycho-educational lectures aimed at promoting healing and reconciliation. Although the researchers measured the reduction of trauma symptoms after the intervention, they also measured changes in orientation towards members of the other group and found a shift towards more positive views. The study doesn't directly adopt post-traumatic growth theory, but it does provide an example that moves beyond a pure deficit-focussed approach to psychological interventions.

[48] See also Williamson 'Posttraumatic Growth at the International Level', p. 41.

[49] Calhoun and Tedeschi, *Facilitating Posttraumatic Growth*, p. 60.

work of psychiatrists, includes a number of counselling programmes offered by NGOs.[50] When it comes to facilitating post-traumatic growth among Rwandans, this book has demonstrated that historical socio-cultural factors should be taken into consideration, particularly the destruction of indigenous culture caused by colonialism. As Chapters 2 and 3 highlighted, both men and women are responding not just to the genocide but to the longer-term traumas of colonialism, neo-colonialism, dictatorship and patriarchy.

Another important socio-cultural factor that should be taken into consideration in a Rwandan therapy setting is gender. In men, it would help to appreciate Rwanda's military history in order to understand that, for men, the goal of unity rather than reconciliation might be a more meaningful starting point for improving social cohesion in Rwandan society. In women, individual strength and courage are commonly observed agentic growth themes. While it may be important to highlight and promote such positive change, it is equally important to have an understanding of the destruction experienced in women's interpersonal lives to ensure that the drive of communion is not forgotten. The benefits generated by changes in gender relations may prove useful for promoting both agentic and communal post-traumatic growth in women. For example, making women aware of

---

[50] Alongside the treatment offered by psychiatrists, there are a number of ongoing counselling/psychosocial projects in Rwanda. For example, Irish charity, Trocaire, was running a trauma counselling programme which, in 2004, evolved into a national NGO in its own right called the Rwandese Association of Trauma Counsellors (ARCT). Among its activities, ARCT offers training for trauma counsellors and has, in the past, focused on adolescent trauma, offering a 'Trauma Awareness, Healing, and Group Counselling' programme in selected secondary schools. This project placed counsellors in schools who held daily office hours and offered group and individual therapy sessions. Similarly, AVEGA offers individual and group-based counselling programmes for genocide widows which aim to confront issues such as depression and psychological trauma by building confidence and challenging the social stigma surrounding widows and victims of sexual violence. Other organisations offer similar programmes for widows and orphans such as Asoferwa, Benishyaka and Icyuzuzo. Favila argues that these programmes have helped address the need for mental health care in Rwanda but only offer 'a minimum training in trauma counselling at a very basic level' and 'have not provided an effective long-term solution to the widespread trauma created by the genocide'. Favila, 'Treatment of Post-Traumatic Stress Disorder in Post-Genocide Rwanda', p. 4. For a summary of the programmes, see Favila, 'Treatment of Post-Traumatic Stress Disorder in Post-Genocide Rwanda', pp. 12–13.

changes in law which give them more rights could enable women survivors to feel more empowered.[51] Additionally, it is important to
make women aware of and encourage them to get involved in the
numerous women's groups which actively support women and survivors materially, educationally or socially.[52] In their testimonies, many
women link their changes in self-perception to the empowerment provided by training or housing offered by these groups. Moreover,
given that most of the negative interpersonal problems arise from no
longer having friends and family for support, these groups have, in
many cases, taken on the role of providing such social support.[53]
Involvement in women's groups is, thus, likely to promote both agentic and communal growth.

For both men and women, it is important to distinguish genuine
psychological growth from stigma avoidance. It is possible that, to
avoid being associated with the negative stereotypes of survivors
as psychologically unstable, some survivors present a façade of
strength without actually experiencing it. It is, therefore, important
for clinicians and other practitioners working with survivors to
confront these social stigmas and create an atmosphere in which
survivors feel accepted and comfortable to display vulnerability, as
this, according to Calhoun and Tedeschi is what ultimately leads to
strength.[54] It is particularly useful to promote a positive image of
survivors and encourage them to adopt empowering stigma management strategies such as rejecting the stigma and seeking action
to remove it.[55] Breaking down the stigma by encouraging such strategies as well as promoting the cultural acceptance of displays of vulnerability are likely to improve not only growth in self-perception, but
also interpersonal growth. As Shih observes, individuals who adopt
empowerment strategies are more likely to identify with other members

---

[51] Many of the new laws that benefit women which were introduced after the
genocide do not necessarily reflect what happens in practice (such as laws
extending the rights of pregnant and breastfeeding mothers in the workplace,
laws of inheritance guaranteeing that women have the same rights as men to
inherit property, laws against gender-based violence, laws against
discrimination against women, etc.). See Chapter 3.
[52] Burnet, *Genocide Lives in Us*, p. 216.
[53] Ibid., pp. 193 and 216.
[54] Calhoun and Tedeschi, *Facilitating Posttraumatic Growth*, pp. 78–9.
[55] Shih, 'Examining Resilience and Empowerment in Overcoming Stigma',
pp. 180–1.

of the same group.[56] Given that one of the negative interpersonal factors observed was the avoidance of other survivors, it would appear
that such strategies may promote both agentic and communal growth.

One domain of growth that has not been addressed in this book is
that of spiritual or religious growth. As I have discussed elsewhere,
religion is a factor cited by survivors as promoting post-traumatic
growth as it can provide them with a sense of meaning and empowerment as well as a source of social support from fellow churchgoers.[57]
As seen in Chapter 4, however, religious appraisals can also put pressure on survivors to forgive perpetrators in a manner that is consistent with the government's ideology of forced apologies. Although
this may go against the interests of their group, given the sensitivity
of spirituality, I am inclined to agree with Calhoun and Tedeschi who
suggest that 'the clinician should tolerate and respect the client's perception' because 'the ultimate arbiter of posttraumatic growth in
spiritual and religious matters is the client'.[58] Given the very personal
nature of spirituality and the sensitive nature of politics in Rwanda, a
wiser approach would be to break down aspects of the stigma engen-
dered by dominant ideologies in Rwanda, rather than try to promote
criticism of the government or question survivors' religious beliefs.

Facilitating Collective Post-Traumatic Growth

As I argue in Chapter 4, there is a need to take the fundamental
human drives of agency and communion into consideration when
defining what we mean by 'post-conflict reconstruction', particularly
given that more men than women are experiencing both drives and
more women than men are experiencing neither. The promotion of
growth at the collective level falls not only to the clinician or trauma
practitioner but also to policy makers, NGOs and other institutions.
The main inhibitory factor for growth at this level is the lack of
access to public discourse. Survivors are typically not in positions of
political, economic or religious power and, thus, have relatively little
access to public discourse. Another factor which inhibits collective

---

[56] Ibid., p. 181.
[57] Caroline Williamson, 'Posttraumatic Growth and Religion in Rwanda:
Individual Well-Being vs. Collective False Consciousness', *Mental Health,
Religion & Culture*, 17. 9 (2004), 946–55.
[58] Calhoun and Tedeschi, *Facilitating Posttraumatic Growth*, pp. 57 and 121.

post-traumatic growth is the adoption of silent coping among survivors. Silent coping has emerged in Rwanda for two main reasons. First, it is a culturally appropriate coping mechanism because it saves the individual from appearing weak, insane or being associated with any of the other negative attributes associated with survivors (discussed in Chapter 1).[59] Second, it is quite literally a survival mechanism. Though survivors may be freer to speak than members of the Hutu population, criticising the Rwandan government, or denouncing perpetrators is still dangerous and may result in repercussions. Bampiriye, for example, explains her frustration at the silence of other survivors at Gacaca:

There are some people who won't even give their testimony. If you give it, people accuse you of slandering them. Indeed, when you give your testimony, you believe it will help you but you end up testifying on behalf of the people who took part in the killings. I saw this: we went to Gacaca and you explain the way they tried to kill this person or how he was attacked but he ends up fighting against you because you said what you saw ... There are survivors who are afraid of accusing killers and instead call them innocent.

The women and men who have given their testimonies to the Aegis Trust are in many ways exceptional. Most people in Rwanda still fear to speak openly about politically contentious issues because doing so may put their lives at risk. Burizihiza, for example, has to live in a military camp because she has experienced several attempts on her life as a result of her outspoken performances in Gacaca and in the media on issues surrounding rape and the genocide. Burizihiza boldly confronts the stigma surrounding genocide victims, particularly the stigma of sexual violence, and seeks justice and truth. However, this is at great sacrifice to her personal security. Issues of security make the facilitation of growth at the collective level extremely difficult. Of course it is desirable, psychologically speaking, for survivors to gain justice and dispel the negative stereotypes surrounding their identities. However, doing so is potentially dangerous. There are no easy solutions to such problems in Rwanda, but there are some signs of hope. For example, although it has received much criticism from human rights organisations and the international community, Clark believes that Gacaca constituted 'one of the most revolutionary traditional

---

[59] Burnet, *Genocide Lives in Us*, p. 78.

justice approaches pursued anywhere in the world'.[60] Because of the sense of popular ownership over Gacaca and the agency it accorded to all Rwandans via its *modus operandi* of popular participation, Clark suggests that Gacaca has 'proven effective in many communities at initiating processes of restorative justice, healing, forgiveness and reconciliation'.[61] Indeed, Bernard Rimé and colleagues found that, although participation in Gacaca increased negative emotions and other symptoms of PTSD among survivors, it also reduced feelings of shame and enhanced social integration. For example, survivors reported reduced perceptions of out-group homogeneity; increased non-ethnic self-identification; and increased positive stereotypes of out-group members (Hutu).[62] While Gacaca came under criticism in many of the survivors' testimonies, there are those, such as Kayiraba, who have made the most of this institution for achieving positive outcomes:

How Gacaca has helped me is that, I now have a place where I can express myself. I now have a place where I can say, 'My husband and my children were killed', 'So and so destroyed our house' 'So and so stole from our house!' I was working at the level of the cell, but now I work at the level of the sector. I often judge trials involving the death of people, not trials involving stealing wealth. Gacaca has helped survivors in general. We used to accompany each other, that is the first thing AVEGA told us. 'Accompany each other, sit next to your colleague, help each other.' They now call us 'those ones'.

It is clear from this statement from Kayiraba's testimony that Gacaca has helped her pursue individual drives of agency and communion by providing her with employment and enabling her to stand together with other women. It is also apparent, however, that Gacaca has enabled Kayiraba to fulfil motivations of communion at the collective level, by providing justice for survivors and promoting steps towards reconciliation. Now that the Gacaca programme has finished, it is

---

[60] Clark, *The Gacaca Courts, Post-Genocide Justice and Reconciliation in Rwanda*, p. 355.

[61] Ibid., p. 342.

[62] Bernard Rimé, Patrick Kanyangara, Vincent Yzerbyt and Dario Páez, 'The Impact of Gacaca Tribunals in Rwanda: Psychosocial Effects of Participation in a Truth and Reconciliation Process after a Genocide', *European Journal of Social Psychology*, 41 (2001), 695–706 (pp. 703–4).

up to other organisations to help promote collective post-traumatic growth.

The Aegis Trust is one such organisation which contributes to the needs of survivors by providing them with access to public discourse. Clark highlights truth-telling as an important step towards personal healing and gaining a sense of release, referring to this function of truth as 'therapeutic truth'.[63] The testimonies collected by the Genocide Archive of Rwanda provide survivors with the opportunity to reconstruct their life narratives which may in turn lead them to catharsis. Unlike the ICTR or Gacaca, the Genocide Archive of Rwanda allows survivors to give their version of events without coercion and without their stories being contested by opposing parties. During the recording phase, both the cameraman and interviewer are survivors themselves, and usually conduct the interviews in survivors' homes or chosen location. Survivors are, therefore, provided with a comfortable environment in which they can speak openly, which may ultimately help them on the path to healing.

As well as enabling survivors to make sense of their experience and gain a sense of release, the testimonies serve an important role in healing by providing a forum for remembering lost loved ones.[64] Survivors frequently express difficulties in coming to terms with losing their families because often they have never seen their bodies and are unaware of the circumstances in which they died. The Genocide Archive of Rwanda thus plays a vital function in providing a form of digital memorial. The interviewer always encourages survivors to give full names of all those who died and to describe their characters in as much detail as possible so as to provide the deceased with an identity and sense of humanity. Another type of healing described by Clark is 'healing as belonging' which refers to the experience of greater psychological and emotional wholeness through reconnecting with a community and gaining a sense of acknowledgement.[65] Knowing that their testimony has been recorded and can be accessed by others may

---

[63] Clark, *The Gacaca Courts, Post-Genocide Justice and Reconciliation in Rwanda*, p. 187.

[64] Clark suggests that healing may be facilitated through collective mourning and remembering which provides a form of memorial to lost friends and relatives. Clark, *The Gacaca Courts, Post-Genocide Justice and Reconciliation in Rwanda*, pp. 264–5.

[65] Ibid., pp. 258 and 271.

also provide survivors with this form of healing. Thus, the Genocide Archive of Rwanda contributes in many ways to achieving post-traumatic growth at the national level.

When it comes to facilitating growth at the international level, the responsibility lies beyond Rwanda's borders. Chapter 5 showed that survivors are attempting to engage in a dialogue with the international community, but external factors are impeding their success. A significant impediment to this growth is the dominant ideology that prevails in the West which portrays survivors as passive victims. While the translation of testimonies held in the Genocide Archive of Rwanda is making them accessible to an increasingly international audience, this ideology affects the process of translation.[66] It appears to be internalised by the Rwandan translators who often mitigate survivors' criticisms of the West, obstructing the possibility of genuine dialogue.[67] If the Genocide Archive of Rwanda is to fulfil its role as a vehicle for disseminating the voices of individual Rwandans, it is essential that the testimonies housed therein be translated with accuracy and a sense of ethical responsibility. Therefore, translation should be considered a priority in the process of documenting survivors' experiences. The Aegis Trust has now employed an in-house translator rather than outsourcing this service,[68] which will hopefully lead to investment in training. In future, translation should be conducted with a greater awareness of potential ideological pitfalls. A foreignising, non-fluent translation strategy would be most appropriate, intentionally disrupting target-language cultural values and enabling survivors to seek agency and communion.[69]

Even with inaccuracies, however, at least the translated testimonies at the Genocide Archive of Rwanda do not replace the original audio-visual interviews; they appear as either subtitles or accompanying transcripts so it is obvious to viewers/readers that they are translations. Moreover, despite the problems of translation, thanks to the work of the Aegis Trust, the testimonies of survivors are becoming increasingly accessible from around the world. Not only have many been made available via the online digital archive, but also the Aegis

---

[66] Williamson, 'Posttraumatic Growth at the International Level', p. 41.

[67] Ibid., p. 46.

[68] I met the newly hired translator during my research trip to the Genocide Archive Rwanda in July 2015.

[69] Venuti, 'Translation as Cultural Politics', p. 69.

Trust's American partner, the University of Southern California's Shoah Foundation, has now incorporated fifty testimonies into its Visual History Archive. Some of the testimonies will also be added to the Institute's public web portal, called the Visual History Archive Online (vhaonline.usc.edu). While the voices of survivors may be mistranslated to some extent, such projects provide them with a much larger audience which would not have been possible without the work of the Aegis Trust.

The dominant ideology in the West is more obstructive in the presentation of survivors' testimonies in *We Survived* and other similar collections. Chapter 5 suggested that this editorial intervention was perhaps deemed necessary at the time as the book was intended to promote the work of the Aegis Trust and thus sought to avoid interrupting dominant understandings of events which might appear subversive. However, aside from a brief acknowledgement in the opening pages, *We Survived* offers no information about the translation and editing process.[70] As such, it might be perceived to contain the unrestricted voices of Rwandan survivors.

There are two steps that publishers of survivors' testimonies could take to promote post-traumatic growth at an international level. First, Rwandans need to be more involved in the editing process. In his work on the testimonial encounter between American and Rwandan students, Dauge-Roth encourages a process of 'co-witnessing'.[71] Specifically, American students created a 'performance based on the correspondence they had maintained throughout the semester with survivors', but the Rwandan survivors subsequently 'read the draft and amended its content according to their sense of appropriateness and how they desired to be perceived'.[72] While this may not be easily achievable for published testimonies, as often those who testify do not understand the target languages, survivors' participation is essential for their narratives to be conveyed accurately. Second, if publishers of survivors' testimonies are to fulfil their ethical responsibility to survivors, then the role of translation and editing needs to be made more visible, acknowledging that these testimonies are in fact only a form of 'indirect witnessing'.[73] Collections of edited

---

[70] I contacted Whitworth to discuss the editing process but received no reply.
[71] Dauge-Roth, 'Fostering a Listening Community', para. 22.
[72] Ibid., paras 19–20.
[73] Ibid., para. 6.

testimonies should, therefore, include a preface explicitly stating the strategies adopted by translators and editors and explaining the challenges posed by the process.

This book, and Rwanda in general, also holds lessons for scholars of trauma and their role in facilitating post-traumatic growth. At both individual and collective levels, art and creative practice can play a helpful role but only in a context of creative freedom. As a number of scholars have observed, theory influences art. Joanna Spiro observes, for example, how writers 'feel the weight of Lanzmann's interdiction' to represent the Holocaust through fiction.[74] Similarly, Alan Gibbs argues that the genre of trauma literature is looked on approvingly by critics when it conforms to theoretical orthodoxy. I, therefore, advocate a new reading of trauma in the humanities, moving beyond trauma theory's narrow, Eurocentric prescriptivism and instead recognising the ability of survivors to rebuild their lives after trauma and, in some cases, experience a higher level of psychological or social functioning.

By listening to the voices of survivors to gain an understanding of their needs, it may become possible to facilitate an environment in which post-traumatic growth can take place individually and collectively. Efforts to rebuild the fabric of Rwandan society should, therefore, not simply be left to the individuals who suffered, but a concerted effort should be made by policy-makers, NGOs, educational institutions, trauma professionals and academics to promote positive change so that a brighter future for Rwanda can be achieved.

---

[74] Joanna Spiro, 'The Testimony of Fantasy in Georges Perec's *W ou le souvenir d'enfance*', *The Yale Journal of Criticism*, 14. 1 (2001), p. 34.

Bibliography

Abrahamsen, Rita, 'African Studies and the Postcolonial Challenge', *African Affairs*, 102. 407 (2003), 189–210.

Abraido-Lanza, Ana F., Carolina Guier, and Rose Marie Colón, 'Psychological Thriving among Latinas with Chronic Illness', *Journal of Social Issues*, 54 (1998), 405–428.

Adorno, Theodor W., *Prisms*, trans. by Samuel, and Shierry Weber (Cambridge: MIT Press, 1987).

Adorno, Theodor W., 'Commitment', in Rolf Tiedemann, ed., *Can One Live after Auschwitz: A Philosophical Reader*, trans. by Rodney Livingstone et al. (Stanford: Stanford University Press, 2003), pp. 240–258.

African Rights, *Rwanda: Death, Despair and Defiance* (London: African Rights, 1995).

African Rights, Rwanda: Broken Bodies, Torn Spirits: Living with Genocide, Rape and HIV/AIDS (African Rights Report, 2004).

Allport, Gordon W., *The Nature of Prejudice* (Cambridge, MA: Addison-Wesley, 1954).

American Psychiatric Association (APS), *Diagnostic and Statistical Manual of Mental Disorders (DSM-III)* (Washington, DC, 1980).

Amnesty International, Rwanda: 'Marked for Death', Rape Survivors Living with HIV/AIDS (Amnesty International Report, 2004).

Andermahr, Sonya, 'Decolonizing Trauma Studies: Trauma and Postcolonialism', *Special Issue of Humanities* (2015). www.mdpi.com/books/pdfview/book/196 [accessed 04 December 2017].

Baines, Erin K., 'Body Politics and the Rwandan Crisis', *Third World Quarterly*, 24. 3 (2003), 479–493.

Bakan, David, *Duality of Human Existence: An Essay on Psychology and Religion* (Chigago, IL: Rand McNally, 1966).

Balaev, Michelle (ed.), *Contemporary Approaches in Literary Trauma Theory* (Basingstoke: Palgrave Macmillan, 2014).

Bernabé, Jean, Patrick Chamoiseau, and Raphael Confiant, *In Praise of Creoleness* (English and French Edition), trans. by Mohamed B. Taleb Khyar (Paris: Editions Gallimard, 1993).

Bisschoff, Lizelle, and Stefanie Van de Peer, 'Representing the Unrepresentable', in Lizelle Bisschoff, and Stefanie van de Peer eds., *Art and Trauma in Africa: Representations of Reconciliation in Music, Visual Arts, Literature and Film* (London: I.B.Tauris & Co Ltd, 2011), pp. 3–25.

Bloom, Sandra L., 'By the Crowd They Have Been Broken, By the Crowd They Shall Be Healed: The Social Transformation of Trauma', in Richard G. Tedeschi, Crystal L. Park, and Lawrence G. Calhoun, eds., *Posttraumatic Growth: Positive Changes in the Aftermath of Crisis* (Mahwah, NJ: Lawrence Erlbaum Associates, Inc. 1998), pp. 179–214.

Bonanno, George A., 'Loss, Trauma, and Human Resilience: Have We Underestimated the Human Capacity to Thrive after Extremely Aversive Events?', *American Psychologist*, 59. 1 (2004), 20–28.

Bornstein, Marc H., Joseph Tal, and Catherine Tamis-LeMonda, 'Parenting in Cross-Cultural Perspective: The United States, France, and Japan', in Marc H. Bornstein, ed., *Cultural Approaches to Parenting* (Hillsdale, NJ: Lawrence Erlbaum Associated, 1991), pp. 69–90.

Boseley, Sarah, 'Rwanda: A Revolution in Rights for Women', Guardian, 28 May 2010. Retrieved from: www.guardian.co.uk/world/2010/may/28/womens-rights-rwanda [accessed 04 December 2017].

Brown, Laura S., 'Not Outside the Range: One Feminist Perspective on Psychic Trauma', in Cathy Caruth, ed., *Trauma: Explorations in Memory* (Baltimore, MD: Johns Hopkins University Press, 1995), pp. 100–112.

Brown, Laura S., *Cultural Competence in Trauma Therapy: Beyond the Flashback* (Washington, DC: American Psychological Association, 2008).

Buckley-Zistel, Susanne, 'Remembering to Forget: Chosen Amnesia as a Strategy for Local Coexistence in Post-Genocide Rwanda', *Africa: The Journal of the International African Institute*, 76. 2 (2006), 131–150.

Burnet, Jennie E., 'Gender Balance and the Meanings of Women in Governance in Post-Genocide Rwanda', *African Affairs*, 107/428 (2008), 361–386.

Burnet, Jennie E. *Genocide Lives in Us: Women, Memory and Silence in Rwanda* (Madison, WI: Wisconsin University Press, 2012).

Butler, Judith, *Frames of War: When Is Life Grievable* (London: Verso, 2010).

Calhoun, Lawrence G., Arnie Cann, and Richard G. Tedeschi, 'The Posttraumatic Growth Model: Sociocultural Considerations', in Tzipi Weiss, and Roni Berger, eds., *Posttraumatic Growth and Culturally Competent Practice: Lessons Learned from Around the World* (Hoboken, NJ: John Wiley & Sons Inc, 2010), pp. 1–14.

Calhoun, Lawrence G., and Richard G. Tedeschi, *Facilitating Posttraumatic Growth: A Clinician's Guide* (Mahwah, NJ: Lawrence Erlbaum Associates, Inc. 1999).

Calhoun, Lawrence G., and Richard G. Tedeschi, eds., *Handbook of Posttraumatic Growth: Research and Practice* (Mahwah, NJ: Lawrence Erlbaum Associates Publishers, 2006).

Calhoun, Lawrence G., and Richard G. Tedeschi, 'The Foundations of Posttraumatic Growth: An Expanded Framework, in Lawrence G. Calhoun, and Richard G. Tedeschi, *Handbook of Posttraumatic Growth: Research and Practice* (Mahwah, NJ: Lawrence Erlbaum Associates Publishers, 2006), pp. 3–23.

Calhoun, Lawrence G., and Richard G. Tedeschi, *Posttraumatic Growth in Clinical Practice* (New York: Routledge, 2013).

Caruth, Cathy (ed.), *Trauma: Explorations in Memory* (Baltimore, MD: Johns Hopkins University Press, 1995).

Caruth, Cathy (ed.), *Unclaimed Experience: Trauma, Narrative and History* (Baltimore, MD: Johns Hopkins Press, 1996).

Chauvin, Luc, James Mugaju, and Jondoh Comlavi, 'Evaluation of the Psychosocial Trauma Recovery Program in Rwanda', *Evaluation and Programming Planning*, 21. 4 (1998), 385–392.

Chu, Valerie, 'Within the Box: Cross-Cultural Art Therapy with Survivors of the Rwanda Genocide', *Art Therapy: Journal of the American Art Therapy Association*, 27. 1 (2010), 4–10.

Clark, Phil, *The Gacaca Courts, Post-Genocide Justice and Reconciliation in Rwanda: Justice without Lawyers (Cambridge Studies in Law and Society)* (Cambridge: Cambridge University Press, 2010).

Comrade, *Socio-Economic Analysis and Conditions of Street Children in Kigali* (Unpublished report, Kigali).

Courtemanche, Gil, *Un Dimanche à la piscine à Kigali* (Montréal: Editions du Boréal, 2000).

Couser, Gil Thomas, 'Making, Taking, and Faking Lives: Ethical Problems in Collaboative Life Writing', in Todd F. Davis, and Kenneth Womack, eds., *Mapping the Ethical Turn: A Reader in Ethics, Culture, and Literary Theory* (Charlottesville, VA: Virginia University Press, 2001), pp. 209–226.

Craps, Stef, *Postcolonial Witnessing: Trauma out of Bounds* (London: Palgrave Macmillan, 2013).

Craps, Stef, and Gert Buelens, 'Introduction: Postcolonial Trauma Novels', *Studies in the Novel*, 40. 1 & 2 (2008), 1–12.

Crocker, Jennifer, Brenda Major, and Claude Steele, 'Social Stigma', in Daniel T. Gilbert, Susan T. Fiske, and Gardner Lindzay, eds., *The Handbook of*

Social Psychology, 3 vols (Boston, MA: McGraw-Hill, 1998), II, pp. 504–553.

Dauge-Roth, Alexandre, *Writing and Filming the Genocide of the Tutsis in Rwanda: Dismembering and Remembering Traumatic History* (Lanham/Plymouth: Lexington Books, 2010).

Dauge-Roth, Alexandre, 'Fostering a Listening Community Through Testimony: Learning with Orphans of the Genocide in Rwanda', *Journal of Community Engagement and Scholarship*, 5. 2 (2012), http://jces.ua.edu/fostering-a-listening-community-through-testimony-learning-with-orphans-of-the-genocide-in-rwanda/ [accessed 15 October 2013].

de Brouwer, Anne-Marie, and Sandra Ka Hon Chu, *The Men Who Killed Me: Rwandan Survivors of Sexual Violence* (Vancouver: Douglas & McIntyre, 2009).

Des Forges, Alison, Leave None to Tell the Story: Genocide in Rwanda (Human Rights Watch Report, 1999).

Des Forges, Alison, and Timothy Longman, 'Legal Responses to Genocide in Rwanda', in Eric Stover, and Harvey M. Weinstein, eds., *My Neighbour, My Enemy: Justice and Community in the Aftermath of Mass Atrocity* (Cambridge: Cambridge University Press, 2004), pp. 49–68.

de Saint-Exupéry, Patrick, *Complices de l'Inavouable: La France au Rwanda* (Paris: Éditions des Arènes, 2004).

Devlin, Claire, and Robert Elgie, 'The Effect of Increased Women's Representation in Parliament: The Case of Rwanda', *Parliamentary Affairs*, 61. 2 (2008), 237–254.

Dowden, Richard, 'The Media's Failure: A Reflection on the Rwanda Genocide', in Allan Thompson, ed., *The Media and the Rwanda Genocide* (London: Pluto Press, 2007), pp. 248–255.

Dudman, Jane, 'Lessons from Rwanda's Female-Run Institutions', The Guardian, 1 July 2014. Retrieved from: www.theguardian.com/society/2014/jul/01/lessons-rwanda-female-run-institutions-mps [accessed 04 December 2017].

Dyregrov, Atle, Leila Gupta, Rolf Gjestad, and Eugenie Mukanoheli, 'Trauma Exposure and Psychological Reactions to Genocide among Rwandan Children', *Journal of Traumatic Stress*, 13. 1 (2000), 3–21.

Eagly, Alice, *Sex Differences in Social Behaviour: A Social-Role Interpretation* (Hillsdale: Erlbam, 1987).

Economist, The, 'Aid to Rwanda: The Pain of Suspension', The Economist, 12 January 2013. Retrieved from: www.economist.com/news/middle-east-and-africa/21569438-will-rwandas-widely-praised-development-plans-now-be-stymied-pain [accessed 04 December 2017].

Eltringham, Nigel, *Accounting for Horror: Post-Genocide Debates in Rwanda* (London: Pluto Press, 2004).

Eltringham, Nigel, 'The Past is Elsewhere: The Paradoxes of Proscribing Ethnicity in Post-Genocide Rwanda', in Scott Straus, and Lars Waldorf, eds., *Remaking Rwanda: State Building and Human Rights after Mass Violence (Critical Human Rights)* (Madison, WI: University of Wisconsin Press, 2011), pp. 269–282.

Fanon, Frantz, *Les damnés de la terre* (Paris: François Maspero, 1961).

Favila, Isaura Zelaya, 'Treatment of Post-Traumatic Stress Disorder in Post-Genocide Rwanda' (Global Grassroots Report, 2009), www.globalgrassroots.org/pdf/PTSD-Rwanda.pdf [accessed 04 December 2017].

Felman, Shoshana, 'Education and Crisis, or the Vicissitudes of Teaching', in Shoshana Felman, and Dori Laub eds., *Testimony: Crisis of Witnessing in Literature, Psychoanalysis and History* (New York: Routledge, 1992).

Fletcher, Narelle, '(Re)Telling the story of the 1994 Tutsi genocide in Rwanda: Une Saison de machettes (Machete Season) by Jean Hatzfeld', in J. Shaw, P. Kelly, and L. Semler, eds., *Storytelling: Critical and Creative Approaches* (Basingstoke: Palgrave Macmillan, 2013), pp. 66–79 (version cited from www.academia.edu/7566816/_Re_Telling_the_story_of_the_1994_Tutsi_genocide_in_Rwanda_Une_Saison_de_machettes_Machete_Season_by_Jean_Hatzfeld [accessed 04 December 2017], pp. 1–12.

Freud, Sigmund, *Beyond the Pleasure Principle*, trans. by James Stachey (New York: Dover Publications, 2015).

Gibbs, Alan, *Contemporary American Trauma Narratives* (Edinburgh: Edinburgh University Press, 2014).

Gilbert, Catherine, 'Making the Impossible Possible?: Collaboration in Rwandan Women's Testimonial Literature in Névine El Nossery, and Amy L. Hubbell, eds., *The Unspeakable: Representations of Trauma in Francophone Literature and Art* (Newcastle: Cambridge Scholars Publishing, 2013), pp. 115–136.

Gilligan, Carol, *In a Different Voice: Psychological Theory and Women's Development* (Cambridge, MA: Harvard University Press, 1993).

Gishoma, Darious, Jean-Luc Brackelaire, Naason Munyandamutsa, Jane Mujawayezu, Achour Ait Mohand, and Yvonne Kayiteshonga, 'Supportive-Expressive Group Therapy for People Experiencing Collective Traumatic Crisis During the Genocide Commemoration Period in Rwanda: Impact and Implications', *Journal of Social and Political Psychology*, 2. 1 (2014), 469–488.

Godard, Marie-Odile, *Rêves et traumatismes: Ou la longue nuit des rescapés* (Éditions Érès: Paris, 2003).

Goffman, Erving, *Stigma: Notes on the Management of Spoiled Identity* (Englewood Cliffs, NJ: Prentice-Hall, 1963).

Goldstein, Joshua S., *War and Gender: How Gender Shapes the War System and Vice Versa* (New York: Cambridge University Press, 2001).

Gready, Paul, 'Beyond "You're with Us or against Us": Civil Society and Policymaking in Post-Genocide Rwanda', in Scott Straus, and Lars Waldorf, eds., *Remaking Rwanda: State Building and Human Rights after Mass Violence (Critical Human Rights)* (Madison, WI: University of Wisconsin Press, 2011), pp. 87–100.

Greenberg, Jeff, Tom Pyszczynski, and Sheldon Solomon, 'The Causes and Consequences of a Need for Self-Esteem: A Terror Management Theory', in Roy F. Baumeister, ed., *Public Self and Private Self* (New York: Springer, 1986), pp. 189–212.

Hacking, Ian, 'Making Up People', *London Review of Books*, 28. 16 (2006), 23–26.

Hamilton, Heather B., 'Rwanda's Women: The Key to Reconstruction', *The Journal of Humanitarian Assistance* (2000). Retrieved from: www.jha.ac/greatlakes/b001.htm [accessed 04 December 2017].

Hatzfeld, Jean, *Dans le nu de la vie: récits des marais rwandais* (Paris: Éditions du Seuil, 2000).

Hatzfeld, Jean, *Une Saison de machettes* (Paris: Éditions du Seuil, 2003).

Hatzfeld, Jean, *Into the Quick of life: The Rwandan Genocide – The Survivors Speak*, trans. by Gerry Feehily (London: Serpent's Tail, 2005).

Hatzfeld, Jean, *A Time for Machetes. The Rwandan Genocide: The Killers Speak*, trans. by Linda Coverdale, preface by Susan Sontag (London: Serpent's Tail, 2005).

Hatzfeld, Jean, *Life Laid Bare. The Survivors in Rwanda Speak*, trans. by Linda Coverdale (New York: Farrar, Straus & Giroux, 2005).

Hatzfeld, Jean, *Machete Season. The Killers in Rwanda Speak. A Report by Jean Hatzfeld*, trans. by Linda Coverdale, preface by Susan Sontag (New York: Farrar, Straus & Giroux, 2005).

Hatzfeld, Jean, *La Stratégie des antilopes. Rwanda après le génocide* (Paris: Éditions du Seuil, 2007).

Hatzfeld, Jean, *The Antelope's Strategy: Living in Rwanda After the Genocide*, trans. by Linda Coverdale (New York: Farrar, Straus & Giroux, 2009).

Helgeson, Vicki S., 'Relation of Agency and Communion to Well-Being: Evidence and Potential Explanations', *Psychological Bulletin*, 116. 3 (1994), 412–428.

Helms, Elissa, 'Women as Agents of Ethnic Reconciliation? Women's NGOs and International Intervention in Postwar Bosnia–Herzegovina', *Women's Studies International Forum*, 26. 1 (2003), 15–33.

Herrero, Dolores, and Sonia Baelo-Allu, eds., *The Splintered Glass: Facets of Trauma in the Post-Colony and Beyond* (New York: Rodopi, 2011).

Heru, Alison, 'The Linkages Between Gender and Victimhood', *International Journal of Social Psychiatry*, 47. 3 (2001), pp. 10–20.

Hilhorst, Dorethea, and Mathijs van Leeuwen, 'Emergency and Development: The Case of Imidugudu, Villagization in Rwanda', *Journal of Refugee Studies*, 13. 3 (2000), 264–280.

Hintjens, Helen, 'Post-Genocide Identity Politics in Rwanda', *Ethnicities*, 8. 5 (2008), 5–41.

Hintjens, Helen, 'Reconstructing Political Identities in Rwanda', in Phil Clark, and Zachary D. Kaufman, eds., *After Genocide: Transitional Justice, Post-Conflict Reconstrucion and Reconcilation in Rwanda and Beyond* (London: Hurst and Co., 2008), pp. 77–99.

Hitchcott, Nicki, 'A Global African Commemoration – Rwanda: Ecrire par Devoir de Mémoire', *Forum for Modern Language Studies*, 45. 2 (2009), 151–161.

Hitchcott, Nicki, 'Benjamin Sehene vs Father Wenceslas Munyeshyaka: The Fictional Trial of a Genocide Priest', *Journal of African Cultural Studies*, 24. 1 (2012), 21–34.

Hitchcott, Nicki, 'Between Remembering and Forgetting: (In)Visible Rwanda in Gilbert Gatore's Le Passé devant soi', *Research in African Literatures*, 44. 2 (2013), 76–90.

Hitchcott, Nicki, *Rwanda Genocide Stories: Fiction after 1994* (Liverpool: Liverpool University Press, 2015).

Hofstede, Geert H., *Culture's Consequences: Comparing Values, Behaviors, Institutions, and Organizations across Nations*, 2nd Edn (Thousand Oaks, CA: Sage Publications Inc, 2001).

Hogg, Nicole, 'Women's Participation in the Rwandan Genocide: Mothers or Monsters?', *International Review of the Red Cross*, 92. 877 (2010), 69–102.

Hron, Madelaine, 'Gukora and Itsembatsemba: The "Ordinary Killers" in Jean Hatzfeld's Machete Season', *Research in African Literatures*, 42. 2 (2011), 125–146.

Human Rights Watch/Africa, Human Rights Watch Women's Project, Fédération Internationale des Ligues des Droits de l'Homme, *Shattered Lives: Sexual Violence during the Rwandan Genocide and Its Aftermath* (New York, Washington, London, Brussels: Human Rights Watch, 1996).

Ifowodo, Ogaga, *History, Trauma, and Healing in Postcolonial Narratives: Reconstructing Identities* (New York: Palgrave Macmillan, 2013).

Ilibagiza, Immaculée, *[with Steve Erwin], Left to Tell* (London: Hay House Ltd., 2006).

Janoff-Bulman, Ronnie, *Shattered Assumptions: Towards a New Psychology of Trauma* (New York: The Free Press, 1992).

Janoff-Bulman, Ronnie, and Cynthia McPherson Frantz, 'The Impact of Trauma on Meaning: From Meaningless World to Meaningful Life', in Mick Power, and Chris R. Brewin, eds., *The Transformation of Meaning in Psychological Therapies: Integrating Theory and Practice* (Chichester: John Wiley & Sons, 1997), pp. 91–106.

Jefremovas, Villia, *Brickyards to Graveyards. From Production to Genocide in Rwanda* (Albany, NY: State University of New York Press, 2002).

Jones, Adam, 'Gender and Genocide in Rwanda', *Journal of Genocide Research*, 4. 1 (2010), 65–94.

Jones, Edward E., Amerigo Farina, Albert H. Hastorf, Hazel Markus, Dale T. Miller, and Robert A. Scott, *Social Stigma: The Psychology of Marked Relationships* (New York: W. H. Freeman and Company, 1984).

Joseph, Stephen, *What Doesn't Kill Us: The New Psychology of Posttraumatic Growth* (Hachette Digital: London, 2011).

Joseph, Stephen, and Lisa D. Butler, 'Positive Changes Following Adversity', *PTSD Research Quarterly*, 21. 3 (2010), 1–8.

Joseph, Stephen, and P. Alex Linley, 'Positive Psychological Perspectives on Posttraumatic Stress: An Integrative Psychosocial Framework', in Stephen Joseph, and P. Alex Linley, eds., *Trauma, Recovery, and Growth: Positive Psychological Perspectives on Posttraumatic Stress* (Hokboken, NJ: John Wiley & Sons, Inc. 2008), pp. 3–20.

Joseph, Stephen, Ruth Williams, and William Yule, 'Changes in Outlook Following Disaster: The Preliminary Development of a Measure to Assess Positive And Negative Responses', *Journal of Traumatic Stress*, 6. 2 (1993), 271–279.

Jost, John T., and Mahzarin R. Banaji, 'The Role of Stereotyping in System-Justification and the Production of False Consciousness', *British Journal of Social Psychology*, 33. 1 (1994), 1–27.

Kabir, Ananya Jahanara, 'Affect, Body, Place: Trauma Theory in the World', in Gert Buelens, Sam Durrant, and Robert Eaglestone, eds., *The Future of Trauma Theory: Contemporary Literary and Cultural Criticism* (London: Routledge, 2014), pp. 63–75.

Kagame, Alexis, 'La philosophie băntu-rwandaise de l'être' [Bantu-Rwandan Philosophy of Being], *Académie royale des sciences coloniales*, Mémoire, 8, 20 June 1955.

Kagame, Paul, 'Preface', in Phil Clark, and Zachary D. Kaufman, eds., *After Genocide: Transitional Justice, Post-Conflict Reconstruction and Reconciliation in Rwanda and Beyond* (London: Hurst and Co., 2008), pp. xxi–xxvi.

Kaiser, Cheryl R., S. Brooke Vick, and Brenda Major, 'A Prospective Investigation of the Relationship between Just-World Beliefs and the Desire for Revenge after September 11, 2001', *Psychological Science*, 15. 7 (2004), 503–506.

Kameya, Laetitia Umuhoza, *Kami yanjye: Urwibutso rwa data* (Butare, 2009).

Kayitare, Pauline [avec Patrick May], *Tu leur diras que tu es Hutue!* (Bruxelles: André Versaille, 2011).

Kayitesi, Berthe, Rollande Deslandes, and Christine Lebel, 'Facteurs de résilience chez des orphelins rescapés du génocide qui vivent seuls dans les ménages au Rwanda (Association Tubeho)', *Revue Canadienne de Santé Mentale Communautaire*, 25. 1 (2009), 67–81.

Kerstens, Paul, '"Voice and Give Voice": Dialectics between Fiction and History in Narratives on the Rwandan Genocide', *International Journal of Francophone Studies*, 9. 1 (2006), 93–110.

Kierkegaard, Søren, *The Sickness unto Death*, trans. by Alastair Hannay (London: Penguin Books, 1989).

Kitayama, Shinobu, Hazel Rose Markus, and David Matsumoto, 'Culture, Self and Emotion: A Cultural Perspective on "Self-Conscious" Emotions', in June Price Tangney, and Kurt W. Fischer, eds., *Self-Conscious Emotion: The Psychology of Shame, Guilt, Embarrassment and Pride* (New York: Guilford Press, 1995), pp. 439–464.

Koenig, Harold G., Kenneth I. Pargament, and Julie Nielsen, 'Religious Coping and Health Status in Medically Ill Hospitalised Older Adults', *Journal of Nervous and Mental Disease*, 186 (1998), 513–521.

Kwibuka, Eugene, 'Twenty-Two Years Later, Rwandans Talk of Liberation Fruits', The New Times, 04 July 2016. Retrieved from: www.newtimes. co.rw/section/article/2016-07-04/201387/ [accessed 04 December 2017].

Lanzmann, Claude, 'Holocauste, la représentation impossible', Le Monde, 3 March 1994.

Lee, Victoria, and Geoffrey Beattie, 'The Rhetorical Organisation of Verbal and Nonverbal Behavior in Emotional Talk', *Semiotica*, 120. 1/2 (1998), 39–92.

Legatum Institute, Africa Prosperity Report. Retrieved from: https://lif.blob. core.windows.net/lif/docs/default-source/publications/2016-africa-pros-perity-report-pdf.pdf?sfvrsn=2, [accessed 04 December 2017].

Lemarchand, René, 'The Politics of Memory in Post-Genocide Rwanda', in Phil Clark, and Zachary D. Kaufman, eds., *After Genocide:*

Transitional Justice, Post-Conflict Reconstrucion and Reconcilation in Rwanda and Beyond (London: Hurst and Co., 2008), pp. 65–76.

Levene, Mark, 'What Makes Genocide Different from Other Types of War?'. Retrieved from: http://clg.portalxm.com/library/keytext.cfm?keytext_id=188 [accessed 04 December 2017].

Linstrum, Erik, *Ruling Minds: Psychology in the British Empire* (Cambridge, MA: Harvard University Press, 2016).

Longman, Timothy, 'Identity Cards, Ethnic Self-Perception, and Genocide in Rwanda', in Jane Caplan, and John Torpey, eds., *Documenting Individual Identity: The Development of State Practices in the Modern World* (Princeton, NJ: Princeton University Press, 2001), pp. 345–359.

Longman, Timothy, 'Rwanda: Achieving Equality or Serving an Authoritarian State?', in Hannah Evelyn Britton, and Gretchen Bauer, eds., *Women in African Parliaments* (Boulder, CO: Lynne Rienner Publishers, 2006), pp. 133–150.

Longman, Timothy, *Christianity and Genocide in Rwanda* (Cambridge: Cambridge University Press, 2010).

Longman, Timothy, 'Limitations to Political Reform: The Undemocratic Nature of Transition in Rwanda', in Scott Straus, and Lars Waldorf, eds., *Remaking Rwanda: State Building and Human Rights after Mass Violence (Critical Human Rights)* (Madison, WI: University of Wisconsin Press, 2011), pp. 25–47.

Longman, Timothy, and Théoneste Rutagengwa, 'Memory, Identity, and Community in Rwanda', in Eric Stover, and Harvey M. Weinstein, eds., *My Neighbour, My Enemy: Justice and Community in the Aftermath of Mass Atrocity* (Cambridge University Press, 2004), pp. 162–182.

Maccoby, Eleanor E., 'Gender and Relationships: A Developmental Account', *American Psychologist*, 45. 4 (1990), pp. 513–520.

Mannheim, Karl, *Ideology and Utopia: An Introduction to the Sociology of Knowledge* (New York: Harcourt, Brace and World, 1936).

Markus, Hazel Rose, and Shinobu Kitayama, 'Culture and the Self: Implications for Cognition, Emotion, and Motivation', *Psychological Review*, 98 (1991), 224–253.

Marx, Karl, and Friedrich Engels, *The German Ideology* (London: Arthur, 1974).

May, Rollo, *Freedom and Destiny* (New York: Norton, 1981).

Mbaraga, Robert, 'State Pushes Campaign that Critics Say It Is Ethnically Divisive', The East African, 16 November 2013. Retrieved from: www.theeastafrican.co.ke/Rwanda/News/Mixed-reactions-to--Ndi-Umunyarwanda-initiative-/-/1433218/2075366/-/6ktcmf/-/index.html. Retrieved 12 August 2015 [accessed 04 December 2017].

McAdams, Dan P., *The Stories We Live By: Personal Myths and the Making of the Self* (New York: William Morrow & Company, 1993).

McAdams, Dan P., *The Redemptive Self: Stories Americans Live By* (New York: Oxford University Press, 2006).

McCormack, Lynne, 'Primary and Vicarious Posttraumatic Growth following Genocide, War and Humanitarian Emergencies: An Interpretative Phenomenological Analysis', Thesis submitted to the University of Nottingham for the degree of Doctor of Philosophy (2010). Retrieved from: http://etheses.nottingham.ac.uk/2142/1/FINAL_THESIS_-_corrections_%26_dedication_18.11.10.pdf, [accessed 04 December 2017].

McMillen, J. Curtis, and Rachel H. Fisher, 'The Perceived Benefits Scale: Measuring Perceived Positive Life Changes Following Negative Events', *Social Work Research*, 22. 3 (1998), 173–187.

McNally, Richard J., 'Conceptual Problems with the DSM-IV Criteria for Posttraumatic *Stress Disorder*', in Gerald Rosen, ed., *Posttraumatic Stress Disorder: Issues and Controversies* (New York: John Wiley & Sons, 2004), pp. 1–14.

Melvern, Linda, *A People Betrayed: The Role of the West in Rwanda's Genocide* (London: Zed Books, 2004).

Mibenge, Chiseche, 'Gender and Ethnicity in Rwanda: On Legal Remedies for Victims of Wartime Sexual Violence', in Dubravka Zarkov, ed., *Gender, Violent Conflict and Development* (New Delhi: Zubaan Books, 2008).

Morland, Leslie A., Lisa D. Butler, and Gregory A. Leskin, 'Resilience and Thriving in a Time of Terrorism', in Stephen Joseph, and P. Alex Linley, eds., *Trauma, Recovery, and Growth: Positive Psychological Perspectives on Posttraumatic Stress* (Hokboken, NJ: John Wiley & Sons, Inc. 2008), pp. 39–61.

Moskowitz, D. S., Eun Jung Suh, and Julie Desaulniers, 'Situational Influences on Gender Differences in Agency and Communion', *Journal of Personality and Social Psychology*, 66. 4 (1994), 753–761.

Mujawayo, Esther, and Souâd Belhaddad, *SurVivantes* (Paris: Editions de l'Aube, 2004).

Mujawayo, Esther, and Souâd Belhaddad, *La Fleur de Stéphanie: Rwanda entre réconciliation et déni* (Paris: [Éditions] Flammarion, 2006).

Mukagasana, Yolande, *Les Blessures du silence. Témoignages du génocide au Rwanda*(Arles: Actes Sud and Médecins Sans Frontières, 2001).

Mukagasana, Yolande, and Patrick May, *La Mort ne veut pas de moi* (Paris: Fixot, 1997).

Mukamana, Donatilla, and Petra Brysiewicz, 'The Lived Experience of Genocide Rape Survivors in Rwanda', *Journal of Nursing Scholarship*, 40. 4 (2008), 379–384.

National Unity and Reconciliation Commission (NURC), Report on the National Summit of Unity and Reconciliation (2000).

Neugebauer, Richard, Prudence W. Fisher, J. Blake Turner, Saori Yamabe, Julia A. Sarsfield, and Tasha Stehling-Ariza, 'Post-traumatic Stress Reactions among Rwandan Children and Adolescents in the Early Aftermath of Genocide', *International Journal of Epidemiology*, 38. 4 (2009), 1033–1045.

Newbury, Catharine, and Hannah Baldwin, 'Confronting the Aftermath of Conflict: Women's Organisations in Post-genocide Rwanda', in Krishna Kumar, ed., *Women and Civil War: Impact, Organisations, and Action by* (Boulder, CO: Lynne Rienner Publishers, 2001), pp. 97–128.

Newbury, Catharine, and Hannah Baldwin, *Aftermath: Women in Postgenocide Rwanda* (U.S. Agency for International Development, 2000). Retrieved from: http://pdf.usaid.gov/pdf_docs/pnacj323.pdf [accessed 04 December 2017].

Nowrojee, Binaifer, 'A Lost Opportunity for Justice: Why Did the ICTR not Persecute Gender Propaganda?', in Allan Thompson, ed., *The Media and the Rwanda Genocide* (London: Pluto Press, 2007), pp. 362–372.

Nowrojee, Binaifer, '"Your Justice Is Too Slow". Will the International Criminal Tribunal for Rwanda Fail Rwanda's Rape Victims?', in Donna Pankhurst, ed., *Gendered Peace: Women's Struggles for Post-War Justice and Reconciliation* (New York: Routledge, 2008), pp. 107–136.

Organisation of African Unity, *Rwanda: The Preventable Genocide* (Addis Ababa: OAU, 2000).

Páez, Darío, Nekane Basabe, Silvia Ubillos, and José Luis González-Castro, 'Social Sharing, Participation in Demonstrations, Emotional Climate, and Coping with Collective Violence After the March 11th Madrid Bombings', *Journal of Social Issues*, 63. 2 (2007), 232–337.

Pals, Jennifer L., and Dan P. McAdams, 'The Transformed Self: A Narrative Understanding of Posttraumatic Growth', *Psychological Inquiry*, 15. 1 (2004), 65–69.

Park, Crystal L., Lawrence H. Cohen, and Renee L. Murch, 'Assessment and Prediction of Stress-Related Growth', *Journal of Personality*, 64. 1 (1996), 71–105.

Powley, Elizabeth, 'Case Study Rwanda: Women Hold up Half the Parliament', in Julie Ballington, and Azza Karam, eds., *Women in Parliament: Beyond Numbers*, rev. edn (Stockholm: The International Institute for Democracy and Electoral Assistance, 2005), pp. 154–163.

Powley, Elizabeth, *Rwanda: The Impact of Women Legislators on Policy Outcomes Affecting Children and Families* (United Nations Children's Fund (UNICEF) Report, 2006).

Prunier, Gérard, *The Rwanda Crisis: History of a Genocide* (London: C. Hurst & Co., 1997).

Prunier, Gérard, *From Genocide to Continental War: The 'Congolese' Conflict and the Crisis of Contemporary Africa* (London: Hurst Publishers Ltd., 2009).

Radstone, Susannah, 'Trauma Theory: Contexts, Politics, Ethics', *Paragraph*, 30. 1 (2007), 9–29.

Raeff, Catherine, *Always Separate, Always Connected: Independence and Interdependence in Cultural Contexts of Development* (Mahwah, NJ: Lawrence Erlbaum Associates, Inc., 2006).

Rajiva, Jay, *Postcolonial Parabola: Literature, Tactility, and the Ethics of Representing Trauma* (New York: Bloomsbury, 2017).

République du Rwanda, *Enquête Sociodémographique1996, Rapport Final (Abrege)* (Kigali, Rwanda: Ministère des Finances et de la Planification Economique, Office de la Population, et Fonds des National Unis pour la Population, 1998).

Rettig, Max, 'Truth, Justice and Reconciliation in Postconflict Rwanda?', *African Studies Review*, 51. 3 (2008), 25–50.

Reyntjens, Filip, 'Rwanda, Ten Years On: From Genocide to Dictatorship', *African Affairs*, 103. 411 (2004), 177–210.

Reyntjens, Filip, 'Constructing the Truth, Dealing with Dissent, Domesticating the World: Governance in Post-Genocide Rwanda', *African Affairs*, 110. 438 (2010), 1–34.

Reyntjens, Filip, '(Re-)imagining a Reluctant Post-Genocide Society: The Rwandan Patriotic Front's Ideology and Practice', *Journal of Genocide Research*, 18. 1 (2016), 61–81.

Ricci, Sandrine, '*La Parole Mémorielle de Rescapées du Génocide des Tutsi au Rwanda: vers une (Re)Construction du Sens*' (Montréal: Mémoire, Université Du Québec À Montréal, 2008).

Rimé, Bernard, Patrick Kanyangara, Vincent Yzerbyt, and Dario Páez, 'The Impact of Gacaca Tribunals in Rwanda: Psychosocial Effects of Participation in a Truth and Reconciliation Process after a Genocide', *European Journal of Social Psychology*, 41 (2001), 695–706.

Rizzini, Irene, and Andrew Dawes, 'Editorial: On Cultural Diversity and Childhood Adversity', *Childhood*, 8 (2001), 315–321.

Rizzuto, Nicole, *Insurgent Testimonies: Witnessing Colonial Trauma in Modern and Anglophone Literature* (New York: Fordham University Press, 2016).

Rothberg, Michael, 'Decolonising Trauma Studies: A Response', *Studies in the Novel*, 40, 1 & 2 (2008), 224–234.

Rothberg, Michael *Multidirectional Memory: Remembering the Holocaust in the Age of Decolonisation* (Stanford: Stanford University Press, 2009).

Rusagara, Frank, *Resilience of a Nation: A History of the Military in Rwanda* (Kigali: Fountain Publishers Rwanda, 2009).

Ryan, Richard M., and Edward L. Deci, 'Self-Determination Theory and the Facilitation of Intrinsic Motivation, Social Development, and Well-Being', *American Psychologist*, 55 (2000), 68–78.

Samuelson, Beth Lewis, and Sarah Warshauer Freedman, 'Language Policy, Multilingual Education, and Power in Rwanda', *Language Policy*, 9 (2010), 191–215.

Sartre, Jean-Paul, *Being and Nothingness* (New York: Philosophical Library, 1956).

Schaal, Susanne, and Thomas Elbert, 'Ten Years after the Genocide: Trauma Confrontation and Posttraumatic Stress in Rwandan Adolescents', *Journal of Traumatic Stress*, 19. 1 (2006), 95–105.

Schnabel, Albrecht, and Anara Tabyshalieva, 'Forgone Opportunities: The Marginalisation of Women's Contributions to Post-Conflict Peacekeeping', in Albrecht Schnabel, and Anara Tabyshalieva, eds., *Defying Victimhood: Women and Post-Conflict Peacebuilding* (New York: United Nations University Press, 2012), pp. 3–47.

Sedanius, Jim, and Felicia Pratto, *Social Dominance: An Intergroup Theory of Social Hierarchy and Oppression* (Cambridge: Cambridge University Press, 1999).

Seligman, Martin E. P., *Helplessness: On Depression, Development, and Death* (San Francisco: W. H. Freeman, 1975).

Semujanga, Josias, *Origins of Rwandan Genocide* (New York: Humanity Books, 2003).

Sherif, Muzafer, *In Common Predicament: Social Psychology of Intergroup Conflict and Cooperation* (Boston, MA: Houghton Mifflin Company, 1966).

Shih, Margaret, 'Examining Resilience and Empowerment in Overcoming Stigma', *Annals of the American Academy of Political and Social Science*, 591 (2004), 175–185.

Skitka, Linda J., Christopher W. Bauman, and Elizabeth Mullen, 'Political Tolerance and Coming to Psychological Closure Following the September 11, 2001, Terrorist Attacks: An Integrative Approach', *Personality and Social Psychology Bulletin*, 30 (2004), 743–756.

Sommers, Marc, 'Fearing Africa's Young Men: The Case of Rwanda', Conflict Prevention & Reconstruction, World Bank Social Development Papers, 32 (2006).

Soudan, François, 'Paul Kagamé: "Je ne conseille à personne de se mêler des affaires intérieures du Rwanda"' [Paul Kagame: 'I would not advise anyone to interfere in Rwandan internal affairs], *Jeune Afrique*, 14 April 2014. Retrieved from: www.jeuneafrique.com/Article/ JA2778p020.xml1/ [accessed 04 December 2017].

Soudan, François, *Kagame: Conversations with the President of Rwanda* (New York: Enigma Books, 2015).

Spiessens, Anneleen, 'Voicing the Perpetrator's Perspective: Translation and Mediation in Jean Hatzfeld's Une Saison de machettes', *The Translator*, 16. 2 (2010), pp. 315–336.

Spiro, Joanna, 'The Testimony of Fantasy in Georges Perec's W ou le souvenir d'enfance', *The Yale Journal of Criticism*, 14. 1 (2001), 115–154.

Splevins, Katie, Keren Cohen, Jake Bowley, and Stephen Joseph, 'Theories of Posttraumatic Growth: Cross-Cultural Perspectives', *Journal of Loss and Trauma*, 15 (2010), 259–277.

Staub, Ervin, and Laurie Anne Pearlman, Alexandra Gubin, Athanase Hagengimana, 'Healing, Reconciliation, Forgiving and the Prevention of Violence after Genocide or Mass Killing: An Intervention and Its Experimental Evaluation in Rwanda', *Journal of Social and Clinical Psychology*, 24. 3 (2005), 297–334.

Summerfield, Derek, 'Cross Cultural Perspectives on the Medicalisation of Human Suffering', in Gerald Rosen, ed., *Posttraumatic Stress Disorder: Issues and Controversies* (Chichester: John Wiley, 2004), pp. 233–247.

Tadjo, Véronique, *L'Ombre d'Imana* (Paris: Actes Sud, 2005).

Tajfel, Henri, and John C. Turner, 'An Integrative Theory of Intergroup Conflict', in William G. Austin, and Stephen Worchel, eds., *The Social Psychology of Intergroup Relations* (Monterey, CA: Brooks/Cole, 1979), pp. 33–47.

Tal, Kalí, *Worlds of Hurt: Reading the Literature of Trauma* (New York: Cambridge University Press, 1996).

Taylor, Christopher, 'A Gendered Genocide: Tutsi Women and Hutu Extremists in the 1994 Rwanda Genocide', *Political and Legal Anthropological Review*, 22. 1 (1999), 42–53.

Taylor, Christopher, *Sacrifice as Terror: The Rwandan Genocide of 1994* (Oxford: Berg, 1999).

Tedeschi, Richard G., 'Violence Transformed: Posttraumatic Growth in Survivors and their Societies', *Aggression and Violent Behavior*, 4. 3 (1999), 319–341.

Tedeschi, Richard G., and Lawrence Calhoun, 'The Posttraumatic Growth Inventory: Measuring the Positive Legacy of Trauma', *Journal of Traumatic Stress*, 9. 3 (1996), 455–471.

Tedeschi, Richard G., Crystal L. Park, and Lawrence G. Calhoun, 'Posttraumatic Growth: Conceptual Issues', in Richard G. Tedeschi, Crystal L. Park, and Lawrence G. Calhoun, eds., *Posttraumatic Growth: Positive Changes in the Aftermath of Crisis* (Mahwah, NJ: Lawrence Erlbaum Associates, Inc. 1998), pp. 1–22.

Tedeschi, Richard G., and Ryan P. Kilmer, 'Assessing Strengths, Resilience, and Growth to Guide Clinical Intervention', *Professional Psychology: Research and Practice*, 36. 3 (2005), 230–237.

Thompson, Allan, ed., *The Media and the Rwanda Genocide* (London: Pluto Press, 2007).

Thomson, Susan, 'Whispering Truth to Power: The Everyday Resistance of Rwandan Peasants to Post-Genocide Reconciliation', *African Affairs*, 110. 440 (2011), 439–456.

Tickner, J. Ann, *Gendering World Politics: Issues and Approaches in the Post-Cold War Era* (New York: Columbia University Press, 2001).

Triandis, Harry C., and Eunkook M. Suh, 'Cultural Influences on Personality', *Annual Review of Psychology*, 53 (2002), 133–160.

United States Agency for International Development (USAID) Office of Democracy and Governance, 'Rwanda Democracy and Governance Assessment', November 2002. http://pdf.usaid.gov/pdf_docs/PNACR569.pdf [accessed 04 December 2017].

Umutesi, Marie Béatrice, *Fuir ou mourir au Zaïre: le vécu d'une réfugiée rwandaise* (Paris: L'Harmattan, 2000).

Uvin, Peter S., *The Introduction of a Modernized Gacaca for Judging Suspects of Participation in the Genocide and the Massacres of 1994 in Rwanda* (Governance and Social Development Centre, 2000).

Uwimbabazi, Penine, Patrick Hajayandi, and Jean de Dieu Basabose, 'Forums for Reconciliation in Rwanda: Challenges and Opportunities', The Institute for Justice and Reconciliation, Policy Brief, 17 (November 2014).

Van Dijk, Teun, *Ideology: A Multidisciplinary Approach* (London: Sage Publications, 1998).

Vázquez, Carmelo, Pau Pérez-Sales, and Gonzalo Hervás, 'Positive Effects of Terrorism and Posttraumatic Growth: An Individual and Community Perspective', in Stephen Joseph, and Alex Linley, eds., *Trauma, Recovery and Growth* (New Jersey: John Wiley & Sons, 2008), pp. 63–91.

Veale, Angela, and Giorgia Donà, 'Street Children and Political Violence: A Socio-Demographic Analysis of Street Children in Rwanda', *Child Abuse & Neglect*, 27. 3 (2003), 253–269.

Venuti, Laurence, *The Translator's Invisibility: A History of Translation* (London: Routledge, 2004).

Venuti, Laurence, 'La commémoration du génocide au Rwanda: Violence symbolique, mémorisation forcée et histoire officielle', *Cahiers d'études africaines* 175 (2004), 575–592.

Venuti, Laurence, 'Translation as Cultural Politics: Regimes of Domestication in English', in Mona Baker, ed., *Critical Readings in Translation Studies* (London: Routledge, 2010), pp. 67–79.

Vidal, Claudine, 'De la religion subie au modernisme refusé: 'Théophagie', ancêtres clandestins et résistance populaire au Rwanda' [Religion subjected to unwanted modernism: 'Theophagy', Clandestine Ancestors and Popular Resistance in Rwanda], *Archives des Sciences Sociales des Religions*, 38 (1974), 63–90.

Vishnevsky, Tanya, Arnie Cann, Lawrence G. Calhoun, Richard G. Tedeschi, and George J. Demakis, 'Gender Differences in Self-Reported Posttraumatic Growth: A Meta-Analysis', *Psychology of Women Quarterly*, 34 (2010), 110–120.

Waldorf, Lars, 'Instrumentalising Genocide: The RPF's Campaign against "Genocide Ideology"', in Scott Straus, and Lars Waldorf, eds., *Remaking Rwanda: State Building and Human Rights after Mass Violence (Critical Human Rights)* (Madison, WI: University of Wisconsin Press, 2011), pp. 48–66.

Wall, Melissa, 'An Analysis of News Magazine Coverage of the Rwanda Crisis in the United States', in Allan Thompson, ed., *The Media and the Rwanda Genocide* (London: Pluto Press, 2007), pp. 261–273.

Waller, James, *Becoming Evil: How Ordinary People Commit Genocide and Mass Killing*, 2nd edn. (Oxford: Oxford University Press, 2007).

Ward, Abigail (ed.), *Postcolonial Traumas: Memory, Narrative, Resistance* (New York: Palgrave Macmillan, 2015).

Weiss, Tzipi, and Roni Berger, 'Posttraumatic Growth around the Globe', in Tzipi Weiss, and Roni Berger, ed., *Posttraumatic Growth and Culturally Competent Practice: Lessons Learned from around the World* (Hoboken, NJ: John Wiley & Sons Inc, 2010), pp. 189–196.

Weitsman, Patricia A., 'The Politics of Identity and Sexual Violence: A Review of Bosnia and Rwanda', *Human Rights Quarterly*, 30. 3 (2008), 561–578.

Whitworth, Wendy, ed., *We Survived: Genocide in Rwanda* (Laxton: Quill Press, 2006).

Williamson, Caroline, 'Accessing Material from the Genocide Archive of Rwanda', *African Research and Documentation*, 120 (2013), pp. 17–24.

Williamson, Caroline, 'Posttraumatic Growth and Religion in Rwanda: Individual Well-Being vs. Collective False Consciousness', *Mental Health, Religion & Culture*, 17. 9 (2014), 946–955.

Williamson, Caroline, 'Towards a Theory of Collective Posttraumatic Growth in Rwanda: The Pursuit of Agency and Communion', *Traumatology: An International Journal*, 20. 2 (2014), 91–102.

Williamson, Caroline, 'Posttraumatic Growth at the International Level: The Obstructive Role Played by Translators and Editors of Rwandan Genocide Testimonies', *Translation Studies*, 9. 1 (2016), 33–50.

Women's Commission for Refugee Women and Children, *Rwanda's Women and Children: The Long Road to Reconciliation* (New York: Women's Commission, 1997).

World Bank, *Doing Business Report* www.doingbusiness.org/rankings [accessed 04 December 2017].

Young, Allan, *The Harmony of Illusions: Inventing Post-Traumatic Stress Disorder* (Princeton: Princeton University Press, 1995).

Yusin, Jennifer, *The Future Life of Trauma: Partitions, Borders, Repetition* (New York: Fordham University Press, 2017).

Index

CPSIA information can be obtained
at www.ICGtesting.com
Printed in the USA
LVHW021405120921
697665LV00010B/993

9 781108 444590